Anti-Oppressive Social Work Practice

Sara Miller McCune founded SAGE Publishing in 1965 to support the dissemination of usable knowledge and educate a global community. SAGE publishes more than 1000 journals and over 800 new books each year, spanning a wide range of subject areas. Our growing selection of library products includes archives, data, case studies and video. SAGE remains majority owned by our founder and after her lifetime will become owned by a charitable trust that secures the company's continued independence.

Los Angeles | London | New Delhi | Singapore | Washington DC | Melbourne

Anti-Oppressive Social Work Practice

Prospera Tedam

Learning Matters
A SAGE Publishing Company
1 Oliver's Yard
55 City Road
London EC1Y 1SP

SAGE Publications Inc.
2455 Teller Road
Thousand Oaks, California 91320

SAGE Publications India Pvt Ltd
B 1/I 1 Mohan Cooperative Industrial Area
Mathura Road
New Delhi 110 044

SAGE Publications Asia-Pacific Pte Ltd
3 Church Street
#10-04 Samsung Hub
Singapore 049483

Editor: Kate Keers
Development editor: Sarah Turpie
Senior project editor: Chris Marke
Project management: Deer Park Productions
Marketing manager: Camille Richmond
Cover design: Wendy Scott
Typeset by: C&M Digitals (P) Ltd, Chennai, India
Printed in the UK

Library of Congress Control Number: 2020941890

British Library Cataloguing in Publication Data

A catalogue record for this book is available from the British Library

ISBN 978-1-5264-7688-3
ISBN 978-1-5264-7689-0 (pbk)

Contents

Contents

Since launching in 2003, *Transforming Social Work Practice* has become the market-leading series for social work students. Each book is:

- Affordable
- Written to the Professional Capabilities Framework
- Mapped to the Social Work curriculum
- Practical with clear links between theory and practice

These books use activities and case studies to build critical thinking and reflection skills and will help social work students to develop good practice through learning.

BESTSELLING TEXTBOOKS

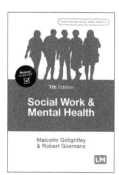

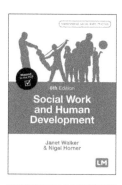

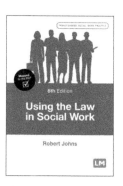

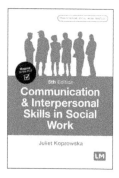

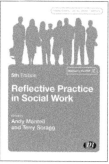

About the Series Editor

DR JONATHAN PARKER is Professor of Society & Social Welfare at Bournemouth University. He has published widely on social work education, policy, theory for practice, disadvantage, marginalization and violence, across the world.

About the author

Prospera Tedam is currently an Assistant Professor in Social Work at the United Arab Emirates University and teachs on undergraduate and postgraduate social work programmes. She moved to the United Arab Emirates in 2018 from Anglia Ruskin University where she was Principal Lecturer in Social Work, overseeing Practice Quality. Prospera has also taught social work at the Open University and University of Northampton, and has research interests in critical race theory, social work with Black and ethnic minority service users, and anti-oppressive practice. Prospera is the editor for the *Journal of Practice Teaching and Learning*, and is an associate editor for *Child Abuse Review*.

Series editor's preface

During recent teaching sessions for student social workers, I have been struck keenly by the changes permeating our contemporary world. Values and ethics lie at the heart of social work and social work education, and we address these throughout all the books in the series. The positions that we take in terms of values and ethics is, to an extent, determined by context, time and experience, and these are expressed in different ways by students coming into social work education today and, of course, by the different routes that students take through their educational experience.

Since the turn of this century, we have witnessed shifts and challenges as the marketised neoliberal landscape of politics, economy and social life may attract little comment or contest from some, and even the acceptance of populist right-wing positions. We have also observed the political machinery directing much of statutory social work towards a focus on individuals apart from their environment. However, on a more positive note, we have also seen a new turn to the social in the #MeToo campaign where unquestioned entitlement to women's bodies and psychology is exposed and resisted. We have seen defiance of those perpetuating social injustices that see long-term migrants alongside today's migrants being abused and shunned by society and institutions, as well as by individuals.

It is likely that, as a student of social work, you will lay bare and face many previously unquestioned assumptions, which can be very perplexing and uncover needs for learning, support and understanding. This series of books acts as an aid as you make these steps. Each book stands in a long and international tradition of social work that promotes social justice and human rights, introducing you to the importance of sometimes new and difficult concepts, and inculcating the importance of close questioning of yourself as you make your journey towards becoming part of that tradition.

There are numerous contemporary challenges for the wider world and for all four countries of the UK. These include political shifts to the 'popular' right, a growing antipathy to care and support, and dealing with lies and 'alternative truths' in our daily lives. Alongside this is the need to address the impact of an increasingly ageing population with its attendant social care needs and working with the financial implications that such a changing demography brings. At the other end of the lifespan, the need for high-quality childcare, welfare and safeguarding services has been highlighted as society develops and responds to the changing complexion. As demand rises, so do the costs, and the unquestioned assumption that austerity measures are necessary continues to create tensions and restrictions in services, policies and expectations.

As a social worker, you will work with a diverse range of people throughout your career, many of whom have experienced significant, even traumatic, events that require a professional and caring response. As well as working with individuals, however, you may be required to respond to the needs of a particular community disadvantaged by local, national or world events, or groups excluded within their local communities because of assumptions made about them.

The importance of high-quality social work education remains if we are adequately to address the complexities of modern life. We should continually strive for excellence in education, as this allows us to focus clearly on what knowledge it is useful to engage with when learning to be a social worker. Questioning everything, especially from a position of knowledge, is central to being a social worker.

The books in this series respond to the agendas driven by changes brought about by professional bodies, governments and disciplinary reviews. They aim to build on and offer introductory texts based on up-to-date knowledge and to help communicate this in an accessible way, so preparing the ground for future study and for encouraging good practice as you develop your social work career. Each book in the series is written by academics and practitioners who are passionate about social work and social services, and aim to instil that passion in others.

Anti-oppressive practice is central to social work. The people we work with are often excluded from or marginalised in our societies; they are made vulnerable by unspoken assumptions or actions by those in powerful positions. Social work walks the interstices between oppressed people and normative society. This can be an uncomfortable position for social workers and is not easy to do in a way that is positively transformative. This book introduces you to core knowledge that will help you to explore some of the ways you can adopt and grow anti-oppressive and transformative practices, and to inculcate the values underpinning social work throughout the world.

Professor Jonathan Parker

June 2020

Foreword

We can all think of a day, time or year where events or encounters have stayed with us. This year, 2020, will go down as one of those years in my book (as well as, I am sure, for many others) and in history books as being memorable but for the wrong reasons – notably, due to the global Covid-19 pandemic as well as the murders of Ahmaud Arbery and George Floyd in the USA.

On 23 February 2020, Ahmaud Arbery, who was out jogging in a neighbourhood, was gunned down in cold blood by a White father and son who thought he matched the description of a burglar who had recently operated in the area.

On 25 May 2020, George Floyd went into a grocery store in Minneapolis to purchase some items. Suspecting that he had paid with a counterfeit $20 note, the store owner called the police who arrived on the scene. Four officers attended the call-out and the lead officer proceeded to restrain the alleged suspect by pressing his knee into George's neck for nearly nine minutes, resulting in his death.

Although there are many others in the USA who have died at the hands of police brutality, in both cases described above, the presence of video evidence has meant that many people around the world watched the murder of these two Black men. The videos have been heartbreakingly painful to watch, yet research by DeGue et al. (2016) suggests that in the USA, Black people constitute 32 per cent of victims who died as a result of the use of lethal force by law enforcement, despite being significantly less likely to be armed. This disproportionality in outcomes for victims of police brutality reminds us about the racial and ethnic inequalities that exist in many parts of our world, and how systems produce and reproduce oppression of people from minority groups.

This was never how I imagined I would introduce this book on anti-oppressive practice in social work, yet I am aware that by not openly challenging these gruesome acts, I am not only undermining the spirit of the contents in this book, but also complicit in oppression. I am therefore delighted that the launch of this book will be in October 2020, which is Black History Month in the UK.

For the Arbery and Floyd families, their unimaginable pain may be bearable due to the outpouring of support from people around the world and the protests to denounce the systemic racism and oppression that resulted in the murder of these two Black men. Social workers have been actively involved in different parts of the world protesting and campaigning to denounce racism and racial oppression.

The officer who pressed his knee into George Floyd's neck is said to be the field training officer for one of the officers who attended the call with him. As a qualified practice educator and an academic with research interests in practice/field education, what is clear is that he was supposed to be modelling best practice, equipping his 'trainee' police officer with the knowledge and skills to work effectively with members of the public and ultimately make a judgement about the trainee's suitability for the role. Yet, when George Floyd gaspingly uttered the words, 'I can't breathe', not a single one of the four officers intervened. This complicity arising from refusing to intervene is an important lesson for us as social workers.

For social work students for whom this book is written, I would like you to reflect on the following statements as you engage with its contents. Imagine that

- you are a social worker in the school where George Floyd's children attend;
- you are the social worker responsible for the community where Ahmaud Arbery lives;
- you are a mental health social worker supporting the bereaved families of Covid-19.

How would you bring hope to the families and communities affected? Has your qualifying social work programme prepared you for the task? These are not easy questions to answer. However, I hope the strategies, tools and ideas presented in this book provide some direction.

Introduction

It gives me great pleasure to present *Anti-Oppressive Social Work Practice*. Writing this book has not been an easy task, not least for the fact that I emigrated to the United Arab Emirates during the writing of the book and had to cope with changes to lifestyle and routine while getting to grips with a different way of delivering the social work curriculum.

Anti-Oppressive Social Work Practice could not have been written at a more appropriate time when the world over, the oppression of people with minority status continues unabated. The outbreak and spread of coronavirus (COVID-19) resulted in the cancellation of events, closure of universities, colleges and schools in many parts of the world. The implementation and in some places the enforcing of social distancing has created what is being referred to as the 'new normal' in terms of how we undertake our work and how we engage with service users and each other. Social work is about social connections and during this pandemic, we have seen the creative ways in which social workers have tried to remain connected to their colleagues, service users and communities, while practising within safe guidelines recommended by the government.

If I am anxious about any of these changes to the 'new normal', it is that acts of oppression and discrimination may also become the 'new normal' because perpetrators can hide behind technology, online and distance processes to keep unsuspecting people out. Access to technology and the internet, and the space to work from home will reveal certain groups in our society as disproportionately disadvantaged. Microaggressions and covert oppression are more likely to go unnoticed during this period because non-verbal cues will be harder to interpret from behind the computer screen or while on the telephone. So, what is my message? My message is one of vigilance for all social workers. Speak out in a constructive way, reach out to understand and support colleagues, friends and service users who are being oppressed by systems, institutions or other people. These are not new requirements; they are core values that underpin our practice and we should not wait for people to lose their lives before we act. The service users we work with rely on us to help them challenge oppressive systems that can result in real change.

This book is about anti-oppressive practice in social work, a concept that can be difficult to understand and confusing to practise. My intention in writing this book is that it will provide social work students with knowledge, skills and values needed to become anti-oppressive in their approach to their peers, colleagues and service users. Although the book is written for social work students, it has wider application to students studying for the allied health professions.

As no single book can address the range of issues involved in becoming an anti-oppressive practitioner, this book serves as a contribution to this broad area of knowledge and practice.

Book structure

Series features

Achieving a social work degree

All chapters are mapped against the Professional Capabilities Framework (PCF) and the subject benchmark statements for social work. For each chapter, four PCF domains and relevant subject benchmark statements are identified.

Case studies and activities

In this book, I present case studies which, from experience, students find useful because they allow you to explore what you have learned and how it applies to real-world situations. There are many activities that also support your learning through more specific questions about concepts in relation to information discussed under specific chapters. The aim of the activities is to get you engaged in discussion with peers or in silent reflection.

Research summaries

Research summaries have been provided to offer you brief overviews of research, relevant to specific chapters. These are useful pieces of information that further help you to build on your existing knowledge while creating your own list of useful references.

Illustrations

Unusually, I have included a few illustrations in this book to help you understand some ideas which can be difficult to explain using only written text. Again, from experience, visual information can be easier to recall and, for the topics in this book, I believe that visual representation will be held in the memory longer than written text. My appreciation to Harry Venning for the artwork.

Further reading

At the end of each chapter, I have recommended two resources which will assist you to extend your knowledge on areas covered in the chapter.

Content

The book has been strategically divided into three main sections aimed at providing students with opportunities to develop the skills needed to work anti-oppressively.

Relevant theoretical concepts are broken down, and the use of case studies and activities should assist the student to reflect on and apply the knowledge they have gained.

Part One: Theories and concepts

Part One comprises five chapters that introduce theories and key concepts around oppression and anti-oppression, valuing diversity, power and powerlessness, and social justice. Some models for practice are proposed and examined.

Part Two: Anti-oppressive practice with individuals, groups and communities

Part Two of the book comprises seven chapters that address anti-oppressive practice with individuals, groups and communities. Gender, age, race, ethnicity, disability, faith and religion are discussed with intersectionality integrated throughout the chapters. The final chapter in Part Two focuses on marginalised groups, and the examples used are refugee and asylum-seeking populations.

Part Three: Developing anti-oppressive practice through learning

This final part of the book, which is also the shortest with three chapters, outlines how anti-oppressive practice can be achieved in practice learning (placements) and post-qualification through learning. Multi-agency working is addressed and strategies for disrupting oppressive practice in multi-agency teams outlined. In Chapter 13, I draw on the key findings from my doctoral research undertaken in 2015. It examines how practice learning settings can perpetuate oppression towards students and service users, and proposes ways in which placement settings can ensure anti-oppressive practice. Importantly, I have offered some suggestions about how students might appropriately challenge oppression during their placements.

Conclusion

I finish the book with some concluding thoughts, summarising the main ideas and dilemmas proposing areas for future research and consideration.

Part One

Theories and concepts

1

Understanding oppression

(Continued)

It will also introduce you to the following standards as set out in the Social Work Subject Benchmark Statement (2019):

5.3   Values and ethics
5.16   Skills in working with others

See Appendix 2 for a detailed description of these standards.

Introduction

Serving as the opening for this book, this chapter does more than introduce the concept of oppression. It provides an opportunity to discuss what is meant by oppression, and considers oppression within the context of social work education and practice. The social work profession has a longstanding interest in equality, fairness and social justice, and it is important that these continue to be at the forefront of our thinking and everyday practice. In this chapter, we will discuss a few definitions of oppression and utilise case studies and activities to stimulate thinking and ideas about anti-oppressive practice. The 'Ally model' of social justice (Gibson, 2014) will be presented as a useful way of supporting anti-oppressive practice, as well as the SHARP framework (Shaia, 2019) to understand oppression in the context of poverty and socioeconomic disadvantage. Experiencing disadvantage has the potential to stigmatise people, and social workers must work at changing social relationships which create stigma, social exclusion and ultimately oppression. These social relationships also include the social worker's own relationship with service users. Anti-oppression must start from an understanding of history and historical processes, which have resulted in ideology and practice that has oppressed groups, individuals and whole societies. Neoliberalism is an ideology that retains and maintains domination, exploitation and power arising from colonial relations and extending to present day. It is therefore not uncommon to see that *the exchange of capital takes precedence over social justice* (Giroux, 2003, p196), something that social work and you, as social workers, must challenge because it essentially means rationing resources at the expense of meeting the needs of service users.

Defining oppression

Locating a universally agreed definition of oppression is no mean feat. However, as Dalrymple and Burke (2006) suggest, one main ingredient in oppression is power and power relations, and for this reason Chapter 3 in this book has been dedicated to the discussion of power and powerlessness. They suggest that oppression is an emotive and complex term, and that any attempt to define oppression in simple terms is to undermine this complexity.

Thompson (2001, p34) defines oppression as

inhuman or degrading treatment of individuals or groups; hardship and injustice brought about by the dominance of one group over another; the negative and demeaning exercise of power. Oppression often involves disregarding the rights of an individual or group and is thus a denial of citizenship.

No one is immune to oppression. However, it is important to note that individual characteristics and social identities can provide privilege or result in disadvantage, which puts them in the category of the oppressor or oppressed. Inhumane or degrading treatment is treatment that dehumanises people. Dominelli (2008) suggests that focusing on one aspect of oppression may be helpful to an individual at a particular point in time, but will not eradicate oppression completely or from groups of people.

In this chapter, I invite you to consider your own understanding of oppression arising from your experiences, observations and engagement with relevant theoretical information and knowledge of oppression. Oppression is nothing to be proud of, yet it is a real experience for many. It is the systematic and sustained abuse and misuse of power over others. Oppression can silence, but it can also be the vehicle for rebellion and emancipation.

Barker (2003, pp306–7) defines oppression as:

*The **social act** of **placing severe restrictions** on an **individual, group or institution.** Typically, a government or political organization that is in power places these restrictions **formally or covertly** on oppressed groups so that **they may be exploited** and **less able to compete** with other social groups. The oppressed individual or **group is devalued, exploited and deprived of privileges by the individual or group which has more power** [my emphasis in bold type].*

This definition by Barker is significant for many reasons and speaks to my own understanding and experiences of being oppressed. First, the 'social act' emphasises the fact that oppression comes to life through human social interactions. Everyone is at risk of being oppressed, devalued or exploited – individuals, groups and institutions – and this is done through covert hidden restrictions or via bold formal controls of those wielding more power.

A second definition of oppression is that by Charlton (1998, p8) which states that

oppression occurs when individuals are systematically subjected to political, economic, cultural, or social degradation because they belong to a social group . . . results from structures of domination and subordination and, correspondingly, ideologies of superiority and inferiority.

Ideologies of superiority and inferiority rely on the use of power to operationalise. There are many practice behaviours which result in people feeling inferior. For example, a situation where a family who are experiencing poverty and socioeconomic disadvantage are told they have too many children and should have considered their financial situation before having 'all these children', is one in which the social worker or professional is abusing their power.

I will continually refer to various portions of the definition by Barker (2003) as a way of drawing your attention to its application to practice.

Activity 1.1

Reflect on your own views and experiences of oppression.

- What does oppression mean to you?
- How have you reached your understanding of oppression?

Write these down and share with a colleague.

It is my view that oppressive practice places barriers between social workers and service users, and that these barriers prevent full and meaningful engagement between a social worker and a service user. In its extreme form, the barrier of oppression not only keeps people out of mainstream life and situations, but also does not allow perpetrators of oppression to see the other side. The illustration below is my take on what oppression could feel like. It is a barrier to freedom and achieving potential; oppression also silences those on the 'wrong side' of the wall. This is a call for you, as social workers, to support the emancipation of those whose voices are muffled and whose visions for a better future are not visible because of where they are.

Figure 1.1 Oppression

Activity 1.2

- Now that you have looked at the illustration, what are some of the words and phrases that come to mind when you hear the word 'oppression'?

List these and consider what they mean to you.
    It would be helpful to undertake this activity with a friend or colleague and compare responses afterwards.

- Which phrases and words do you have in common and where were the differences?
- To what extent did your personal experiences factor into your discussion?

Lister (2008) argues that we need to understand our own experiences of oppression in order to fully appreciate the impact of oppression on others. This mirrors the view by Carniol (2005) who states that it is important to analyse our own social location prior to analysing the social location of others. He emphasises the importance of using our critical consciousness to deepen our awareness of our privilege. It is important that, as social workers, we understand and acknowledge our privilege as a first step towards becoming anti-oppressive practitioners.

Types of oppression

For oppression to exist there must be two categories of people – the oppressor and the oppressed. These terminologies have been brilliantly examined by Paulo Freire (1970) in his famous *Pedagogy of the Oppressed* in which he proposes that in order to work harmoniously, knowledge creation should be a shared endeavour in the context of education and the teacher–student relationship. In a similar vein, social workers should not claim to be the experts and must utilise a shared approach when working with service users to meet their needs. This working together has the potential to minimise oppression in the working relationship.

There are different forms of oppression and these are referred to as the four I's of oppression (Chinook Fund, 2010). They include ideological, institutional, interpersonal and internalised.

1. **Ideological** Any system of oppression begins with a view or idea that one group is better or more important than another group, or other groups of people. The group that feels superior often associates with positive labels such as strong, intelligent, competent, and it ascribes the 'other' group using negative labels such as weak, unintelligent, incompetent.
2. **Institutional** oppression usually comes from larger organisational acts or omissions which result in people with characteristics being over-represented or in receipt of negative or oppressive outcomes. For example, in the UK there are disproportionate numbers of Black minority ethnic people receiving mental health services when compared to other groups. The reasons offered for this are varied; however, institutional oppression is rarely accepted as the main reason.
3. **Interpersonal** oppression is the interaction between people where oppressive language, actions and insinuations are used.
4. **Internalised** oppression works when oppressed people come to believe in their own inferiority. Things reach this point when oppressed groups have nowhere to express their feelings, so keep these inside them (internalised) or direct their frustration towards others of the same group.

What can be done about oppression?

Having examined what oppression is, we turn our attention to what can be done about oppression and, specifically, what social workers can do to minimise or disrupt oppression in their work with service users. While many social workers understand the impact of oppression in theory, fewer are confident about how their own approach to service users and their families might be oppressive (Shaia, 2019).

Let us begin with a reminder of the global definition of social work:

Social work is a practice-based profession and an academic discipline that promotes social change and development, social cohesion, and the empowerment and liberation of people. Principles of social justice, human rights, collective responsibility and respect for diversities are central to social work. Underpinned by theories of social work, social sciences, humanities and indigenous knowledges, social work engages people and structures to address life challenges and enhance well-being.

(IFSW, 2014)

It is right that the international definition is given prominence in this first chapter, as it contains words and phrases that will be unpicked and examined further in this book. For this chapter, the *liberation of people* refers to freeing people from oppression, and this aligns with the aims of this chapter and the book. The answer to the question about what can be done about oppression is 'quite a lot'. However, this will depend on your understanding of oppression, and your ability and willingness to challenge individuals and structures that allow oppression to persist. Challenging individuals and structures will require you, as social workers, to use frameworks, a few of which will be discussed in this book.

According to Yee et al. (2015), a framework for anti-oppressive practice can only be viewed as a *practical tool to understand, critique and improve current practices of social work agencies, including exposing the rules, ideas and belief systems that have become embedded within institutional practices* (p476). The use of the word 'tool' is poignant, and in the context of anti-oppressive practice, it offers social workers a way of working. Essentially, a tool can be used or rejected dependent on who is using it. A tool will only be useful if it is used appropriately. One cannot observe a tool and expect it to work itself; consequently, there must be an active and proactive use of the tool for it to have the potential to yield the desired results. One of these tools is a social justice ally which, according to Griffin (1997, p76), *is a member of the agent group who rejects the dominant ideology and takes action against oppression out of a belief that eliminating oppression will benefit agents and targets.* An ally will be one who is critically self-reflective and continuously looking for ways to relate favourably with people from varying backgrounds and social locations. Becoming an ally should be viewed as a process and not a one-off event because of the multiple social identities that people have.

We will argue that by default, all social workers should be social justice allies. However, this could be viewed as somewhat simplistic because it is not always easy to take a social justice ally position when organisational and structural barriers exist in practice. It may be that, as social workers, you need to develop tools and strategies to disrupt oppressive policies, guidelines and working practices to ensure that they are adhering to Anderson and Middleton's (2011) recommendation of being a critical thinker and provocative. Becoming an ally begins with a motivation to protect friends, family members and colleagues from harm. The altruistic ally, according to Edwards (2006), is one who is motivated by guilt to act, whereas the ally for social justice is one who is pushed to act to address the root causes of systemic oppression, regardless of whether they personally know any 'victims' of oppression. Thus, whether you are an altruistic or social justice ally, the process of self-development by using one's privilege to support and advocate on behalf of others is welcome in social work practice.

Language and oppression

We will argue throughout this book that language perpetuates power and influences power relations which are used to maintain oppression. When women are shamed, mothers are blamed consciously or unconsciously through social worker reports; such language serves to perpetuate the oppression of women. Language can be gendered and can perpetuate different types of oppression. For example, there is growing concern about some of the 'professional' language used by social workers and arguments being made about the need to change this. 'Mother and baby groups' has been changed to 'parenting groups' to reflect the diversity of parents and to acknowledge the role of others in the parenting role. 'Looked after children' or 'children looked after' is being replaced by 'care experienced', and phrases such as 'contact time' are being ditched for a preferred and less oppressive 'family time'. This evidences the dynamic nature of language and the importance of regularly checking with service users how they wish to be addressed.

Continuing the theme of language and oppression, the COVID-19 pandemic is showing little sign of abating (June 2020), and in the UK and USA it has been found to be impacting disproportionately on Black minority ethnic people. The language used in some of the reporting is noteworthy and promotes the view that the reasons for disproportionality are down to individual biological and genetic make-up rather than structural inequalities. The scientific explanation for this is still to be verified; however, there are also concerns that nurses and health professionals from Black and/or other minority ethnic backgrounds are being pushed and made to take shifts on COVID-19 wards in hospitals (*Nursing Times*, 18 April 2020). In addition, in the UK and the USA, Black people are more likely to live in overcrowded neighbourhoods and have jobs which make it difficult to practise social distancing or self-isolation. Such structural and institutional oppression needs to be exposed for what it is and replaced with fairer, more equitable processes of work allocation among health professionals. This also reminds us of the fact that having good health is a privilege, which is often invisible to its bearers. Burke and Parker (2007) argue that the failure to recognise difference of all kinds enables a culture of exclusion and exclusionary behaviours, something that social workers must avoid if they are to work anti-oppressively.

Wilson and Beresford (2000) remind us of the importance of understanding oppression and anti-oppressive practice from the perspective of service users. To this end, Haworth (2019), writing about social work with single fathers in the UK, concluded that single fathers continue to be invisible in social work research and that gendered stereotypes accounted for them experiencing alienation in social work practice encounters. He argues that a more inclusive approach would be in line with social work values, ethics and anti-oppressive practice.

Teaching and learning anti-oppressive practice

In this section, we will examine the way in which anti-oppression is taught on social work programmes and highlight the tensions that can be present in the classroom during such important teaching. There is a shared responsibility between you, the learner, and the educator to consciously and meticulously engage in learning that will enhance your practice in the future. Such learning is expected to be painful, uncomfortable and unsettling; however, it should not be used as a reason not to engage in these discussions (Boler and Zembylas, 2003).

Anti-oppressive practice seeks to negate or minimise the influence of oppression and recognises that oppression does not operate in a vacuum. Social work programmes are, and rightly so, one of the main sites where knowledge and understanding of anti-oppressive practice is valued and taught. There is no clearly defined approach to teaching anti-oppressive practice content in social work programmes around the world; however, there are some principles that can and should permeate all social work programmes. Smith (2010) warns against tokenistic attempts to include marginalised voices in teaching. There is an abundance of literature about the experiences of faculty teaching curriculum on anti-oppression within social work programmes (Chand et al., 2002; Coxshall, 2020) and the research summary below explores this further.

Research Summary

Twenty-one years ago, Coleman et al. (1999), writing about their experiences of teaching anti-oppressive practice to students enrolled on the Diploma in Social Work (DipSW), concluded that there is a need to address not only the cognitive elements of learning, but also the emotional elements involved in teaching about oppression. They also challenged the intentional and unintentional hierarchical approach to teaching oppression in the classrooms and bemoaned the fact that some students were prone to dissociation. Importantly, the research highlighted the traumatic experiences for students and educators in relation to the content of anti-oppressive practice classes, as well as the discussions and debates these generated in the classroom. For example, a student who identified as lesbian attended a mental health class, only to be given a handout in which homosexuality was identified as a personality disorder. This experience is an example of oppression which is damaging and traumatic. This reminds us of Barker's (2003) reference to being devalued as an element of oppression, so, as social work students, you are encouraged to challenge such overt oppression in constructive ways.

Gibson (2014, p204) has argued that social work students' *emotional-affective feelings about groups that are different to their own* is a significant barrier to their learning about social justice and oppression. The teaching content, she argues, is almost always so personal that educators need to be aware of and prepared to address emotional needs, as well as conflicting values and beliefs. In so doing, the model requires social work educators themselves to create an atmosphere of safety by explaining thoroughly the rationale for the discrete areas of teaching. This will go some way to minimise anxiety and discomfort within the classroom, and should result in them being able to transfer this knowledge and behaviour to their various practice settings.

Coxshall (2020) outlines her use of critical race theory as a pedagogic tool and suggests that there are case studies in the recent British history (such as the Grenfell Tower disaster) that students can read about to raise their awareness of oppression, inequality and discrimination.

Activity 1.3

Think about a lecture or seminar you have attended on the topic of anti-oppressive practice.

- What was discussed?
- How would you evaluate:

    1. the teaching;
    2. your understanding of the issues discussed?

On your own or with a colleague, reflect on this and make some notes.

It is important that research which informs your learning is also grounded in anti-oppressive principles. For this reason, McLaughlin (2012) emphasises the need for social work researchers to undertake research that is non-oppressive and aims to emancipate, liberate and change the situations for people in oppressive circumstances. He also makes the case for research into indigenous perspectives, arguing that interventions such as Family Group Conferences that emerged through Maori practices in New Zealand have become invaluable in mainstream social work. In addition, organisations that employ social workers must themselves understand the nuances of oppression and be engaged in management practices that promote anti-oppressive practice.

'Doing' anti-oppressive practice

Having articulated what oppression is, and outlined the forms and types of oppression, we focus now on what anti-oppressive practice is and how social workers can engage with service users in an anti-oppressive way.

According to Dominelli (2002, p6), anti-oppression is:

A methodology focusing on both process and outcome, and a way of structuring relation-ships between individuals that aims to empower users by reducing the negative effects of hierarchy in their immediate interaction and the work they do.

This definition centralises the value of human relationships by empowering service users and minimising the impact of oppression, discrimination and injustice. In Chapter 4, we will examine various models and frameworks which social workers can use to support anti-oppressive practice.

Writing about anti-oppressive practice from the perspective of service users, Wilson and Beresford (2000) states that service users have been minimally involved in the development of anti-oppressive practice, which is both ironic and unfortunate as they are often claimed to be the beneficiaries of anti-oppressive practice. For this reason, it is important for the service user to explain their own reality and experiences, and for you to avoid stereotyped responses to oppressive practice. Instead, you should ensure that you work with each service user to understand their specific and unique experience of oppression.

As a social worker, if you do not know what your service user is entitled to, or you do not understand the legislation that underpins your practice with them, you will most likely be practising oppressively. Here again, we are reminded of the definition by Barker (2003) which refers to oppression as *placing severe restrictions* on individuals. By not knowing the services available to your service users, you are placing restrictions on the direction of the intervention and the scope of possibilities.

Intersectionality

Intersectionality, as a concept, is woven throughout this book as a central theme in understanding and achieving anti-oppressive practice. It is the way in which the inter-connections of social categories such as race, gender, age, ability and class create unique experiences of discrimination and oppression. It is one of the aims of this book to pro-mote the reality that people's lives are complex and their identities diverse. This results in situations where there is always more than one factor that can result in people being oppressed or discriminated against. Conversely, the powers inherent in some of these identities, such as gender, race, ethnicity, disability and sexuality, provide its holders with the power to oppress. If social workers are to gain any real understanding of oppression, then it is imperative that they view situations through the lens of intersectionality.

Activity 1.4

- Who is a 'good parent' and what does good parenting look like from your perspective?

Make a list of what these traits or values might be.

Guidance

You will notice that your views for this activity come from your own experience of being a parent or through being a child, or both. Indeed, you may have formed your views from reading research, legislation or engaging with relevant material. However these views are formed, it is important to note and understand where your oppressive views and ideas may be coming from. There is no single way or type of parenting, yet in many social work endeavours, parenting appears to relate mainly to mothers. This may be a view or approach perpetuated by men; however, it is not uncommon to see female social workers promoting this type of practice. Inequalities exist within households and within relationships; however, taking an oppressive and privileged stance, neglecting the diversity of opinions and views can be unproductive. According to Healy and Mulholland (2007), a social worker must always *try to represent yourself in your writing as thoughtful, objective, experienced and careful about what is being communicated.* This will not only make you accountable, but also evidences the thought and care with which you constructed your recording.

The SHARP framework

Shaia (2019) introduced the SHARP framework to assist social workers to make sense of oppression within the context of poverty and socioeconomic disadvantage in the USA. Arguing that social workers routinely respond to the outcomes of poverty and oppression with little attention to the oppression itself, Shaia proposes this framework to address this anomaly. She examines the term *context blindness* (p18) and makes the case for social workers to examine the contexts of people's lives. She uses an interesting analogy which we will unpick in this chapter. She likens a social worker who is *context blind* to a doctor who treats a patient with radiation poisoning without asking about the environment which caused the radiation poisoning. Such practice could result in the doctor prescribing treatment but sending the patient back to that very same poisonous environment which caused the initial illness. Social workers should endeavour to identify and intervene at the source of the service users' problem, and the SHARP framework enables us do this. There are five core components of this framework:

Structural oppression – This requires you, as the social worker, to interrogate what issues in the service user's ecosystem are impacting on their ability to succeed. These could be lack of access to employment, inadequate or poor housing, unavailability of affordable housing, inadequate access to healthcare.

Historical context – As a social worker, you should consider how a person's history has and is impacting on their current situation and need. For example, how has intergenerational poverty and disadvantage impacted on the service user? How might previous engagement with social workers impact on the service user's willingness or hesitation to engage at this point?

Analysis of role – What role will you, as the social worker have in this situation? The framework argues that there is no neutral position and that social workers are either part of the solution or part of the problem. This analysis of your role will further enable you to reflect on why you are in the role. When you avoid discussing and interrogating issues of oppression and discrimination, you are complicit in their oppression and doing little to disrupt it.

Reciprocity and mutuality – In the fourth component of the framework, you are required to consider what strengths the service user possesses, recognising these as valuable assets which they bring to the helping relationship and the quest for solutions.

Power – Finally, what can the service user do to change their situation and the impact of structural oppression? As a social worker, you should consider supporting the service user to examine how they might change their circumstances through activism or advocacy, recognising that what might seem like small simple actions can have a profound impact. The concept of power and powerlessness is so central to anti-oppressive practice that we have dedicated Chapter 3 to examining it in depth.

The SHARP framework is a useful tool for engaging in anti-oppressive social work as it helps to identify and support service users to counter what may be dominant stereotypical views about them. For minority groups, the SHARP framework employs a social justice perspective, enabling social workers to practise in a careful and systematic, values-informed way towards progress and sustainable change.

Case Study

Mel Johannson is a 44-year-old female on her own with two children after the death of her husband two years ago. She is registered disabled and was made redundant by her employer. She was paid a bulk sum of money which has run out, used mostly on the rent for her house. Her landlord has advised that he does not accept tenants receiving welfare benefits as Mel struggled to pay her rent for the previous month. Mel requests a meeting with her social worker to discuss her options. Social worker Peter insists that Mel remain in her current house as it would be difficult to attempt to find alternative housing. He undertakes a budgeting exercise with Mel and finds that Mel will have less than £200 to live on after all her outgoings. Mel's current property is adapted to meet her mobility needs, and importantly has a garden where her children, aged 11 and 13, often play. Peter is concerned that it will be difficult find a similar property which will meet the family's needs. One week later, Mel's landlord advises her of a planned increase in rent. This is the last straw and Mel becomes anxious and distressed.

Consider how you might use the SHARP framework discussed above to assist Mel.

* What do you consider to be the strengths and weaknesses of this framework?

Commentary

In this case study, you are reminded about how Mel's intersection of identities creates a unique experience for her and her children. Research by the Joseph Rowntree Foundation suggests that there is a growing group of people in the UK who experience poverty due to high housing rental costs. Mel's current unemployment leaves her in a situation where she is in receipt of benefits, much to the dissatisfaction of her landlord, who notifies Mel of a rent increase. You will need to carefully consider the link between housing, disability, single parenthood, unemployment and poverty.

Greater understanding is required of how poverty and employment traps vary by area and rent levels. The significance of the links between housing, poverty and material deprivation deserves greater recognition in policy.

Chapter summary

In this chapter, we have explored the main ideas around the term 'oppression' and have focused on the ways in which oppression manifests in the context of social work. We have argued in favour of the use of the SHARP framework (Shaia, 2019) and how ideas of intersectionality (Crenshaw, 1989) can aid your understanding of the nature and impact of oppression and oppressive practice on service users. Through activities, reflective questions and a case study, you have been encouraged to reflect critically on the forms of oppression and what can be done to minimise and disrupt its presence in social work interactions.

Further reading

Shaia, WE (2019) SHARP: a framework for addressing the contexts of poverty and oppression during service provision in the United States. *Journal of Social Work Values and Ethics*, 16(1): 16–26.

This article provides an excellent introduction to, and discussion of the SHARP framework, examining the context of poverty and oppression from a North American perspective. It has wide application to the UK context.

Wilson, A and Beresford, P (2000) Anti-oppressive practice: emancipation or appropriation? *British Journal of Social Work*, 30(5).

This article highlights the importance of involving service users equally in developing anti-oppressive practice and how the failure to involve services users in this work has detrimental effects on the whole concept.

2

Valuing diversity

(Continued)

It will also introduce you to the following standards as set out in the Social Work Subject Benchmark Statement (2019):

5.3   Values and ethics
5.16   Skills in working with others

See Appendix 2 for a detailed description of these standards.

Introduction

On a daily basis, social workers encounter varying problems, personalities and people, and should work with this variety effectively without prejudice, oppression or discrimination. This chapter aims to extend our understanding and appreciation of diversity in social work and share strategies to enhance our approach to diversity in a way that is empowering and sustainable. There will be a discussion about what diversity is, how it enriches the experience for social workers and service users, as well as how a lack of diversity is oppressive and discriminatory. Using case studies and reflective activities, you will be drawn to the concepts of 'othering' and 'difference'. The idea of cultural competence will be introduced in this chapter with the view to advancing our understanding of how social workers demonstrate and evidence that they value and celebrate diversity. We will outline the ways in which three concepts – exclusion, denial and suppression – work against the core idea of diversity. Suggestions about how social workers might expose, reject, avoid and disrupt such practice will be offered using the SHARE model (Maclean et al., 2018).

What is diversity?

In simple terms, diversity involves the range of human differences. Valuing diversity considers how we can accept and celebrate our differences because, as human beings, each of us has a story, made up of diverse experiences. Our backgrounds, experiences and life lessons make us unique, supporting the well-known phrase that no two people are ever the same. Diversity is a broad concept, often encompassing terms such as inclusion, multiculturalism and difference, to mention a few. Eradicating unlawful discrimination experienced by minority groups and individuals through legislation is a reminder that valuing diversity cannot be left to the good will and preferences of people. Social workers are uniquely placed to understand the need to challenge and disrupt structures, values and views that alienate, oppress, marginalise and exclude people for reasons of their diversity. For example, Black, Asian and minority ethnic people, women, people with mental health problems, Lesbian, Gay, Bisexual, Transgender, Queer and Intersex (LGBTQI) people, the elderly and people with disabilities often bear the brunt of social and structural inequalities. There is also diversity in the specialist areas of social work which practitioners work in. This type of diversity will be highlighted further in Chapter 14 where multi-agency working is discussed.

Why is diversity important?

Everywhere on this earth we find a condition of separateness among groups. People mate with their own kind. They eat, play, reside in homogenous clusters. They visit with their own kind and prefer to worship together. Much of this automatic cohesion is due to no more than convenience. There is no need to turn to out-groups for companionship. With plenty of people at hand to choose from, why create for ourselves the trouble of adjusting to new languages, new food, or to people of a different educational level? It requires less effort to deal with people who have similar presuppositions.

(Allport, 1954, p17)

In 1954, Allport would most certainly have been applauded for stating openly what perhaps the majority of people felt and believed at that time. In 2020, there is evidence that this view is still rife, however, with perhaps fewer people owning up to such thoughts because of public opinion and for fear of being exposed. The statement plays into the hands of people who support reduced cultural and ethnic diversity. As social workers, it may sometimes be obvious to us why diversity is important in the work we do; however, with recent global and national events, it is no longer safe to make such assumptions. Diversity is not a side issue to be addressed occasionally, nor is it one to be left to a few people in a team or organisation. It is something that applies to everyone and should be part of everything we do in practice. Neither we, as social workers, nor the people who use social care services fit into neat and distinct categories; consequently, we see the world from very different perspectives. In order to work effectively in a diverse setting, we need to understand ourselves, recognise our biases and work constructively to overcome them.

Social Work England (SWE) (2020) has identified in their Qualifying and Training Standards (4.3) the need to *ensure that the course is designed in accordance with equality, diversity and inclusion principles, and human rights and legislative frameworks.* This standard demonstrates further the importance of embedding equality and diversity principles from the outset in a trainee social worker's journey while they are in training and well into practice.

In addition, diversity is important because it is one of the nine overarching competences for social workers in the Professional Capabilities Framework for Social Workers in England. According to Parker and Crabtree (2018), the social work profession is preparing its practitioners to serve those who experience discrimination, marginalisation and oppression, and many of these service users will experience this discrimination and oppression on the grounds of many of the areas of diversity.

Social work students prepare to work in a variety of professional arenas and these diverse areas also require diverse skills, knowledge and expertise. Direct work with service users, policy development, management and research are some of these areas. There is a growing need for social work services for persons who have experienced natural or manmade disasters, from victims and survivors of bush fires (Australia), earthquakes (Haiti), hurricanes (USA) to survivors of mass shootings and terrorism (USA, New Zealand) and disasters such as the Grenfell Tower fire (UK). In relation to the Grenfell Tower tragedy in London, Ferguson and Lavalette (2017) suggest that while the building was located in the richest borough in the UK and one of the richest in the EU, the safety of residents appeared not be high on the agenda, as authorities ignored multiple warnings about the quality of material used during the refurbishment of the tower block. The question of class diversity is examined with an overwhelming suggestion that some lives appear to be more important than others. Social workers were called upon to work with survivors and their families, restoring homes and providing appropriate interventions. While reflecting on this, it is important to imagine the extent of diversity manifested in the nature of the families, the expressions of grief and resilience, as well as the varied coping strategies used by the survivors and their families. Working effectively across these differences using the appropriate affective (moods and feelings), cognitive and behavioural skills are required of social workers across the many different areas of practice.

Diversity in social work

The importance of diversity in social work has already been outlined, so we will now move on to examine how social work students and qualified practitioners might acknowledge diversity in practice learning and practice environments. It is important that, as a social work student, you are confronted with case studies that require you to consider intervention and responses from different perspectives.

Activity 2.1

In the table below, I have offered some dimensions of identity and diversity. I invite you to make a list of other dimensions you are aware of and consider the type of oppression and discrimination that bearers of these identity markers might experience.

Also consider which settings or places such oppression might be exacerbated and discuss these with a colleague.

Gender	Marital status
Age	Socioeconomic status
Spiritual beliefs	Sexual orientation
Ethnicity	Race
Parenting status	Employment status
Religious beliefs	Mental health status
Physical size/weight	Nationality

Your list

Guidance

No two people should have the same the list, so it would be interesting for you and your colleague to share what you have written. As students, you may also be regarded as 'traditional' (usually straight from sixth form, potentially younger) or non-traditional (usually older students or who may have been out of formal education for a while). As a traditional or non-traditional student, you may experience *peer othering* (Murtagh, 2019, p793), which can mean that you are unable to join colleagues after classes for social events because you have other commitments, or that you are not invited to an additional IT support session because colleagues feel that you already have that expertise as a result of being a younger 'traditional' student.

Self-reflection is extremely important for social workers at all levels of education and practice because it sets a foundation on which to build. It is important that you are guided not only to look for difference among populations, but also the similarities and intersectional identities that shape complex social inequalities.

Strategies for enhancing diversity

There are many ways to enhance and promote diversity in social work education and practice, and the list below is by no means exhaustive.

- Teach social work students to act as allies.
- Move beyond tokenism.
- Support social workers to use assessment and intervention tools that promote diversity. If these are believed to be Eurocentric, then adaptations and modifications should be made to ensure that these tools are fit for purpose. The ability to make appropriate adjustments to the intervention and/or the manner in which it is used and delivered is an important consideration when thinking about benefits to service users.
- Support students and practitioners to engage with ethically sound media and news outlets – you are what you read!
- Engage in reflective practice as a student and beyond.

Activity 2.2

- What are the first thoughts that come to mind when you hear the word 'diversity'?

Write down your thoughts and discuss with a colleague or reflect on your own.

Difference

Writing strongly about difference, Audre Lorde (1984) argued that there are very real differences between us in terms of race, age and sex. She argues that these differences between us are not separating us, but rather the separation comes from how we respond to those differences. Lorde suggests that we usually respond to differences in three main ways: 1) we ignore the differences; 2) if the differences are difficult to ignore, then we copy them if we think they are dominant, or 3) we destroy them if we believe they are subordinate. It is our refusal to recognise the value of these differences and to examine the distortions that result from our misnaming them and their effects upon human behaviour and expectation *that lead to differentiation* (Lorde, 1984, p115). This strong view by Lorde is a useful starting point in trying to understand that the refusal to recognise difference is what results in discrimination and oppression of people, leading to 'othering'.

Othering

'Othering' is a broadly inclusive conceptual framework that captures expressions of prejudice. According to Nilsen et al. (2017, p40), 'othering' can be conceptually defined as the manner in which social group dichotomies are represented in language via binary oppositions of 'us' and 'them'. Put simply, othering is to view and/or treat someone or a group of people with prejudice based on how different they are from ourselves. As a concept, othering reinforces positions of subordination and domination between and among people. Power relations are central to this concept because being defined as 'other' means not being viewed as 'us/we', nor indeed as ordinary members of society, but rather as outsiders.

Significant damage has been done over the years to unity and cohesion brought about largely by divisionist politics which has exacerbated feelings of 'otherness' in the UK and elsewhere (Meekosha, 2006). Lister (2008) confirms that othering produces and sustains an unhealthy 'them and us' situation. A few groups experiencing othering will be discussed in Chapter 12.

In order to work effectively with difference in social work, the idea of cultural competence has been promoted as a useful and effective skill to enhance outcomes for service users of diverse backgrounds and experiences.

Cultural competence

There are ongoing debates about the utility of the phrase 'competence', as some argue that you can never completely understand and be competent in service users' cultures because of its fluidity. Instead, writers have proposed alternative concepts – for example, cultural humility (Ortega and Coulborn Faller, 2011) and cultural friendliness (Englebrecht, 2006). In this book, I will use the term 'cultural competence' while acknowledging its ambiguity and limitations. One limitation is that the use of the word 'competence' suggests that social workers can get to a point where they become 'experts' in the cultures of service users. I see it as an ongoing process, a tool for anti-oppressive education and practice. I believe that social workers can use their skills, knowledge and expertise competently to work with families from different cultural backgrounds from themselves. Cultural competence requires models that are flexible and although the British Association of Social Workers (BASW) does not have codes of conduct specifically for cultural competence, the National Association of Social Workers (NASW) in the USA does (Laird and Tedam, 2019). In Chapter 12, we will look at the cultural web (Tedam, 2013) and outline how its flexibility allows it to be adapted anti-oppressively in ways to suit the service user, while demonstrating competence in engagement with the service user.

As a valued practice behaviour, cultural competence has received considerable attention in social work and in other allied professional practice discourses for well over two decades. Cultural competence is about having an awareness of one's own cultural identity and positive views about difference. It is the ability to continuously learn and build on the varying cultural and social differences of individual service users, families and groups that make up our communities. Culturally competent social work involves making respectful, reflective and reasoned choices, taking into consideration social and cultural influences on service users' beliefs and behaviours. In Chapter 11, we examine the importance of understanding the diversity of faiths and religious beliefs that social workers work with. Hodge (2013) discussed the importance of routinely including issues of spirituality and religion in assessment, and how this could contribute to the development of a comprehensive understanding of a client, especially in the area of health and mental ill health. It is widely accepted that faith traditions helped to lay the moral foundations of social work; our secular and diverse societies require social workers to demonstrate neutrality in that regard.

Campinha-Bacote (2002, p1) notes that *competence is a process, not an event; a journey, not a destination; dynamic, not static; and involves the paradox of knowing*. It is not unfair to expect to see development in social workers' cultural competence as they grow into sound reflective practitioners who view learning as cumulative and not as individual events. Cross et al. (1989) proposed a definition of cultural competence that emphasises three crucial issues for professionals who want to become culturally competent:

1. Cultural competence includes *knowledge, behaviour and attitudes*. They argue that knowledge in itself is insufficient, and that behaviours and attitudes are important. The knowledge for cultural competence can be understanding historical and structural inequalities and the impact of culture on service users' functioning. For social workers, the behaviour and attitudes referred to here can be said to be ones that promote anti-oppressive practice, avoiding the use of their own cultural beliefs and practices as a benchmark for assessing and intervening with others.
2. Cultural competence is a *skill* that needs to be expressed in behaviour as the capacity to function effectively in multicultural contexts. These skills include communication (speaking, listening, recording) and critical reflexive skills that enable social workers to understand and act on the role of power in the context of cross-cultural work.
3. Cultural competence goes beyond individual professional behaviours and includes *organisations and systemic applications*. A culturally incompetent system can undermine the work of culturally competent social workers where an organisation or team does not have systems in place to address the ever-growing numbers of, for example, Black, Asian and/ or other minority ethnic families who report their involvement with social workers as being of poor standard.

Fook (2012) has suggested that a person's identity is complex – for example, an individual from Africa may express their cultural identity through their belief structure, attire, diet or hairstyle. Even though this individual might identify as African, there are subcultures to which they might further identify with, all of which should be considered to ensure that service users are treated with respect and dignity. Tervalon and Murray-Garcia (1998) have suggested that in order to enhance cultural self-awareness, social workers should interact with diverse clients with the aim of learning from them. Assessments should openly identify forms of oppression, othering and discrimination, and should offer recommendations about how these might be minimised through social work intervention. They further propose some practice behaviours which are congruent with anti-oppressive practice – for example:

- Social workers should view themselves as learners and their service users as experts of their experiences, and should be able to communicate the importance of difference in shaping these experiences.
- Social workers should work to ensure they eliminate personal biases when working with diverse groups of people. This can be achieved through reflecting critically on theirs and colleagues' practice.
- Social workers should recognise when, how and why individual and structural barriers further oppress, alienate and diminish service users' power while maintaining privileged status for some.

Thomas (1995) has suggested that managers in particular have been seen to respond to diversity in a number of ways.

Exclusion – By exclusion, managers minimise diversity by keeping diverse people out or by not retaining them once they have been included. For example, if the selection criteria for a place on a social work programme in the UK requires 'UK' experience in the social care industry, then such a criterion would automatically exclude people who may have recently migrated to the UK, as well as people who may have no social care work experience. Another example of exclusion would be if the majority of students who withdraw, defer or are withdrawn all happen to belong to a specific group – for example, male students, students with disabilities, Asian, Black or other minority students.

Denial – In this context, denial refers to not seeing or not acknowledging the whole person. In social work practice, there is an emphasis on holistic assessments that require practitioners to assess and intervene with the 'whole person' in focus. To deny the race, ethnicity or any other dimension of diversity of a service user is to show disregard for their full identity. Therefore, it is important to avoid gender blind, colour blind and any other denial approaches. When a social worker claims not to see or be influenced by a service user's race, the Asian, Black or other minority service users' perspectives and experiences become invisible. This invisibility is both oppressive and discriminatory. It is important for social workers and educators who are promoting diversity and anti-oppressive practice to be open, honest and upfront about their commitment to social justice through confronting exclusion, denial and suppression of diversity.

Suppression – is about holding down or restricting someone, something or a feeling. In this context, diversity is suppressed when people with specific characteristics are expected to minimise their difference – for example, a social work student who is asked not to wear their traditional clothes to placement. What is being proposed here is that social workers should actively work against the exclusion, denial and suppression of diversity while at university and once qualified in practice.

Case Study

Ged is a female social worker in Romanshire county where the ethnic make-up is over 80 per cent White British. A 35-year-old female of Black British heritage, Janita, requires support to leave an abusive relationship. Ged informs her of a refuge in the area where she could go with her 5-year-old daughter who is of dual heritage. Janita asks Ged whether there are any 'Black' women in the refuge because that would 'really be good', to which Ged responds 'No, but you will be OK'.
   Reflect on the following questions on your own or with a colleague.

* How do you interpret Ged's response to Janita?
* How else could you have responded to Janita if you were the social worker?
* If you were Janita, how might you interpret Ged's response?

Commentary

It is important that you understand the wider issues around domestic abuse and the anxiety, fear and other feelings and emotions that may be at play in this case study. Janita is already feeling anxious about issues of race and ethnicity – hence her direct question about whether there are any Black women in the refuge. Ged's response is one that could be perceived as colour blind and this denial leaves Janita potentially invisible, which in itself is oppressive. Ged may be well-meaning and her comments are possibly borne out of her knowledge of the refuge; however, in the absence of outlining this to Janita, we have to err on the side of caution and interpret her response as dismissive and potentially oppressive.

Diversity pie chart

When I first came across this 'diversity pie chart' I was intrigued about how it was used often to provide a visual and powerful representation extent of diversity in each area or workplace setting. Such a pie chart would identify the breakdown of the population by age, gender or ethnicity, for example. In the activity to follow, you are encouraged to build an image of the diversity pie chart of your university, your course, team or organisation. You may begin to notice a pattern which will assist to understand diversity, and whether structural oppression and discrimination have contributed to what you see. It is also important that people do not simply become a part of the pie chart, but be given a meaningful piece of the pie by way of inclusion.

Activity 2.3

In this activity, consider the following statements and share or write down your views on the following statements.

- When I am being interviewed for a position I often ask about the diversity within the programme, team or organisation.
- I would never question or be concerned about lack of diversity at the top management level of my university, team or organisation.
- How do you demonstrate and evidence that you value diversity?
- Whose voices are heard and whose are not heard in your university, social work programme, team or organisation?

Guidance

Essentially, the aim of this activity is to gauge how comfortable you are in asking direct questions about diversity at your university, team or organisation. To become truly anti-oppressive, you should be able to ask these questions genuinely and insist on a response if a satisfactory one is not given. From the perspective of being a student, it is important to understand whether your programme team reflects the student diversity and, if not, what is being done about it.

The SHARE model

The SHARE model, developed for social work and beyond (Maclean et al., 2018), proposes a multisensory approach to a range of interventions. It has wide application to learning, education and assessing service users in practice. In this chapter we will see how the SHARE model can be applied to the area of valuing diversity at organisational and institutional levels. The acronym SHARE represents seeing, hearing, acting, reading and evaluation, which, when used in organisations, can be effective in exposing practices that work against enhancing and valuing diversity. Social workers should reflect on the following questions in relation to each of the elements of the model.

Seeing

- How much diversity do you see in your team or organisation?
- How visible is this diversity at all levels of your organisation?
- What are you not seeing – support groups for specific 'minorities'?

Hearing

Listening to the voices of those who may be different is an important step towards correcting any misconceptions that exist about particular areas of difference.

- At our universities and social work classrooms, how much of this is adhered to?
- What stories do you hear about other people in the team or organisation?
- What stereotypes, judgements and unconscious bias statements and comments are made about colleagues, service users and others?

Acting

- What can you do about this?
- What should you do about this?
- What have others done about this?
- Is it institutional, systemic?
- Are there policies, laws and guidelines you could refer to?

Reading

- What policies or practices are in place to celebrate diversity?
- What does research tell us about diverse work places?
- Can you 'read' between the lines'?

Evaluation

- Can you use the other elements of SHARE to reach an understanding of how diversity is positioned in your team or organisation?
- Do you know the underrepresented groups in your team/organisation and is there a strategy to change this?
- Are current strategies working?

Chapter summary

Valuing diversity is the cornerstone to working anti-oppressively. By taking a broader approach to how we view others, social workers are less likely to stereotype or discriminate against particular groups in society. Diversity enriches societies and social workers who value this will enhance their practice in this changing and increasingly diverse world. As a social worker, you must approach service users with sensitivity and respect, while strongly challenging oppressive practice aimed at devaluing difference and diversity.

Further reading

Laird, S and Tedam, P (2019) *Cultural Diversity in Child Protection: Cultural Competence in Practice.* London: Red Globe Press.

In this book, the authors offer accounts and analyses of Serious Case Reviews (SCRs) to support students and practitioners in understanding how to work across diversity.

Maclean, S, Finch, J and Tedam, P (2018) *SHARE: A New Model for Social Work*. Litchfield: Kirwin Maclean.

The model proposed in this book can be used to identify and disrupt oppression and discrimination in a variety of ways. For example, it can be used effectively for teaching and learning purposes, as well as to promote diversity and anti-oppressive practice.

3

Power and powerlessness

Achieving a Social Work Degree

This chapter will help you develop the following capabilities from the Professional Capabilities Framework (2018):

2. Values and ethics
5. Knowledge
6. Critical reflection and analysis
8. Contexts and organisations

See Appendix 1 for the Professional Capabilities Framework and the description of the 9 domains.

(Continued)

(Continued)

It will also introduce you to the following standards as set out in the Social Work Subject Benchmark Statement (2019):

5.6   The leadership, organisation and delivery of social work services
5.15   Communication skills

See Appendix 2 for a detailed description of these standards.

Introduction

This chapter will examine the concepts of power and powerlessness, both as generic concepts and specifically in relation to social work education and practice. Beginning with a discussion about what these terms mean, the chapter will address the relevance of this understanding for anti-oppressive social work, as well as the various types of power. I will propose the Power Flower (Arnold et al., 1991) as a useful tool for understanding, visualising and acknowledging our own power.

What is power?

In simple terms, 'power' refers to the possession of influence, authority or control over others or circumstances. This influence, authority or control can be used in ways that are consistent with social work values and social justice, or as a means of oppression.

There appear to be two main discourses around power – one discourse that sees power as a relational entity between and among two or more people. The second assumption is the one advocated by Foucault that sees power as operating within social relations at the most micro level. This suggests that power is not possessed but rather exercised; power is productive and repressive, and finally that power comes from the bottom up. These ideas of power by Foucault are useful in that they emphasise that power is not something that people own, but rather something that is created through social interactions and used in different settings and situations (Fook, 2012). Power is the ability to make decisions over and above other people.

Social work practitioners require clear and effective strategies of dealing with the consequences of power and not just the power itself. Smith (2010) argues that it is important to embed issues of power in practice and not to leave it as a secondary issue when the practitioner finds time in their busy schedule. In this regard Foucault (1998, p93) articulates the

omnipresence of power: not because it has the privilege of consolidating everything under its invincible unity, but because it is produced from one moment to the next, at every point, or rather in every relation from one point to another. Power is everywhere; not because it embraces everything, but because it comes from everywhere.

The importance of understanding power and powerlessness for social workers

Experienced social workers may have developed the skills to work within the context of power in their engagement with service users. They will be aware of the situations that call for the exercise of power and possibly control; however, research by Bundy-Fazioli et al. (2013) found that social workers were often hesitant about when and how to exercise their professional power in a manner that would not be experienced negatively by service users. Bar-On (2002) has argued that due to social work being a political activity, it is impossible for it to be devoid of power. It is therefore essential that social workers understand the effects of power at societal and structural levels. The media in the UK has tended to report social workers and social work interventions in a negative light, particularly in child safeguarding cases where reporting has implied the misuse or abuse of power.

Activity 3.1

Schraer (2016) reported in *Community Care* about a social worker who was struck off by the Health and Care Professions Council (HCPC) for abusing his power by way of using threatening language to foster carers and coercing them to provide a positive review to his employers about his engagement with them. Go to the *Community Care* website and read the article "'Recommend me or you'll never see your children again': Social worker struck off for abuse of power'. The article is also accessible via this link: www.communitycare.co.uk/2016/02/03/recommend-youll-never-see-children-social-worker-struck-abuse-power/ (accessed 7 June 2020).
   What are your thoughts about:

- The behaviour of the social worker?
- The action taken against the social worker?
- The impact on the service user?

Social workers therefore need to have an understanding of what aspects of their role makes them feel powerless, because it is only when they feel empowered that they will be able to effectively assist service users. Braye and Preston-Shoot (2003, p114) concluded that *if practitioners are not part of the solution, they must be part of the problem*. Consequently, an understanding of where they are positioned within the power structure is an important first step to acknowledging what needs to be done in terms of working effectively on the one hand and maintaining loyalty and effective management on the other.

Foucault (1998, p93) suggests that power is everywhere, not because it embraces everything, but because it comes from everywhere. In this regard, Smith (2008a) argues that there are a number of ways in which power might be conceptualised. These are:

- Representations of power.
- Modes of power.
- Sites of power.

Representations of power

Here, Smith (2008a) argues that there are four ways in which power may be conceptualised: the *potential of power, power as possession, power as process* and *power as product*. The *potential of power* refers to the capacity to individuals, groups and communities to realise change or influence outcomes, while the *power as possession* implies a much more fixed view. Child protection social workers, for example, utilise this as representing a social institution that possesses legal authority. *Power as process* recognises the power inherent in group processes. The Family Group Conference is an example of social work practice that uses a creative and collaborative approach to decision making with service users. Finally, *power as a product* recognises that it is an outcome of social relations. An example of this are 'experts by experience' groups who promote their own power by coming together as a group and self-advocating. These representations of power should be an important consideration for social workers who seek to work in non-oppressive ways with service users.

In addition to these representations of power, French and Raven (1959) offer a five-fold typology of power:

1. Referent power.
2. Expert power.
3. Reward power.
4. Coercive power.
5. Legitimate power.

Referent power

Referent power is a result of one person taking a liking to another and therefore holding on to whatever they say as the truth. Celebrities are good examples of this form of power which they use to sway the public into purchasing particular goods and services. We also see this type of power being used when, for example, celebrities endorse a particular cause, which subsequently encourages others to support that cause.

Expert power

Expert power is gained through demonstrating expertise, and professional and practice competency. Social workers, in adhering to the requirements and standards of the profession will exercise expert power in their work with children, families, groups and communities.

Reward power

This form of power usually, but not always, comes from the ability to get others to do something for you for a fee or some form of reward. In social work, this is usually effective in situations where people engage in behaviour change for some reward – for example, adherence to parenting advice in child welfare or child protection cases to prevent further professional involvement.

Coercive power

This form of power is the opposite of reward power mentioned above, and is more punitive and works with threats and punishment. Using the same example as in reward power are a family who are threatened with the removal of a child for non-compliance with required changes to their parenting.

Legitimate power

This form of power comes from a vested recognition of the title or position of a person, which ultimately promotes trust and respect. It can be argued, however, that this trust and respect is perhaps not directed at the person but rather at the position and title that they occupy. Social work is legitimised by being a profession requiring registration and criminal clearance to practise in many parts of the world.

Informational power

This final and sixth form of power was included much later by Raven (1965) and refers to power which is gained as a result of having information that is needed by others. As a social worker, you will have enormous amounts of power by virtue of what you know (information) and that is why it is important to share information with service users so that they can make informed decisions. Withholding relevant information from service users is not in their best interest and is oppressive.

Modes of power

Although a useful categorisation of power by French and Raven (1959), there appears to be three modes through which power is operationalised. These are *personal power*, *positional power* and *relational power*, which will be discussed below.

By *personal power*, Smith (2010) is referring to power at a level consistent with identity and the self which manifest in domination of the 'other'. The concept of 'otherness' is examined in more detail in Chapter 2; however, it is important that social workers understand the ways in which power works at a personal level.

The second way in which power is transmitted is through one's position. *Positional power* therefore is vested in people in specific roles, job titles and responsibilities. Teachers, social workers, nurses and many other professionals have power vested in their roles. During collaborative, multi-agency work, it is important that you, as a social worker, fully understands that each profession will be using their own positional power as a means to propose interventions for service users and their families. Where there is a clash or disagreement of this power, service users are likely to be disadvantaged through decision making that may not be in their best interests or which may reflect the power struggles among the professionals. This is similar to expert power by French and Raven (1959).

The third mode of power by Smith (2010) is *relational power*, which is dynamic and fluid rather than fixed. Here, power is understood to be shaped by human interactions that shape every changing relationship.

Sites of power

It is important for social workers to understand how service users, carers and family members respond to a lack of power. Equally, it is vital that social workers acknowledge and reflect on their own use of power when working with the different groups of service users. The uses and abuses of power permeate all professional practice spheres and, as Gardner (2008, p50) stated, *power can easily be abused, but exercising power is not intrinsically oppressive.*

When we share power with the families and communities we work with, this can result in positive outcomes for all involved. It is, however, important to remember that the misuse of power at all levels (individual, organisational and systems) can impact negatively on the experiences and outcomes for service users.

In the following section, I will discuss the uses and abuses of power in the areas of child safeguarding, mental health and homelessness.

Child safeguarding

Child protection interventions are undertaken within power-laden contexts right from the beginning of social workers' involvement and intervention, right through to closure and exit from the family. Consider the following telephone discussion between a social worker and a mother.

Case Study

Social worker	Good morning, am I speaking to Jane Cornell?
Mother	Yes, this is Jane.
Social worker	My name is Gracie Loom and I am a Senior Practitioner in the Ellet Child Protection Team.
Mother	Uh, hmmm.
Social worker	We have received concerns about the safety and welfare of your children and we would like to come out to see you today to discuss these concerns.

Mother	Today? I was planning to go and visit my father who is in a care home.
Social worker	Well, I think you should rearrange that visit to the care home. This is very important.
Mother	Sorry, who did you say shared their concerns?
Social worker	We received an anonymous call from a concerned member of the public. Is 2pm this afternoon a good time to come, since the children are on school holidays?
Mother	Um, yes.
Social worker	OK, see you later. Ensure all children are home when I arrive. I would like to see and speak to them as part of my investigation.
Mother	What investigation? You said it was a discussion.
Social worker	I would rather not discuss the details over the phone. I will explain when I visit. Goodbye.

Commentary

The telephone discussion above between a social worker and a parent gives us the opportunity to reflect on the power game being played out here. Whether consciously or unconsciously, the social worker sends the message that she holds the power of disclosure – she cannot tell the mother about who made the referral. She then tells her to cancel her appointment to see her father in a care home and then drops the term 'investigation' into the conversation, which immediately causes the mother to become anxious. Finally, the social worker cautions the mother to ensure that the children are home when she arrives. This phone discussion is only one example of power displayed at the start of involvement with a family in the area of child protection. The formal investigation, assessment and intervention stages will carry varying levels of use of power by social workers, other professionals and, in some instances, service users and families. For example, Bernard and Greenwood (2019) found that there was a power differential when working with issues of neglect with affluent families in England. This was because social workers were more likely to feel intimated by social class, educational and career achievements of the service users, thus causing them to incorrectly assess the parent–child circumstances. This indicates therefore that the issues of power are not only a concern that service users should have about social workers, but also one that social workers should consider carefully with regard to their service users.

Mental health

The age-old discourse around 'care' versus 'control' in mental health practice is one that centres around power, and the use of power by social workers and other mental health practitioners. Tew (2006) suggests that issues of power are intrinsically linked to mental ill health, from eating disorders where people feel a sense of power to control what they eat, to the area of recovery where people are left thinking about how they might reclaim spaces from which they may have previously been excluded – for example, at work, within the family or in a relationship. Writing about the use of power by nurses in the mental health field, Cutcliffe and Happell (2009) identify several areas where power is used over service users. These areas include the removal of personal freedom, forced administration of medication, deciding what will and will not be discussed, use of language, and deciding what might be in the client's best interest and what course of action should be taken. In social work, it is well known that service users from Black minority ethnic groups are overrepresented in mental health services in the UK (Jupp, 2005; Memon et al., 2016) and in the USA, African American men suffering from schizophrenia and bipolar disorder are more likely to be in prison than White men (Holden et al., 2012).

The area of mental health is one that illuminates issues of power in the practice and delivery of social work services. Anti-oppressive practice in mental health social work would require practitioners to develop and enhance their skills in reflection in order that they are better able to recognise and understand the sometimes *invisible manifestations of power* (Cutcliffe and Happell, 2009, p116) inherent in their practice. Consideration of anti-oppressive practice at the personal, cultural and societal levels will be critical.

Research by Memon et al. (2016) found that Black and minority ethnic service users felt that they were often *being talked down to* (p5) and did not have the power to make decisions about matters that were affecting them. One service user remarked: 'We have to follow what the professional said; if we do not want to follow what they are saying, it is our problem.' This feeling of helplessness was exacerbated when, as a consequence of being assertive, one service user was *taken off the list* and denied further services (p5).

Building trust and maintaining healthy, respectful relationships with mental health service users is a crucial first step towards enhancing anti-oppressive practice in the field of mental health. It is also important that social workers in this area understand what gives rise to inequitable service provision to specific minority groups, as well as identifying what steps they can take to enhance anti-oppressive practice.

Stigma is another area where professional social work intervention can support and advocate on anti-oppressive practice through anti-stigma work. A study by Arboleda-Flórez and Stuart (2012) found that stigmatisation is degrading and devalues people with mental ill health. Social workers need to be aware of how their own behaviours and attitudes could reproduce stigma within families and communities and should introduce robust anti-stigma practice that will not only be beneficial to service users, but will also enhance the image of the social work profession.

Homelessness

Sheikh and Teeman (2016) state that rough sleeping and homelessness will rise to 32 per cent by 2026 in the UK, and that homeless families and individuals are confronted with a few other challenges and difficult circumstances. In the area of homelessness, Johnsen et al. (2018) propose five types of power utilised as social control, which comprise *measures which seek to mould the behaviour of targeted individuals* (p1106). People who are homeless in the UK face multiple challenges and these challenges are exacerbated by other areas of their lives and functioning – for example, addictions and substance abuse, poverty, mental ill health, and many others. For this reason, social workers who may be working in this area are expected to reflect on their own biases and assumptions about homelessness and the causes.

- *Force* strips people of the right to choose and can lead to behaviour change because of the sanctions and punishments associated with non-compliance.
- *Coercion* overlaps with force because there is a threat that benefits will be removed if people are deemed to be non-compliant. The possibility of harsh penalties for non-compliance results in homeless people being left with no choice but to conform for fear of harsh penalties. In the UK, homeless people are said to be more likely to receive Designated Public Place Orders (DPPOs) for street drinking and other public disorders.
- *Bargaining* impacts behaviour by offering incentives usually of a positive nature to affect behaviour change. In order to bargain, one needs a certain degree of power.
- *Influence* involves gentle nudges or persuasion to affect change. Techniques of influencing do not include force or coercion, but rather the use of discussions and dialogue to alter people's beliefs, values and the desire to change.
- *Tolerance* is the final type of power in the area of homelessness, and this refers to the absence of any planned or defined coercion to conform. It involves an acceptance of the status quo. In relation to homeless service users, tolerance is about services being welcoming regardless of the circumstances of the homeless person.

Considering homelessness on a more global level, parts of the world that have experienced natural or man-made disasters will require their social workers to work within a different power context. Hurricane Katrina, which occurred in New Orleans in the USA in 2005, resulted in 49.6 per cent of citizens becoming homeless, with loss of lives and livelihood. The government response to this crisis was condemned by many, and social workers stepped in to work with many people who were left homeless by the hurricane.

Powerlessness

It is the case that many groups who consider themselves as minority groups experience a lack of power in relation to control and influence in their various spheres of life. Social workers also experience powerlessness when they are bound by institutional and organisational policies and guidelines which effectively prevent them from taking certain courses of action that they feel is beneficial to service users they are working with. Every one of us will feel powerless at some point in our lives, either at work or in the private spheres of our families. Recognising how it feels to be powerless is a useful experience for social workers.

Activity 3.2

Think about a situation or circumstance which left you feeling powerless.

- How did that make you feel?
- What did you do about it?

Discuss this with a colleague or reflect on your own.

We will now turn our attention to a practical tool to assist you in identifying how close you are to the dominant source of power.

The Power Flower was first introduced by Arnold and colleagues in 1991 and is presented as a daisy flower divided into 16 segments with each segment representing a category of our social identity. There are many different ways to use this activity, and the process described here is one that I have found to be effective. The flower has three layers. At the centre of the flower, write your name. The innermost layers show broad identity categories such as race, religion, sexuality and gender. The petals in the middle should contain your personal identities – for example, on the race petal, I would write 'Black'. Finally, the outermost petals represent social identities, which in our view experience privilege and power. Again, using the petal which represents race, I would write 'White'. We can already see that in my community, the dominant race is White and I am Black, placing me in the minority position in relation to race. The rationale behind this exercise is to enable you to visualise how close or distant you are from the dominant identities in our communities.

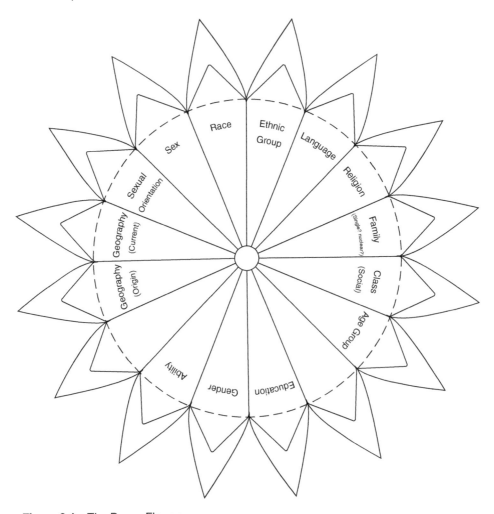

Figure 3.1 The Power Flower

Source: The Power Flower from Arnold et al., 1991. Used with permission of the publisher.

Activity 3.3

Complete the Power Flower above for

- yourself;
- your service users.

Discuss or reflect on what you see and propose strategies for working anti-oppressively with what you have discovered.

- Were there any surprises or confirmations about the power and privilege of yourself and others?

Privilege, authority and influence in social work

Privilege is something that a person is either born into or acquires during the course of their life which gives them power over others. There is a close relationship between privilege and authority. Privilege has been described as invisible to people who have it because they come to normalise it. People who are privileged are often the ones with the power and authority in society. The BASW Code of Ethics requires social workers to use authority in accordance with human rights principles. This requires social workers' understanding of the authority inherent in their role and ensures that this authority is used in a responsible, accountable and respectful manner at all times (BASW, 2019, online).

As a profession committed to social justice, it is imperative that we interrogate the ways in which social work is positioned to challenge unearned privilege and the misuse of authority which are in contradiction to anti-oppressive practice principles.

According to Fook (2012, p55),

People do not fit easily into 'powerful' or 'powerless' groupings, sometimes having membership of both at the same time. The very same experience can be empowering for some and disempowering for others.

Activity 3.4

- In what situations and contexts are you most aware of your own privilege?
- In what situations and contexts are you most aware of your own power?

Chapter summary

The social work profession challenges the exercise of power which is oppressive, discriminatory and damaging. Acknowledging and understanding the impact of their own informal and coercive power is crucial, as is recognising how their teams and organisations may perpetuate the oppressive use of power through their policies and guidelines. It remains unclear about the extent to which social work qualifying programmes prepare students for working constructively with power and understanding the role of power in their daily interactions with service users and their families. It may well be that, as a student, you fail to understand how power is exercised in practice, or you may be unaware of the power that your role as a social worker gives you.

In this chapter, I have tried to demonstrate how complex and contested the concept of power is, and the different ways in which it manifests in social work interventions and interactions. Power is not a commodity to be given away; hence, when social workers talk about empowering service users, it is not 'giving' power, but rather it is supporting service users to gain control of their lives and the decisions affecting them. Within the context of anti-oppressive practice, power will continue to be an ever-present consideration for social work students and practitioners alike.

Further reading

Bundy-Fazioli, K, Quijano, LM and Bubar, R (2013) Graduate students' perceptions of professional power in social work practice. *Journal of Social Work Education*, 49(1): 108–21.

In this article the authors assert that it is important to understand the power that underpins the helper–helpee relationship, and that social work students need to better understand the uses and abuses of power in their practice.

Tew, J (2006) Understanding power and powerlessness: towards a framework for emancipatory practice in social work. *Journal of Social Work*, 6(1): 35–51.

This article provides information for social workers to map out and work with issues of power and powerlessness more effectively in their everyday practice.

4

Models of anti-oppressive practice

Achieving a Social Work Degree

This chapter will help you develop the following capabilities from the Professional Capabilities Framework (2018):

2.   Values and ethics
5.   Knowledge
7.   Skills and intervention
9.   Professional leadership

See Appendix 1 for the Professional Capabilities Framework Fan and a description of the 9 domains.

(Continued)

(Continued)

It will also introduce you to the following standards as set by the Social Work Subject Benchmark Statement (2019):

5.3   Values and ethics
5.16   Skills in working with others

See Appendix 2 for a detailed description of these standards.

Introduction

In earlier chapters, we have examined the concepts of oppression, diversity, power and powerlessness, and located them within the context of anti-oppressive social work practice. One of the aims of this chapter is to recommend anti-oppressive models and practice frameworks, and guide you in your use during intervention with service users. The persistence of inequality and social injustice in our communities means that, as social workers, we should be relentless in our efforts to disrupt practices, cultures and structures that perpetuate oppression which results in inequality. As anti-oppressive practice is central to ethical social work practice (Burke and Parker, 2007), social workers are open to discussions about divisions in society and the impact on people who become service users. In particular, social workers are concerned with helping to change oppressive structures and influence more inclusive and supportive structures for service users.

Research Summary

Oppression is both a process and an outcome, which means that actions and interactions of people leads them to hold increased power, which perpetuates oppression, which in turn is a result of that process. Collins and Wilkie (2010) argue that there are controversies about how anti-oppression works in practice. This view is supported by Jeffery (2007) who suggests that anti-oppressive practice is an elusive concept because it is more easily articulated theoretically yet difficult to practise. Challenging and confronting oppression is central to anti-oppressive practice and, according to Collins and Wilkie (2010), empowerment and partnership with service users are needed to demonstrate anti-oppressive practice.

As social workers, we must be cautious against promoting the idea of a hierarchy of oppressions, as all forms of oppression are dangerous and dehumanising. Instead, the idea of intersectionality, which has already been discussed earlier sets the tone for understanding the importance of multiple identities and the implications of this understanding for social workers. This is why this book attempts to address the many and interrelated aspects of human identity and the asymmetric power relations that give rise to oppression and oppressive practices. The aim of this chapter, therefore, is to offer some ideas about how to 'do' anti-oppressive practice and to move it from the theoretical to the practical.

Models for anti-oppressive practice

Models in social work assist in explaining and using theories. It is important that you know about and have a range of models for working in different circumstances, including with service users experiencing a range of difficulties.

To practise anti-oppressively as a social worker, you must understand your contribution to oppression and oppressive practice. It is this understanding that will enable you to create reflective spaces to give time for sense making in this important area. When people stand to benefit from oppression, they are unable to see beyond their personal gains, and this is why you must socially locate yourself and not claim neutrality (Cowie, 2010).

Recommended models for enhancing anti-oppressive practice

In this section, we will examine three existing models that can be used to enhance anti-oppressive practice. They are the PCS model (Thompson, 1997), Social GGRRAAACCEEESSS (Burnham, 2012) and the MANDELA model (Tedam, 2012). I will also introduce the 4D2P practice framework as a means of not only identifying where oppression has occurred, but also working proactively to disrupt it, thus beginning the real work of changing attitudes in relation to oppression, power and privilege. Using case studies and activities, this chapter will support you in the application of the models and framework to contemporary social work practice.

PCS model

This model by Professor Neil Thompson (1997) is a significant and well-known contribution to the area of anti-discriminatory practice in social work and beyond. In recognising that discrimination is not just an individual issue, the PCS examines discrimination within cultural and social contexts as well. This tripartite model encourages social workers to examine and understand discrimination from the P (personal), C (cultural) and S (structural) perspectives.

Personal level (P)

At the personal level (P), you will need to understand yourself, your views, opinions, feelings, attitudes and actions. You must reflect upon where these ideas have come from, and how family and home environments may have shaped your views and perspectives. It is also important for you, as the social worker, to consider how stigma might operate at this level.

Cultural level (C)

The cultural level (C) requires you to examine those shared ways of thinking, seeing and doing (Thompson, 1997, p20) and how these are shaped through language. The cultural level requires you to explore those cultural influences that are shared by many others about what is considered normal – for example, those views which may impact on the effective participation of service users. Some cultural values may perpetuate ideas about what is right and wrong, good and bad. While this is not necessarily problematic, as a social worker, your role should be to explore these views because they are value judgements that emerge from somewhere and, if left unchallenged, these shared practices become a norm, and consequently acceptable and accepted.

Structural level (S)

Thompson views this level as one where oppression and discrimination are institutionalised. At this level, the agents of power are usually the managers, executives and CEOs who can be difficult to challenge because of hierarchy.

Activity 4.1

You are on placement and a colleague invites you to come along to observe her practice. The team received a referral today concerning three children from a Traveller community. You agree that this would be a useful learning opportunity as you have never worked with anyone from this community before; however, there are many stereotypes about Traveller families and you have picked up some of these from watching TV programmes.

Outline how you might apply the PCS in this case. In particular, consider the following and discuss these with another student colleague.

P   What are your initial feelings?
C   What are the stereotypes held by other people about Travelling communities?
S   What are the structural considerations and how might these reinforce the personal and cultural?

Understanding your own prejudices will go some way towards you being able to empathise with the Traveller family and their possible anxiety about using social care services. Thompson uses circles purposely to explain that personal attitudes are embedded within the cultural landscape of norms and group rules, which are further located within the wider structural levels controlled by those with power and authority. As social work students, this PCS model is a powerful analytical tool to be used to identify and explore discrimination. It should be used to disrupt oppression and oppressive practice.

Social GGRRAAACCEEESSS

Developed by Burnham (2012) GGRRAAACCEEESSS is an acronym which stands for Gender, Geography, Race, Religion, Age, Abilities, Appearance, Culture, Class, Ethnicity, Education, Employment, Sexuality, Sexual Orientation and Spirituality. This model approaches difference and diversity from a social perspective, recognising that structural forces that create oppression need to be addressed and explored when working with individuals, families and groups in ways that promote social justice while mitigating against discrimination and oppression. The framework seeks to *assist practitioners in being mindful about a range of differences, and generating a desire to extend their practice beyond their current abilities* (Burnham et al., 2008, p530). We all have visible and invisible aspects of our identity which will impact on us in different ways and at different times in our lives. These elements of our identity influence the way we relate to others around us. In the context of social work, it is important to identify our own implicit biases and use our skills, knowledge and values to creatively and anti-oppressively respond to service users who are different from ourselves. Activity 4.2 invites students to use the model by themselves or with a colleague. Examine each component of the model in relation to your own identity.

Activity 4.2

Either on your own or with a colleague, complete a social GGRRAAACCEEESSS profile of yourself and reflect on what you have written.

* When was the last time you considered your identity to this extent?
* What do you think has changed and what has not?
* Were there any difficult or uncomfortable elements of this framework? If so, what were they?
* Are there any other aspects of identity you feel is missing and could add?

Guidance

From my personal experience and previous research findings (Tedam, 2014), I would include another 'A' to GGRRAAACCEEESSS indicating Accent, as this opens up another layer of discussion and acknowledgement. According to Harrison (2012), the value of language as linguistic and cultural capital is an important one because it facilitates economic and social mobility. In the context of anti-oppressive practice, we should be concerned about how accents, speech, tone, pitch and similar markers of identity can result in otherness and disadvantage. Lindemann (2002) articulates quite clearly that in any dialogue there is a joint responsibility on both the speaker and the listener to ensure that communication is not unclear or misunderstood, and that when foreign accents are criticised as difficult to understand, the burden of responsibility is located firmly with the speaker, contrary to anti-oppressive practice principles.

Case Study

Clive Misontwa is a 16-year-old boy who migrated to Scotland with his mother and stepfather two years ago. Clive's birth father died when Clive was 10 years old and his mother remarried Karl a year later. Clive's mother, Mrs Murani, is 40 years old and employed part-time as a housekeeper/cleaner in a local hotel. Originally from Zambia, the family moved to Edinburgh where Mrs Murani is studying for a PhD in Music at the local university. Clive has two half-sisters (Claudette who is 5 and Reena who is 4 years old). The family live in a two-bedroom flat and Clive has a camp bed in the living room while his two sisters share a room.

Recently, the Head of the sixth form at Clive's school asks to meet with his parents due to his increasingly disruptive behaviour in school. Of particular concern was a report from the work experience supervisor that Clive was asked to leave his work experience placement for falling asleep on the job and causing loss of money to the business due to incorrect sales at the till. Clive is alleged to have become involved in a verbal exchange with a work colleague and exhibited some violence, which resulted in the termination of his work experience.

On his return to school, Clive continued to display challenging behaviour and is now at risk of exclusion. You speak to Clive, advising him that you will need to involve his parents in a future meeting. Clive informs you that you only need to invite his mother and insists his 'step-father', Karl, is not welcome at this meeting.

- You are a student social worker on your first placement in Clive's sixth form. How might you approach a discussion with Clive?
- What are some of the areas you would need to discuss with the family?
- How and where might oppressive practice emerge in this case?

Commentary

Clive is 16 years old, so as a social worker you need to understand what is likely to be behind the behaviours he is displaying. A review of your human development notes may be useful. However, you should not make any assumptions and should seek to discover who Clive is and what his concerns are. It is important not to make assumptions based on what you know or have heard about 'Black boys', as this is likely to prejudice your decisions and be oppressive. There is a discussion to be had about family dynamics, the impact of Clive sleeping on a camp bed in the living room and his half-sisters having a bedroom to themselves. Additionally, his mother works part-time and is a student, but there is no information about what Karl does, if anything.

Before you address the reason for your involvement (Clive's risk of exclusion from school), you need to enable Clive to discuss his concerns and explain how things developed thus far.

The MANDELA model

The MANDELA model, which was developed by Tedam (2012), focuses on developing, building and maintaining relationships between and among people (Tedam and Zuckowski, 2014). The development of this model became necessary to address what appeared to be relationship difficulties between Black and minority ethnic social work students and their practice educators (PEs), often resulting in them failing practice placements at worst or experiencing delays in progression. Research evidence bore out these conclusions not only in the UK (Bartoli et al., 2008), but also in Canada (Razack, 2001) and Australia (Gair et al., 2014). Further investigation into this situation revealed that these difficulties occurred more frequently involving Black students of African origin. The reasons for this are varied and complex. However, findings from the afore-mentioned research concluded that there was the need for supervisory relationships between Black and minority ethnic students and their PEs to be anti-oppressive, anti-racist and person-centred. In this chapter, I have adapted the MANDELA model to direct social work practice and emphasised the ways in which the model can assist practitioners to develop and maintain good working relationships with service users. In this regard, Coulshed (1991, p2) expressed the importance of good working relation-ships as follows:

> *People do not come to social work looking for a relationship and while it is no substitute for practical support, nevertheless social workers are one of the few groups who recognize the value of relating to others in a way which recognizes their experiences as fundamental to understanding and action.*

Interactions between service users and social workers can unearth many challenges, not least how to be open and honest with service users without creating a hostile environ-ment, as hostility can easily become an avenue for oppressive practice. Thus, in order to enhance meaningful, non-oppressive partnerships between service users and social workers, the use of the MANDELA model is recommended.

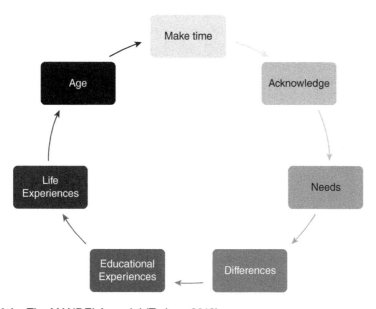

Figure 4.1   The MANDELA model (Tedam, 2012)

The model is presented as a cycle, which means that elements may be revisited as many times as appropriate during an interaction or in the context of relationship building. The cyclical nature gives it flexibility and also means that any changes that occur in a person's lifetime can be updated and included in the next round of its use. As a tool for anti-oppressive practice, the MANDELA model has the potential to draw out sensitive and important discussions which enable social workers to enter into the lives of service users in a measured and respectful way. It is a model that places power in the hands of service users by enabling and encouraging them to lead discussions meaningfully, enhance cooperation and minimise the potential for oppressive practice. Social workers do not practise in a vacuum, and it is clear that they work in systems that are often underpinned by different sets of beliefs that require us to begin from a position of 'not knowing'. The model begins by urging practitioners to make time for their service users. Being person-centred, the model supports the view that service users will be different in the lengths of time required for visits, discussion, assessment and interventions.

Make time

In the fast and busy world of social work, practitioners can struggle to find sufficient time to get to know service users and to fully understand their needs. The starting point of this model specifies the importance of time. The process of relationship building is one that takes time if it is to be done effectively. That said, there are situations where the service user is compelled to see the social worker and, in such situations, relationship building can be problematic. Such service users have been referred to as *involuntary* (Trotter, 2015) or *resistant* (Trevithick, 2000). Assessments and other activities identified as part of the intervention should not be rushed. A rushed assessment may not enable practitioners to gain all the necessary information to make an informed analysis and reach fair and informed recommendations. Such practice invariably results in oppressive practice, which is neither welcome nor ethical in social work practice. Making time enables social workers to accept their own lack of knowledge about a service user, while seeking to learn about their circumstances, wishes and ideas for intervention. If you are faced with a practice educator or manager who asks you how much time you need for an assessment, I would expect that you are not able to put a timescale, but rather to say that it is dependent on the nature and type of concerns raised. However, I must add a word of caution here, because it does not give you unlimited time, but instead it offers you the opportunity to consider the service user's needs fairly.

Acknowledge needs

The model then requires social workers to acknowledge the needs of service users. Understanding service users' needs is at the very heart of social work, and social workers should possess the skills required not only to hear from the service users about their daily and perhaps obvious needs in terms of services, but also to identify any unmet needs. A report by Ipsos Mori (2017) highlighted extensive areas of unmet needs in relation to older people's social care. The links between unmet need and well-being have been established in research and provide an interesting basis upon which to utilise the MANDELA model as a tool to uncover what may be the hidden or previously undisclosed needs of people who use social care services.

Some areas to consider here are the service user's personal needs in terms of childcare and other caring responsibilities, as this should guide your choice of meeting dates and times. The service user's spirituality and faith needs should be explored so you can consider, for example, whether to visit on Fridays if they are a practising Muslim family. If you are a male social worker, you need to establish whether it is acceptable to meet with the mother or other female service users on their own.

Differences

Here, the concern is with the range and variety of differences in life chances and social inequalities arising from individual (or group) characteristics. Differences exist across all facets of our social lives, and at the centre of this book is how to work in a non-oppressive way with service users and their families. Cultural and other beliefs and attitudes configure the meanings we attribute to an event or events. Although understanding and valuing differences are key in social work interactions, social workers need to be careful about not turning this discussion into one that implies 'othering'. Differences in gender, race, religion, ethnicity, faith sexuality, class, ability and age should be discussed here. Some of the previously discussed concepts (diversity, othering), for example, can be examined here.

Educational experiences

The role and place of education and educational experience is a useful area for exploration and discussion with service users. It is important here not to make any assumptions about the literacy or otherwise of service users. Social workers should clarify with service users their preferred mode and language of communication. It is important for social workers not to equate English language proficiency with level of education, as the two are not the same. A service user for whom English is an additional language may be well educated and fluent in other languages. Graddol (2004) estimates that by 2050, native speakers of English will be approximately 5 per cent of the global population, and this is important information for social workers. It is also important to confirm with service users so you are better placed to provide them with interpreting support, if needed.

Life experiences

A service user's life experiences, like our own, will be varied and diverse. For example, experiences of poverty, homelessness, bereavement, loss, abuse, migration, divorce, separation, trauma, ill health, wealth, war, relocation, marriage, discrimination, are all life experiences that will have shaped the service user and their family. Enabling the service user to discuss these in whichever format, in detail or summary, makes it possible for them to consider how these experiences have influenced or impacted on their current situation. This element of the model allows the practitioner to critically consider the family's socioeconomic, political, social and wider environmental conditions, and the ways in which these have impacted on their previous or current well-being and functioning. In addition, this discussion will assist the social worker to identify the appropriate intervention and their approach to working with the service user. This element of the model reinforces the fact that you cannot rush your meetings and discussions with service users.

Age

Social workers will engage with service users of varying ages, so this is an important area to understand and acknowledge. In the UK, age is a protected characteristic under the Equality Act 2010 (HMSO, online) and social workers cannot discriminate against any service user because of their age. Social workers have reported the difficulties that can arise because they are younger (or appear to be younger) than the service user. In particular, Holmström (2012), writing about age and social work, found that overall, younger people faced discrimination as student social workers and as students on placement from qualified social workers and staff. Some 3 per cent of service users discriminated against younger students. Chapter 7 is devoted to the discussion of age-related discrimination and oppression, and some of the ideas proposed in that chapter can be used here. You should consider whether or not your service user is older, younger or similar age to you. How does that influence you and the dynamics of the relationship? For example, in some communities and cultures, older people are not challenged and their views are always agreed with as a sign of deference. How might age impact on the relationship? The following case study gives you an opportunity to apply the MANDELA model.

Case Study

Dean is a 68-year-old man of mixed heritage who was married to Mildred until her death ten years ago. The wider family, including his four children, have had very little contact with Dean since he disclosed to his family that his is gay and moved in with his new partner Jay (62 years) over three years ago. In particular, Dean's oldest son, Richard, who is a Church minister, has found his father's sexuality difficult to understand. Jay has recently been diagnosed with early onset dementia and Dean is not coping with Jay's diagnosis. You are a social worker in the voluntary sector and the couple are referred to your organisation for a range of supports. Your organisation has just launched their domiciliary care service and you are keen to discuss this option with Jay and Dean.

- Using the MANDELA model, consider how you might structure your meeting/assessment interview with Jay and Dean.
- Which elements of the model might be most useful and why?

Commentary

There are many ways to use the MANDELA model in this case scenario and the first one must always be to give the couple (Jay and Dean) sufficient time to speak, and to share their concerns, feelings and emotions. As a social worker, you cannot and should not rush this stage. While it is good practice to specify timings for service users, the social worker in making time for Jay and Dean should be flexible, enabling them to use as much time as they need to discuss their concerns with you. In a situation where this cannot be done in one visit, you should offer them another appointment.

Acknowledging their needs requires you to consider their individual needs, as well as their shared needs. For example, Jay is the one with the diagnosis and will have different needs from Dean. Dean appears to be the one struggling at the time of the referral, so it is important that you consider his needs as well. He is estranged from his children, because after his wife died ten years ago, he 'came out' to his family. It is reasonable to assume that isolation and loneliness will be a contributory factor in the current situation. However, it is for you, as the social worker, to establish that through interview and interaction.

In this situation, I would move to the Age element of the model because of the situation in hand, which is 'early onset dementia', and examine how this diagnosis impacts on some people earlier than others.

The area of difference will require the social worker to examine the issue of diversity. Dean is said to be of mixed heritage. What does that mean and how does it affect the current situation (positively or negatively)? Are there any differences in faith and beliefs that might impact on the couple's current situation? Are there differences in the way in which early onset dementia is understood by the people involved and their families? Cox (2007) reminds us that culture shapes our responses to dementia and other cognitive impairments, and also influences the roles that caregivers will have. It is important that difference is not merely tolerated (Lorde, 1984), but rather acknowledged and celebrated.

What does Dean know about early onset dementia? How much does Jay understand and know about his diagnosis? What level of education do they have and what are the gaps in their knowledge about early onset dementia? Are they able to read and understand any information and leaflets given to them to read?

The 4 Ds and 2 Ps of anti-oppressive practice

In an attempt to contribute new ideas about how we might understand oppression and work anti-oppressively in social work, I have devised a practice framework called the 4 Ds and 2 Ps of anti-oppressive practice (4D2P framework). The aim of this practice framework is to assist social workers to understand the steps through which they can evaluate their own non-oppressive practice on an ongoing basis. According to Stanley (2017), practice frameworks can promote effective professional practice in social work, so it is important that your use of this framework is discussed during supervision with your supervisor or manager.

Features of the framework

One of the strengths of this framework is its proactive and challenging approach to anti-oppressive practice. The 4D2P is aligned with the broad social work values and ethical principles of human rights, social justice and professional identity. For example:

- Respecting the service user's right to self-determination.
- Upholding and promoting human dignity and well-being.
- Identifying and developing strengths.
- Challenging unjust policies and practices.
- Recognising diversity.
- Being prepared to whistleblow.

(BASW, online)

In addition to social work values, the 4D2P framework supports all nine domains of the professional capabilities framework and the six main professional standards by Social Work England (SWE, 2020). In the next section, we will see how these features align with the steps in the framework.

Stages of the framework

The 4D2P framework is an overarching framework designed to achieve anti-oppressive practice when working with service users. It is a user-friendly framework that enables social workers to evidence anti-oppressive practice in their daily encounters with service users. At all levels of practice (student through to experienced practitioner) there can be anxiety about evidencing how you have worked anti-oppressively with service users. The 4 Ds are discuss, discover, decide and disrupt. The 2 Ps are power and privilege.

Discuss

In this first step, you are trying to understand what has brought the service user to your service or provision. This begins with a discussion about their circumstances, during which you will be collecting and recording relevant information. At this stage, communicating using non-oppressive language is important. As discussions are two-way processes, it is also important that we advise service users who may themselves use inappropriate or oppressive language. Anti-oppressive practice at this stage will require you to locate a safe space for discussions. Discussions should be non-judgemental, fair and respectful. A discussion involves talking with others, so if you find yourself doing all the talking, you will need to adjust your strategy and draw on your rapport building skills. During the discussion, you will have to acknowledge your power and privilege, and make a conscious effort not to let that undermine your discussion. It is also during this discussion phase that service users may allude to or directly inform you about their experiences of oppression. Covert oppression may be more difficult to identify, hence the importance of a discussion that is sincere and open.

- SWE Standard 2   Establish and maintain the trust and confidence of people.
- SWE Standard 5   Act safely, respectfully and with professional integrity.

Discover

There is a lot to discover about yourself and others in relation to oppressed individuals, groups and communities, and this framework makes it possible to discover who you are, what your values are, your beliefs and views about other people. These are all important areas because what you find out about your service users and the reasons why you are intervening in their lives are all a process of discovery, according to the 4D2P framework. The second part of the discovery process involves identifying the presence of oppression and moving to a point where a decision needs to be made about the next course of action to be taken. Again, you will have to acknowledge how our privilege and power can impede our work at this stage.

- SWE Standard 1   Promote the rights, strengths and well-being of people, families and communities.
- SWE Standard 4   Act safely, respectfully and with professional integrity.

Decide

At this stage, you need to decide what your next course of action might be, and it is important to remember that this stage may be protracted because you might be required to seek guidance from others – for example, line managers, more experienced practitioners, colleagues. bell hooks (1996) asserts that oppression is the absence of choices; consequently, the decision-making process must ensure the voice of service users. For example, if you are a social worker with no disabilities, you have to address the mobility needs of the people you are working with. Understanding and reflecting on your own power and privilege is central to decision making in the sense that it allows you to be inclusive in your approach to interaction and decision making.

- SWE Standard 3   Be accountable for the quality of your practice and the decisions you make.

Disrupt

This stage of disruption involves using the decisions reached to ensure that your service user is no longer oppressed, or at the very least that you are not contributing to their oppression. The aim is to disrupt oppression and oppressive systems, and it is interesting to note that although a single individual cannot create and sustain oppression, it can sometimes take one person to disrupt and change oppressive practices. As social workers, we cannot stand by and witness oppression and discrimination targeted at colleagues or service users. Disrupting oppression can also involve guiding and supporting service users to navigate systems and processes that are oppressive. Minority individuals and groups are less likely to have the access to the power to disrupt oppression and oppressive structures; consequently, this stage of disrupting oppression provides you, the social worker, with the opportunity to assist service users address life challenges while supporting them to enhance their own well-being.

- SWE Standard 6   Promote ethical practice and report concerns.

While using this framework, you will need to continuously reflect on the 2 Ps (privilege and power) which must be at the fore of your anti-oppressive practice. This framework is generic and can be used for working with all forms of oppression – ageism, sexism, racism, to mention a few.

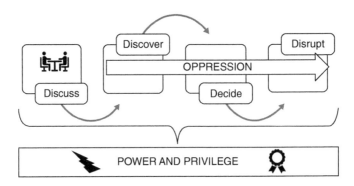

Figure 4.2   The 4D2P framework for anti-oppressive practice

The figure above is the visual representation of 4D2P and shows the 4D process as well as the 2P considerations which should underpin our use of the framework.

Case Study

St Paul's House in Ethicshire is home to four male children, two aged 14 and the other two aged 15 who can no longer live at home with their parents because they are displaying challenging behaviour and are at risk of harm. Three of the boys are of African-Caribbean ethnicity and one is White British. None of the African-Caribbean boys have been to school because they are in a children's home away from their families and have been told there are no spaces in the school nearest to them. You are a social work student on placement and although you have asked other colleagues why the three boys are not accessing education, you have not received a satisfactory response. You decide to speak to each boy on their own to understand what may be going on.

Application of 4D2P

Discuss

During your discussion, one of the boys informs you that he completed the relevant forms but has heard nothing in reply. The second boy tells you that his key worker said he would be unlikely to be admitted to the school in the catchment area because he has a history of disruptive behaviour in school. The third boy informs you that he has a statement of special educational needs and the school said they could not meet his needs at this point in the school year as all their support resources have been allocated. The third boy adds that their White peer (who is 15) also has special educational needs; however, he managed to get a place in the local school despite arriving at St Paul's about a month later than him. Throughout your discussion, your language should be encouraging, empowering, respectful and age appropriate.

Discover

With each discussion, you discover additional information which points to unfair and discriminatory practice both in St Paul's home and at the local school. You are a White female social work student with perfect attendance and behaviour records from when you were in school and you had no additional needs. This is a privileged position to be in; however, you will need to have this in your thoughts as you move on to the next stage of this framework.

Decide

How might you approach the situation at hand? What decisions have you reached? It is quite clear that something is amiss here and you will need to acknowledge oppressive practice and the presence of discrimination. The school and the management of St Paul's need to explain why another child with a statement of special education needs and who arrived at St Paul's weeks after the African Caribbean boy was given a place. You will need to know the relevant national legislation and policies about children, education and special educational needs. You will most likely need to ask the school for their policies and read the policies of St Paul's home. This means confirming who made those decisions and why.

Disrupt

What steps will you take towards disruption of the oppression? A meeting or discussion with the school as well as the management of St Paul's should be considered. It is also important that you understand whistleblowing and the potential for you to report this practice to the authorities.

Throughout your intervention in this case, you will need to reflect on your privilege and power, being conscious that this could influence your decisions and the potential to disrupt any oppressive practices.

Making sense of the models and practice framework

There are compelling moral, ethical and professional arguments supporting anti-oppressive practice in social work. However, there can be intrinsic and extrinsic barriers, making this difficult to achieve. First and foremost, there is variance in the delivery of content relating to oppressed individuals, groups and communities in social work courses. Where these kinds of knowledge are minimally disseminated in social work classrooms, there is the risk of graduating social workers unknowingly perpetuating oppression despite having good intentions (Friere, 2000). Some aspects of social work have been seen to have controlling functions, notably in the areas of child protection and mental health, so these are areas where social workers are required to understand the impact of the power they hold and how anti-oppressive practice intersects with the controlling functions of social work. Resource constraints in social work is an extrinsic barrier to anti-oppressive practice when time is highly precious, especially where practitioners work to tick boxes or where the use of electronic media is replacing face-to-face contact with service users.

All four models discussed in this chapter promote anti-oppressive practice through enabling social workers to recognise how inequalities are maintained through assumptions. All four models are flexible, requiring you to utilise deep learning strategies in order to understand the forces that shape our assumptions prior to and during our interaction with service users. As language is central to the formation of relationships, the use of these models will assist in forming and maintaining relationships with service users. The 4D2P practice framework moves us from discussions about oppression to the disruption of oppression and oppressive structures, while also offering hope that at the very least, the social workers' reflection on their privilege and power is significant progress.

The notion of hopeful practice (Boddy et al., 2018) enables you, as a social worker, to support service users to cope by developing strategies to improve their quality of life. Hope is therefore a motivator to achieve and is a tool for recovery, and service users who are hopeful should not be labelled as being in denial. This implies that hopeful social work can be an anti-oppressive strategy for practice.

Chapter summary

In this chapter, we have looked at models and frameworks, which I believe can and do have potential to enhance anti-oppressive and anti-discriminatory practice in social work. Like many models, frameworks and tools, the social worker must be able to use them confidently and competently in order to achieve the best outcomes for service users. The social work profession needs reflexive practitioners who are able to use law and best practice to ensure that service users experience fair and non-oppressive interactions and interventions. Dalrymple and Burke (2006) suggest that the relationship between social work and the law can be problematic; however, the law directs and guides practice in the areas of prevention, protection and intervention. A critically reflexive practitioner will understand, for example, the oppressive and unequal relationship between social work and people seeking asylum.

Oppression and anti-oppressive practice need to become more visible in social work supervision, whether between student and their practice educator, social worker and manager, or any other form of supervision in social work practice.

Further reading

Collins, S and Wilkie, L (2010) Anti-oppressive practice and social work students' portfolios in Scotland. *Social Work Education*, 29(7): 760–77.

This article reports the findings from research about how students addressed issues of anti-oppressive practice in their placement portfolios. The research found that some aspects of social divisions and forms of oppression such as gender, age, disability and language received considerable attention, while others such as 'race', class, sexuality and religion received less attention.

Parker, J (ed.) (2020) *Introducing Social Work*. London: Sage.

The whole book is relevant and useful to student social workers. However, Chapter 7, 'Anti-Oppressive Practice Skills', would be supportive to your reading of this chapter.

5

Social justice

(Continued)

It will also introduce you to the following standards as set out in the Social Work Subject Benchmark Statement (2019):

5.4   Service users and carers
5.12   Information gathering
5.16   Building relationships and working effectively with others

See Appendix 2 for a detailed description of these standards.

Introduction

In this chapter, we will examine the concept of social justice and trace its historical development more generally as well as specifically in relation to its emergence into social work. We will explore how social workers can contribute to promoting social justice in their daily work with service users, which will be the main concern of this chapter.

Historically, social justice has been one of the underlying principles of the profession of social work, long before the term made it into the international definition in 2012 (IFSW, 2014). The concept of social justice entered mainstream social work education and practice discourse as a critical consideration in work with vulnerable individuals, groups and communities. I acknowledge that the term 'vulnerable' is contested, so, for the purposes of this chapter, it refers to people in need of special protection or support who may be at risk of harm, maltreatment or abuse. Social justice is the fair, just and respectful treatment of all people, while recognising that unfairness, corruption and inequalities are the leading causes of war, conflict, inhumane treatment, suffering, pain, exploitation, and many other ills that confront our world today.

Social justice is defined as *promoting a just society by challenging injustice and valuing diversity*. Social justice exists when *all people share a common humanity and therefore have a right to equitable treatment, support for their human rights, and a fair allocation of community resources*. In conditions of social justice, people are

not to be discriminated against, nor their welfare and well-being constrained or prejudiced on the basis of gender, sexuality, religion, political affiliations, age, race, belief, disability, location, social class, socioeconomic circumstances, or other characteristic of background or group membership

(Toowoomba Catholic Education, 2006)

According to Irizarry et al. (2016), social work has a history of working with people who have felt humiliated by institutional structures that have also simultaneously promoted injustices towards them, not only in their individual capacities, but also within groups and their communities. Social justice is considered a vital element of contemporary life, as well as a critical component for removing barriers that people face because of race, ethnicity, gender, age, disability, religion or culture.

Historical development of social justice

It is necessary to examine the importance of the historical and philosophical development of social justice to understand how its use and meaning may have changed over time.

Social justice is said to have its roots in the Christian religious doctrine which espoused the value of helping the less fortunate, who are usually oppressed and powerless. Orstein (2017) has argued that human behaviour has previously been grounded in self-interest and with an appetite to amass more. Early civilisations appeared to function with two main groups: people with power and wealth, and those without. People with power and wealth were not seeking to lose their status or power, and those with little or no power and wealth were unable to challenge or oppose what was the status quo. While many unequal relationships continue to exist the world over, the focus of this chapter is the way in which this impacts on the work undertaken by social workers.

Nations all over the world have defined their own versions of social justice – for example, Oguz (2017), in a study about teachers' perceptions of social justice in Turkey, found that teachers believed that social justice was just a concept on paper but not practised in any meaningful way due to the lack of equal opportunity for many in that country, particularly in the areas of education, employment, housing and shelter. It is, however, almost unanimous that in order to adhere to social justice, governments are viewed as the primary source of development in that policies and legislation can address social injustice and inequalities to provide a form of distributive justice, which ensures equitable and fair distribution of social goods and services.

John Rawls (1999) argued that justice is the first virtue of social institutions (p3) and sought to differentiate between justice and fairness, arguing that he recognised them as distinct but interrelated.

The two principles of justice

The first principle is the *equality principle* where social and economic inequalities are rearranged to benefit disadvantaged people, while the second principle, the *liberty principle*, is where each person has equal rights to an extensive system of equal basic liberties. Thus, for Rawls, the equality principle requires the rearrangement of social and economic goods to be guided by considerations of opportunity and by the differences that arise from individual circumstances.

In 2007, the General Assembly of the United Nations proclaimed 20 February as the World Day of Social Justice and invited all member states to devote the day to promoting national activities in accordance with the goals and objectives that sought to reduce poverty and inequality, while promoting collaboration and the understanding of social justice as a growing value for determining world development. This gives a louder, more discernible status to the place of social justice in the world.

A social justice framework for social work: SPEAR

According to Taylor et al. (2017), there is an ongoing and longstanding debate about what constitutes social justice in social work. This debate has been centred around issues of 'care vs. control', 'macro vs. micro' and 'individualised vs. community based' practice (p49). These debates represent binary thinking, which has resulted in difficulty in ascertaining where socially just outcomes have been achieved for service users.

Gale and Densmore (2000) explored social justice from an educational perspective, and classified explanations of social justice as distributive, retributive and recognitive. The recognitive stance, as the name implies, acknowledges and values all members of society as being involved in discussions about matters that affect them. They developed the SPEAR framework, based on the principles of recognitive social justice which they view as contributing directly to achieving an anti-oppressive practice environment in social work. SPEAR represents **S**elf-determination, **P**articipation, **E**quity, **A**ccess and **R**ights.

Self-determination

Self-determination as a concept is built on the values of autonomy and respect for the dignity and worth of all people. It is a democratic process to ensure and insist that people have control over the discussions about their lives and any processes involved in the intervention being proposed. In trying to work anti-oppressively, it is important that service users' perspectives, opinions and views are given due consideration and, where their views may be at odds with the recommended intervention, social workers should take the time to explain the reasons behind the chosen intervention. It is recommended that social workers utilise facilitative helping processes, which affirm service users' worth and value, while supporting self-discovery (Heron, 2001).

Participation

Participation in the social justice framework refers to service users being participants in the design and decision making in relation to their care. Any form of participation should not be based on privilege or previous opportunity, but rather should be an open invitation to users of social care services. By recognising the utility of participation, social workers are assisting with the delivery of social justice in terms of understanding the need for service users to be integral to their own care and recovery. There should be no artificial barriers for participation.

Equity

In order to redress imbalance and unfairness, it is imperative that social differences are understood to enable social workers to apply strategies that often disrupt participation. For service users who may be unable to attend interventions due to difficulties with transportation, social workers can negotiate other ways of supporting them to engage with relevant programmes and projects, and against which they will be assessed as the intervention progresses.

Access

Users of social work services should have access to resources they need to ensure that they are able to contribute as best as they can to their own well-being. It should be noted that social justice occurs when political, cultural, economic and social rights and resources are accessed by citizens. Any criteria for access should be clear, transparent and fair.

Rights

These relate to people being rights holders in terms of the right to dignity, respect and various freedoms. Service users should be afforded the opportunity to receive equitable interventions and services that meet their needs. Barriers such as social class, gender, race, ethnicity, sexual orientation and nationality cannot be used to further disadvantage these groups in terms of eligibility for services.

Activity 5.2

As we have already seen, social justice is a concept with many different interpretations. In this activity, I invite you to consider the following questions.

- What does social justice mean to you?
- When did you first become aware of the concept/term?
- What do you think social workers can do to promote social justice in their everyday interactions with service users?

Social justice is a way of ensuring that society functions better, more smoothly and in a much fairer way. Miller (1999) provided what is now a common and straightforward definition of social justice. He argued that *how the good and bad things in life should be distributed among the members of a human society* (p1). This definition pretty much encapsulates the essence of social justice from the perspective of equity. Members of society should bear the brunt of poverty collectively and in the same way gain from the benefits of wealth and affluence together.

In terms of social work education, the aim would be to provide students with an understanding of and appreciation for the value of social justice when working with service users. Students need to acquire the requisite knowledge and skill base to identify social injustices and to advocate on behalf of service users who may require this support to articulate their views to empower service users.

Social workers need to be able to use their skills and expertise to build a climate where everyone feels a sense of belonging and inclusion, and, in the words of bell hooks, *there must exist a paradigm, a practical model for social change that includes an understanding of ways to transform consciousness that are linked to efforts to transform structures* (1996, p193).

Social justice, like many other concepts in social work, is an ongoing process involving the use of opportunities to promote its value in contemporary society and social work. The term has been viewed as having political connotations, yet social work as a profession works within political systems, and challenges these systems and processes if in any way they oppress, suppress or disadvantage the vulnerable populations we work with.

Becoming a social justice advocate

The aim of this chapter has been to extend our understanding of social justice within the context of anti-oppressive practice in social work. To be truly anti-oppressive in our daily social work practice, we require in-depth understanding of social justice and what constitutes social injustice for people who use our services. To do this, it is important that social workers understand the impact of structural inequality which breeds social injustice and engage efforts to reform or dismantle systems of oppression. The vison would be one in which *the distribution of resources is equitable, and all members are physically and psychologically safe and secure* (Bell, 2007, p3). Social justice advocacy can be defined as planned efforts aimed at encouraging change in legislation, public attitudes and policies to create a more socially just society, and it could be argued that social workers are positioned strategically to play such a role. The case study below outlines one example of social justice advocacy aimed at minimising oppressive practice.

Case Study

In July 2018, Elin Ersson, a Swedish student studying social work, boarded a plane from Gothenburg bound for Turkey. She became aware that a passenger on board was being deported to Afghanistan and decided to protest the deportation. Her protest came in the form of a refusal to sit down until the man was removed from the flight. As she was standing upright, the flight was unable to take off. Many hailed the efforts of this lone social work student, and the profession soon acknowledged and praised her for her determination to uphold what was considered to be right and just. However, the student was faced with charges *for crimes against aviation law* in Sweden and fined approximately £250. The social justice sentiment in this case appears to be strong. A student social worker is in tears because she perceives what is happening to another person as unjust and unfair. She does all she can in the circumstances to prevent the deportation. In the process she becomes a 'hero', at least in the eyes of other social workers who ensured that her message went viral on social media platforms.

- If you were in Elin's place, would you have acted in a similar way?
- Why or why not?

Discuss this case study with a colleague and write down your thoughts.

Commentary

The case study presents you with the opportunity to fully reflect on the motivation and outcome of the actions by Elin Ersson. Her actions challenge us to consider the roles of ordinary citizens in promoting social justice in the many facets of life that we meet on a daily basis. Elin livestreamed her protest on Facebook because she felt strongly that the person facing deportation was at risk of being harmed in Afghanistan.

The idea of consumer or customer contribution is very much related to this. For example, when customers decide to buy Fair Trade products from the supermarket, they are contributing to upholding social justice and fairness for the many whose labour results in the items we buy and use. The boycott of products and goods produced due to unfair hiring and labour practices, modern slavery, child labour as well as low wages move many of us to become, sometimes unconsciously, promoters of social justice.

As has already been mentioned, many service users we work with will be experiencing various levels and forms of unjust and unfair treatment, among others. Some of this unfair and unjust treatment will undoubtedly come from within some of our own organisations, agencies and service areas in the form of eligibility and other criteria for services and interventions. In addition, many of us will have experienced various forms of injustice arising from our social locations.

The Just Practice framework

The Just Practice framework is another example of social justice advocacy and was developed by Finn and Jacobson (2003). It proposes that for social work to be truly socially just, practice needs to have the following: meaning, context, power, history and possibility. They argue that these components provide social work students with a framework that connects social work to social justice, discussed below.

Meaning

Human beings interpret the world according to how they perceive it and consequently the term 'justice' can be conceptualised in a myriad of ways. The term is socially and culturally mediated and users of social care services must make sense of the situations they are going through in order to fully comprehend their circumstances. As a social worker, you will not be able to interpret the service user's life for them, and must first recognise that their understanding of fairness and justice will assist them in making sense of social justice.

Context

You are being trained to understand human behaviour within contexts. Consequently, it is difficult to make sense of social justice without the appreciation of context. Finn and Jacobson (2003) suggest that to ignore the context of service users' lives will not prepare social workers adequately for social justice advocacy and will be oppressive.

Power

Chapter 3 was devoted to the discussion of power and powerlessness, so these will not be repeated here. To be a true social justice advocate, social workers employed at all levels and in all organisations and agencies need to question sources of power and the structures that not only legitimise, but also sustain them. How people are able (or unable) to influence others in the context of social work is an important consideration.

History

History is significant in that it enables us to look to the past with the view to understanding how we have arrived at where we are today. Social workers can draw upon historical information about how people living in previous centuries and all over the world navigated their socially unjust worlds and circumstances. Social work has in its history the development of the profession from religious ideals to what is now largely secular ideals.

Possibility

Social workers generally believe that change in a service user's circumstance is possible, so this last element of the just framework requires social workers to focus on what a socially just society would look like. How might you frame and reframe your encounters with service users? It is important to identify new ways of dealing with structural and other forms of disadvantage which often impact on users of social care services.

Knowledge and skills for social justice in social work

Social workers possess many skills required for engaging in practice behaviours that are often associated with social justice. These skills include working inclusively, understanding diversity advocacy, empowerment and community awareness raising. There are several theoretical perspectives that enable social workers to confront oppression with the view to changing practice. Wherever you may be located in terms of service user group, specialism or geography, it is worth undertaking a community profile in order to understand any socioeconomic inequalities that may exist and to begin to identify strategies to work with and on behalf of these groups. The profile of a community is summary of the community in terms of the levels and types of needs and the resources available to meet the needs of the community. That children from Black and ethnic minority groups are over-represented in the looked-after systems of care across the UK (Bernard and Harris, 2016), for example, requires further examination. Social workers in areas where this is apparent are required to question this pattern within the context of social justice and understand how they might contribute towards changing such patterns.

Social justice and supervision

The functions of supervision in social work have been widely written about (Bogo, 2006; Kadushin and Harkness, 2014), yet few have addressed specifically the nature, type and frequency of social justice learning or the way this addresses the educational function of supervision.

Asakura and Maurer (2018) have emphasised the importance of supervisors being able to initiate discussions about social justice in their clinical supervision sessions by recognising clinical supervision as a pedagogical process of modelling, direct observation and feedback, as well as self-directed learning. Inherent in the supervisory relationship is one of power differential and it is important that supervisors model social justice principles by the way they relate to their supervisees. The position of Manager, Supervisor or Team Leader provides these role bearers with authority over social work practice with service users and their families.

Supervision has multiple roles and traditionally the focus has been on emotional and support for well-being, knowledge and skill development, and administrative tasks, without an obvious focus on social justice in practice. The protected private space in which supervision occurs offers supervisors the opportunity for engaging in a process that enhances reflexivity and critical reflection on issues of social justice. These reflections can be about their own professional relationship as supervisor and supervisee, and the ways in which power differentials may or may not influence the supervisory process. In addition, recognising their critical reflections about the dynamics between social workers and their service users would most certainly include discussions such as the service users' rights to self-determination, use of social work values and ethics, as well as the recognition of difference, oppression and diversity in practice interventions. Depending on how well supervisors understand and are transparent about their own social location and the privileges they have in relation to gender, race, ethnicity and class, the idea of social justice can be readily embedded into the shared teaching and learning space.

While sites for supervision have been identified as appropriate for discussions of social justice, there is a dearth of research evidence that supervision discussions about social justice translate into ideas relevant for social work practice. This provides an opportunity for future research into social justice discussions in practice supervision.

Practice learning/placements can provide useful opportunities for social justice to be advocated. Student social workers should be able to challenge discriminatory practices that serve to undermine and exclude service users while advocating on their behalf to ensure that their voices are heard and their needs considered. The value of doing social justice work as a student social worker cannot be overstated, and is likely to require competence, confidence and the willingness of practice educators to make this a reality.

The problem with social justice

This might seem like a contradiction in terms, because for most of us there is no problem with social justice. The problem only arises when people appear not to regard social justice and, as Nussbaum (2000, p33) rightly suggested, social justice is *not something you talk about when you have nothing to say*. It has been suggested that areas of social work practice such as child protection and child welfare work present contradicting views in terms of social justice. One perspective is that children are protected from harm and exploitation. On the other hand, the process of protecting children is often fraught with what can be perceived as oppressive or unjust policies and processes. These competing outlooks on social justice in child protection work may require a more robust interrogation of policy, the interpretation of policy and social work practice competence. Being able to challenge practice and interrupt oppressive systems will be a positive step in contributing to anti-oppressive social work practice.

Chapter summary

Globally and in the UK, there appears to be no slowing down in the manifestations of poverty exacerbated by unfair policies, budget cutbacks and general austerity measures. These have resulted in hardship for the many social care service users who experience varying levels of oppression due to changes in eligibility for services and resources. Social workers must stay true to the profession and engage in social justice advocacy wherever possible.

This chapter has sought to extend our knowledge about social justice and its relationship with anti-oppression in social work practice. It recognises the international definition of social work as making explicit the need to work in way that is congruent with social justice ideals.

The chapters that follow will examine a range of diversities in relation to race, ethnicity, faith and spirituality, age, gender, marginalised groups, persons with disabilities, as well as the importance of having an intersectional approach to understanding difference and diversity.

Further reading

Finn, JL and Jacobson, M (2003) Just Practice. *Journal of Social Work Education*, 39(1): 57–78.

This article proposes the Just Practice framework, which is presented as a social justice-oriented approach to social work. The five key themes have been discussed in this chapter and offer another framework for you to consider when working with service users.

Gale, T and Densmore, K (2000) *Just Schooling: Explorations in the Cultural Politics of Teaching*. London: Open University Press.

This book analyses the various ideas used in classrooms that assist in understanding the diversity of students with regard to their gender, race and social class and their learning dis/abilities, and addresses the question of whether it is possible to have a 'socially just' education system.

Part Two

Anti-oppressive practice with individuals, groups and communities

6

Gender

(Continued)

It will also introduce you to the following standards as set out in the Social Work Subject Benchmark Statement (2019):

5.2   Social work theory
5.4   Service users and carers
5.16   Skills in working with others

See Appendix 2 for a detailed description of these standards.

Introduction

In all societies across the world, gender diversity is a fundamental differentiation among its members (Laird and Tedam, 2019). In this chapter, we will examine the various discourses around gender, and articulate how these discourses assist or hinder your involvement and intervention as a social worker. Using case studies and activities, this chapter will encourage you to reflect on new learning, while consolidating existing knowledge and practice competence. The chapter will begin with a discussion about the gender composition within the profession of social work, and examine key concepts such as feminism, masculinity, transgender and the ways in which intersectionality help us to understand the diverse experiences of people. Social work practice with fathers will be explored and the use of the SHARE model (Maclean et al., 2018) proposed as a framework for understanding and disrupting gender oppression.

Globally, in relation to the people who teach social work, it has been recognised that there are more women than men in social work. Reporting the figures from the USA, the Council of Social Work Education (CSWE, 2017) found that the majority of social work students (Bachelor's: 85 per cent; Master's: 85 per cent; PhD: 74 per cent) were female, as well as 72 per cent of faculty. In the UK, Moriarty and Murray (2007) indicate the low numbers of men entering social work education, commenting that this reflects the relatively low average salary for men. There is also research by the GSSC (2010) which found that men constituted only 13 per cent of social workers in the UK. The Australian case presents a similar picture, with 83 per cent of all professional social workers in Australia being women in 2006 (Pease, 2011).

Conversely, it is also suggested that the social work curriculum and teaching content has a dominance of male social work theorists, quantitative and masculinist approaches to research. In the following section, I will explain some key terminology in order to aid our understanding of gender oppression.

The term 'gender'

According to Skehill (2009), the subject of gender is an interesting one for students studying social work, yet it has been found to be a difficult subject to address. This is because of the different perspectives around the concept itself. Gender is a set of characteristics, behaviours and practices associated with the sexual categories of male and female. Gender is also socially constructed in that its understanding is fluid and changes over time. The power relations that exist between men and women give rise to discussions about men being complicit in the oppression of women for the most part through being silent. In order to draw attention to this unequal power relationship between men and women, feminist writers in social work have argued that the knowledge base, education and social work practice itself must recognise the importance of using a gender-sensitive frame of reference in their practice with service users and carers. According to Newberry-Koroluk (2018), gendered narratives, stereotypes and expectations *emerge in social work classrooms and field placements before they emerge in post-graduation practice* (p448). Such a claim is relevant for social work educators in order that they are conscious of gendered power dynamics from the outset. The aim would be to use this consciousness to model and demonstrate equity, non-oppression and inclusion for students of all genders while guarding against favoritism or reinforcing male privilege. It is also imperative that social work classrooms are spaces where well-being is nurtured through respect, inclusion and dignity. The social work curriculum should include issues of power, its objective and subjective forces, and how it may be channelled into resisting oppression while pursuing liberation (Prilleltensky, 2008). Feminist approaches may assist social work students to achieve this.

Examining feminism

According to Szymanski (2005), there is no universally agreed definition of feminism because there are many different types and models. The most widely agreed underlying principle of feminism is the recognition of women as equal to men. According to hooks (2000), *Feminism is a movement to end sexism, sexist exploitation, and oppression* (pviii). Before I examine the various forms of feminism, it is important to understand how and why feminist thinking is important to social work education and practice. It is the view of Barretti (2001) that despite the gaps, there is a close relationship between social work and feminism. The types of feminism we are going to discuss includes *liberal feminism*, which maintains that gender discrimination against women exists due to ignorance and a lack of awareness. Liberal feminists believe that as the world advances, changes will emerge in the relationship between men and women.

Marxist feminists

Marxist feminists hold the view that gender oppression is a result of capitalism which has placed women's work at the lower margins of remuneration at best or for no pay at worst. This disadvantage begins in the domestic family and private spheres, and often results in women reproducing and socialising the future generations of women into similar situations and circumstances.

Radical feminists

Radical feminists view the oppression of women as being driven by men because they run the main institutions in society. This theory posits that male domination and power are constructed and maintained through social, political and cultural practices and systems which reinforce female inferiority. Radical feminism also turns on its head the characteristics that are valued in men. Examples of these values include being controlling, competitive, macho and aggressive, which are blamed for wars and hunger on a larger scale, and rape, poverty and abuse within a family context. They believe that these are the ways through which men retain power over women.

Postmodern feminists

This is a combination of postmodern and feminist theories. As a starting point, postmodern feminists dismiss all feminist thought which gives a single explanation for women's oppression. They subscribe to and promote the idea of difference, multiplicity and plurality. Feminists argue that social work practice must be informed by the different forms of feminism already discussed above, and that feminism has contributed to the development of social work and practice in many parts of the world, at least in the USA, the UK and Australia.

Black feminism

Black feminist thought contends that White middle-class women have been the focus of feminist theory and that it is important that feminist theory incorporates the experiences of Black women. Black feminists insist on *self-definition*, which is the power to name one's own reality and *self-valuation*. Collins (1990) argues that if a Black woman chooses to relate to her race, then her identity and struggles as a woman are lost. It could be argued that the same is true when she elevates her gender as the focus of her struggles and race is lost. Black women often engage in activism and the application of critical race theory assists in understanding and theorising the experiences of Black people. In anti-oppressive practice, recognising how social workers from Black and minority ethnic or Asian backgrounds navigate practice where Black service users experience multiple oppressions is an important consideration.

The section above has highlighted some of the different forms of feminism and has attempted to examine the different lenses through which feminists view gender and gender discrimination. We will now look at men and masculinity within the context of social work and anti-oppressive practice.

Activity 6.1

- Can you name any writers who are at the forefront of gender theorising in social work?
- Who are they and what do you like about their writing?

Guidance

You may have writers whose work you engage with and use in your assignments and coursework. These do not have to be social work writers, but it is important that you begin to identify people who write about gender and how their writing connects with you – for example, Audre Lorde and bell hooks are two Black feminist writers whose work I often read.

Men and masculinity

According to Christie (2001), in female-dominated professions such as social work, there may be fear of feminisation and stigmatisation among the male minority and this could be the reason why the profession continues to attract more women than men. This brings into question what it means to be a man, or indeed the nature of masculinity.

Alvesson (1998, p972) defines masculinity as the

values, experiences and meanings that are culturally interpreted as masculine and typically feel natural for or are ascribed to men more than women in the particular cultural context.

Traditional male attributes such as leadership and technical skills have tended to form the image of traditional masculinity, according to Lupton (2000). Cree (2001) suggests that what are considered normative masculine behaviours have always included success and status, creating an emotional distance, and avoiding what are perceived as feminine behaviours. This view is supported by Lupton (2000, p35) who found that men *suffer a challenge to their masculinity* by *performing a role which is regarded by society as one which woman normally undertake.* Every culture or society will interpret and measure masculinity using different yardsticks. However, there is a common theme about certain roles and tasks being viewed as feminine. As a social worker, you must avoid these stereotypes and ensure that your practice with males is fair, transparent and non-oppressive. In this regard, social work with fathers is an important area for considering and applying anti-oppressive and non-discriminatory principles.

Research by Pease (2016) makes the case for Patriarchy Awareness workshops for men, arguing that men need to understand patriarchy to enable them to acknowledge their complicity in the oppression of women. This is a useful proposal which you may wish to include in your menu of interventions in relation to gender-based oppression and violence.

Fathers and absent fathers

There appears to be limited research around single fathers in social work, with the available literature often presenting a negative image of them being passive or uninvolved (Scourfield et al., 2012). In some cases, the conclusion of fathers being perpetrators even before an assessment is undertaken can undermine the role of father and feed into negative gender stereotypes. Gendered assumptions can influence social workers' assessments and interventions when working with fathers who may be within the home or absent, and these often result in barriers to support. In their everyday decisions about the adequacy of parenting, according to Nygren et al. (2019) it is important to reflect on and challenge what are dominant gendered norms within the family, understand that not involving fathers might increase risks for children and that fathers are a resource that can, for example, provide care to children when mothers are in prison (Flynn, 2012).

Social workers are often working in families where the absence of fathers often contributes to disadvantaging those families. Single fatherhood, according to Haworth (2019), is not a straightforward term, rather its definition is used in different ways by different individuals, depending on the context. A male lone parent is likely to face difficulties when applying for a role as foster carer, for example, much more than a female lone carer or parent. Nygren et al. (2019) found that the policy on the inclusion of fathers in social work was not translated into practice in England, Sweden, Ireland and Norway. Consequently, as social workers we should reflect on and challenge dominant gendered norms within the family, and recognise that not involving fathers could negatively impact on children in terms of the loss of a primary carer, loss of their home and potentially create unstable care arrangements (Flynn, 2012).

In the case study below, you will read an example of Jonathan, a single father who attends a meeting at his children's school.

Case Study

Jonathan is a single father of three children – sons Peter and Robert, age 8 and 10, and daughter Clare, age 5. The children's mother passed away two years ago and Jonathan has been the sole carer for the children since then. The family recently moved to this area. Jonathan's mother Corrine (the children's grandmother) occasionally supports Jonathan with caring for the children. Clare's class teacher is concerned about her progress in school and involves the special education needs coordinator (SENCO) at the school, who agrees that a meeting is required. The letter is addressed to Mother/Carer of Clare Dodds. The school involves Children's Social Care in this meeting following concerns about all three children being picked up late from school regularly.

The SENCO welcomes everyone to the meeting and during introductions the social worker asks where the mother of the children is because it is important to have her in this meeting. Jonathan reports that the school should have records that he is the sole carer for the children. There are five people at the meeting, four of whom are female (the SENCO, the social worker, the class teacher and the Deputy Head). Jonathan is the only male. The social worker asks Jonathan to describe his daily care routine for the children and why he is late collecting them from school. Jonathan carefully describes the daily routine and stops occasionally to acknowledge the people in the room.

The SENCO asks Jonathan whether he assists the children with their homework and if he has noticed that Clare may have some difficulties.

- Consider how you might progress discussions and contributions to this meeting.
- What questions would you ask and why?

Commentary

This case study requires you to think about who was at this meeting and how you might ensure that Jonathan feels welcome in that space, being the only male in the room. The original letter inviting the family to this meeting was addressed to the children's late mother. There is a clear message of a lack of attention to detail when the social worker asks about the children's mother who has been dead for about two years. This is not a good start to the meeting, and it may be that Jonathan feels overwhelmed as the meeting progresses. The question about why Jonathan collects the children late from school could be more sensitively asked. Jonathan may be feeling powerless and restricted, components of Barker's (2003) definition of oppression, so it is important to revise your approach.

Transgender

The term 'transgender' historically referred to a person who wanted to change their social gender through a change of habitus and gender expression, perhaps also with the use of hormones but usually not surgery (Stryker, 2017). The umbrella term 'trans' is used to describe people whose gender is not the same as, or does not sit comfortably with, the sex they were assigned at birth (Stonewall, 2017).

Burdge (2007) has argued that the transgender community has its own unique culture and language with which they communicate. Referring to them as an at-risk population, Burdge (2007) suggests that social workers must possess the knowledge and skills to work with transgender service users in ways that are empowering and anti-oppressive. Like other minority groups, transgendered people face negative social environments that can make them feel alienated and lead to depression and low self-esteem. For children and young people, family and home environments may not offer them the acceptance and support required to keep them safe and enhance their well-being, and may instead unconsciously reject them. This could force them to run away from home and put themselves at risk of exploitation while they are on the street. As a social worker, you therefore have a role to play in ensuring the safety of transgendered people in school, in family environments and among their peers. You can achieve this through education and awareness raising, and supporting therapeutic interventions with families of transgendered young people with the view to helping the family understand and appropriately support their transgendered child or young person. For hospital social workers, the role could extend to supporting gender reassignment or hormone therapies that may be considered by service users or carers. Anti-oppressive frameworks are characterised by values of inclusion, equity and social justice. According to Baines (2011, p26), attempts to explain both *how power works to oppress and marginalise people, as well as how power can be used to liberate and empower them* requires all forms of oppression to be addressed in order to work towards greater social justice. Gender discrimination does not arise from a single, obvious source; instead, it is perpetuated through political, biological, psychological, economic, educational and social inequalities, which can be on a micro, mezzo or macro level.

Gender and anti-oppressive social work

In this section, we have outlined areas of practice where gender-based discrimination can occur. As students, you will be expected to question the absence of gender considerations in your coursework. When working on a case study or relevant topics during your studies, you will be required to identify where gender discrimination may exist and how you might analyse these issues for effective anti-oppressive practice. In practice and team settings, you should respectfully challenge oppressive attitudes and behaviours such as unfair work allocation, sexist 'jokes', homophobia, sexual violence or harassment of all forms.

Hicks (2015) has argued for consideration and analysis of gender within everyday social work contexts. From receiving initial information about people in need of services through to assessments, and in identifying appropriate interventions, it is crucial that social workers understand the personal, structural and broader contexts around the implications of gender. For example, a social worker's analysis of the role of two heterosexual parents in raising children should be carefully considered.

Gender equality means taking into account men's and women's priorities, needs and interests while recognising the diversity within these groups. Social workers should avoid stereotypical language and recommendations that reinforce gender stereotypes – for example, when a boy is asked to 'take care of your sister', 'be the man' or 'man-up' without due regard to other factors such as age and experience.

On the other hand, it may be the case that in some families – for example, those of a strict Muslim faith – the husband may request that he is present for any interaction between his wife and a male social worker, or his presence may result in the wife not speaking during the interaction. Such a situation would warrant an understanding of the dynamics at play in this interaction, which may be perceived to be culturally appropriate to the family but not necessarily congruent with the requirements of family social work.

Social workers should avoid a line of questioning that borders on heteronormativity (the belief that sexual or marital relationships should be between man and woman) – for example, asking a female if she has a boyfriend or husband. Similarly, asking a man if they have a wife or girlfriend should be avoided.

Burke and Harrison (2016, p46) assert that an awareness of one's own position in relation to others is an important skill to possess when trying to work anti-oppressively. It is also crucial that social workers encourage oppressed groups to challenge oppressive behaviours, attitudes and practices as much as possible.

Barnoff et al. (2006) have noted that the lack of resources can be used to disguise genuine resistance to anti-oppressive work. Consequently, genuine barriers for anti-oppressive practice at organisational and agency levels should be highlighted and addressed. In addition to this, denying, minimising and victim blaming all reinforce and perpetuate gender discrimination. People deny gender discrimination by insisting that victims are overreacting; gender oppression does not exist in their space by being silent and not challenging or acting. Social workers must recognise and name their own positionality in the spirit of sound ethical, anti-oppressive practice. According to Fook (2012), we occupy multiple locations, thus possessing multiple perspectives. I am Black, female, social worker, African, academic, mother, daughter, sister, wife, Catholic. I use specific elements of these multiple locations depending on what questions I am being asked or what I am doing. For example, if a question was asked of me in relation to faith and religion, my social location as a practising Catholic might be at the fore.

Activity 6.2

On your own or with a colleague, describe the multiple locations which you occupy.

The SHARE Model

For social workers seeking a practical and flexible model to examine gender discrimination and oppression, the SHARE model (Maclean et al., 2018) offers opportunities. The SHARE model (Seeing, Hearing, Acting, Reading, Evaluating) has already been discussed in Chapter 2. To recap, when working with families, social workers need to acknowledge what they are seeing as part of the intervention as well as what they hear. What social workers see in relation to gender and gender discrimination may impact on their view of families, service users or carers. What they hear will ultimately inform the action they take. What is being said about the males, females, transgendered people in the context of work? How are they described, talked about and viewed? Social workers will need to take action or intervene with families where there is likely to be gendered practice and expectations. For example, where a social worker is unfamiliar with or has little or no experience working with transgendered people, it is important to be open about this knowledge and skills gap in order to avoid oppressive practice arising from ignorance or lack of experience. You may need to undertake additional reading to enhance your understanding. Once the case proceeds beyond a certain stage, you will need to evaluate the outcomes of your intervention using a gendered and intersectional lens to ensure that their intervention has been devoid of oppressive practice.

Activity 6.3

- What are your knowledge gaps at this stage of your studies in relation to transgendered people?
- What skills do you need to work with transgendered people?

Discuss these questions with a colleague or write down your thoughts.

There can be no discussion of the implications of gender on its own; instead, the understanding of intersectionality is important and has been a theme throughout this book. Intersectionality accounts for the many ways that structural forces intersect in women's lives and has had an undeniable influence on feminist theory. Anti-oppressive practice is intersectional practice and requires a critical understanding of power relations. Patriarchy upholds and supports gender oppression which, according to Gellman (2006), emanates from the Bible where women are considered inferior to men. Intersectional theory asserts that people are often disadvantaged by multiple sources of oppression arising from their race, identity, sexual orientation, religion, class, gender and other identity markers. Intersectionality recognises that identity markers (e.g. 'male' and 'Black') do not exist independently of each other, and that each informs the others, often creating a complex convergence of oppression.

Activity 6.4

Having read the case study about Jonathan and his children earlier in this chapter, you receive the following additional information:

1. The children's mother died while seeking asylum in the UK.
2. Jonathan is a transgender parent.

- How might you use this new information?

Consider incorporating the SHARE model.

Guidance

I will apply some of the elements of the SHARE model and invite you to consider how you might apply the other elements with Jonathan and his family.

In the case of Jonathan and family, this new information is important, and it is good practice to update your records to reflect this additional information. To avoid oppressive practice, you will need to read (R) up on what it means to be transgender and seek to hear (H) directly from Jonathan about how you might support him. It may be that before this information you were considering referring him a parenting group or other specific services. Considering the new information, this will need to be carefully and sensitively explored before you act (A).

Chapter summary

This chapter has outlined a number of key terminologies in the area of gender which are important for social workers to understand and draw upon when working with service users. Recognising the factors that perpetuate gender discrimination is the first step towards disrupting it in social work education and practice. I have sought to emphasise the centrality of understanding and acknowledging one's positionality and the power (or powerlessness) invested in those multiple positions we occupy. For social workers attempting to work in an anti-oppressive way, avoiding gender stereotypes through our language and practice is an effective strategy, alongside calling out gender discrimination wherever we are faced with it.

Further reading

Baines, D (2011) *Anti-oppressive Practice: Social Justice Social Work* (2nd edn). Manitoba: Fernwood Publishing.

This edited book examines anti-oppressive practice and focuses on the complexities and challenges of 'doing' anti-oppressive social work practice. Its strengths lie in the broad scope of the text and the range of chapter authors who emphasise the need for allies and activism to disrupt oppression.

Burdge, B (2007) Bending gender, ending gender: theoretical foundations for social work practice with the transgender community. *Social Work*, 52(3): 243–50.

This article examines gender-based oppression and the resulting psychosocial difficulties experienced by many transgendered individuals who are an at-risk population.

7

Age

Achieving a Social Work Degree

This chapter will help you develop the following capabilities from the Professional Capabilities Framework (2018):

1. Professionalism
5. Knowledge
6. Critical reflection and analysis
7. Intervention and skills

See Appendix 1 for the Professional Capabilities Framework and a description of the 9 domains.

(Continued)

(Continued)

It will also introduce you to the following standards as set out in the social work subject Benchmark Statement (2019):

5.2   Social work theory
5.3   Values and ethics
5.5   Nature of social work practice in the UK

See Appendix 2 for a detailed description of these standards.

Introduction

A quick Google scholar search using the key words 'age and anti-oppressive practice' brings up pages of literature related to social work practice with older people and the elderly. While issues of age relate to everyone, it has been acknowledged that where age influences decision making in social work, or results in differential (often negative) treatment on the basis of age, then the term 'ageism' can be ascribed to that experience of discrimination for older people. The term 'age discrimination' is more appropriately used for discrimination of young(er) people.

In this chapter, we will examine the ways in which oppression impacts on people across the life span and how ageism is experienced in the context of social work. Theories of ageing will be discussed and the chapter will conclude with a suggestion of effective strategies of delivering anti-ageist social work with service users.

Age and ageing

The United Nations (2015, p2) report on *World Population Ageing* notes that:

> *between 2015 and 2030, the number of people in the world aged 60 years or over is projected to grow by 56 per cent, from 901 million to 1.4 billion, and by 2050, the global population of older persons is projected to more than double its size in 2015, reaching nearly 2.1 billion.*

This reality requires social workers to become fully equipped with the necessary skills, expertise and knowledge about older people, whether as service users or as members of families who are engaged with social care services. It is fair to conclude that with the growth in the ageing population around the world, experiences of marginalisation, disadvantage, discrimination and oppression will be on the increase, and must become an area of concern for social workers.

Research Summary

In the UK, the Joseph Rowntree Foundation (2016) reported that older people accounted for 62 per cent of all hospital bed days and also 52 per cent of admissions requiring hospital stays of more than seven days (p7). This is important evidence for social workers who may need to advocate on behalf of older service users.

Research has found that social work students prefer children and families placements and not adult services, and this should be of concern to social work educators (Field et al., 2016) because this could imply that they may be unwilling to work with older people in their future careers or that they may lack the skills and knowledge required to work with older people. This makes the case for ensuring that anti-oppressive social work practice in relation to age is comprehensively addressed on qualifying social work programmes.

In the UK, age is designated a protected characteristic, making age-related discrimination unlawful, yet it remains to be seen how effective this legislation has been in protecting older people. Cox and Pardarsani (2017) suggest that while all older people are potentially vulnerable to discrimination, older women, immigrants and LGBTQI (lesbian, gay, bisexual, transgender, queer or questioning, and intersex), older people are a subgroup with heightened susceptibility to discrimination, reminding us yet again of the multiple oppressions associated with intersectionality.

Ageism

Ageism can be viewed as a set of oppressive beliefs held about people due to their age. Ageism, according to Butler (1980, p8) can be understood through three interrelated aspects:

1. prejudicial attitudes towards ageing, old age and the aged;
2. discriminatory practices against older people and the elderly;
3. institutional and systemic policies and practices which sustain biases and stereotypes about the elderly in ways that undermine their dignity whilst reducing scope for living and maintaining happy fulfilled lives.

These prejudicial attitudes are reinforced in everyday cultural production, in social and professional practices, in social policy and within the structure and function of institutions. During the Covid-19 pandemic, for example, Brooke and Jackson (2020) found that public discourse devalued older people through media reportage and where in some cases the deaths of older people in nursing homes were not reported. This could create the impression that older people's lives were insignificant or that their deaths were expected.

A study by Ben-Harush et al. (2016) found that ageism was common among social workers based in healthcare settings. This appeared to be the case at the start of their training when social workers expressed their views about not needing to spend much time with older service users. The study also found that social workers believed that it was acceptable for older service users to willingly end their lives.

Jackson et al. (2019) examined the association between well-being and age discrimination and found that overall, age discrimination towards older adults in England impacted negatively on their overall health and well-being.

Hughes and Mtejuka, cited by Thompson (1995), define ageism as

The social process through which negative images of and attitudes towards older people, based solely on the characteristics of old age itself, result in discrimination.

Older people experience stereotyping, which homogenises their experiences despite the fact that age is one characteristic and occurs in people individually and differently. There is no one formula for ageing, and greying cannot and should be used as a determinant of ageing.

Unfortunately, addressing age-related discrimination is not likely to be easy, because ageist stereotypes are pervasive and deep-rooted in society. A two-pronged approach aims both to reduce discriminatory behaviour across the population and to mitigate the effects of discrimination on health and well-being among older people.

Theories of ageing

According to Jin (2010), many theories of ageing exist, and while they often interact and complement each other, they do not appear to be conclusive or globally applicable. These theories are biological, sociological and psychological theories of ageing. 'How' we age and 'why' we age are two very important considerations for theorising ageing, and social workers should be aware of these distinctions when working with older people. Biological theories generally refer to physical representations of ageing where 'wear and tear' and natural processes are unstoppable. Body functions and vital organs begin to slow down or deteriorate due to longevity.

Activity and *disengagement* are two main theories used to explain ageing from a sociological point of view. Activity theory is credited to Havighurst and Albrecht (1953) who stated that keeping occupied and busy in later life led to satisfying and fulfilling lives, and although other theorists such as Maddox (1965) disagreed with the detail of this theory, it is broadly agreed that staying active as an older adult is desirable and meaningful.

In contrast to activity theory, Cumming and Henry (1961) proposed disengagement theory claiming that as people age, they contribute less and less to their families and communities, therefore effectively disengaging from social activities and thus spending more time reflecting on their lives, achievements and disappointments. Here, too, critics such as Schroots (1996) argue that disengagement theory does not adequately account for the differences in class and socioeconomic status, which may provide opportunities to disengage for some older people and not others.

The aim of providing a basic summary of the biological and sociological theories of ageing is to serve as a reminder to social work students and practitioners that their perceptions of ageing and their theoretical underpinning about what ageing is will influence their ability to work in an anti-ageist way with older people.

Activity 7.1

Look up other theories of ageing – for example, *continuity theory* by Robert Atchley.

- What are the main arguments of those theories?
- How might these be useful for you as a social worker?

Write down your thoughts and discuss these with a colleague.

The cultural context of ageing

It has long been argued that social and cultural beliefs shape our understanding and perception of age and ageism. While old age is perceived positively in countries and cultures around the world and in the UK, countries such as Japan view ageing as much more of a loss to independence and autonomy. Sin (2007), for example, looks at the experience of Asian-Indians ageing in Britain and concludes that factors such as migration history, ethnicity and gender among others, exacerbate parental expectations of support from their children. The study found the situation of White British respondents to be different in that they did not feel that children should be expected to provide for their ageing parents. They stated that for reasons such as distance and other family circumstances, this added caring responsibility should not be an expectation.

According to Higgs and Gilleard (2015) their review of ageing in the UK found that the gendered natured of ageing should be analysed in order to understand the way in which the key social and cultural drivers affect older people. They argue that older women are more likely to live in poverty after retirement or after the bereavement of a spouse, whereas older men are more likely to have access to pensions and property, which often puts them at an advantage compared to ageing females.

Healthcare systems influence the way that ageing is perceived in different counties. For example, the healthcare system (NHS) in the UK ordinarily implies that older people are eligible for free healthcare and treatment, whereas in the USA about 41 million Americans remain uninsured for healthcare (Clarke and Smith, 2011). Social workers will need to be mindful of the diversity of older people they might be working with and should consider carefully the issue of intersectionality. Older people in the UK may be first-generation immigrants, so it is crucial that this is considered within the wider scope of work and engagement. This could also mean being aware of the different health- and help-seeking behaviours, the gendered nature of helping and perhaps English language proficiency. It has been established that many older people are comfortable with herbal and alternative forms of treatment (Laird and Tedam, 2019). For these reasons, social workers should understand culture as representing the sum of all behaviours that are effective in adapting to one's environment. This will enable them to work in a non-oppressive and non-ageist way with older service users.

The social work role in addressing ageism in practice

Marshall's text (1990), *Social Work with Old People*, is one of the few resources dedicated to this area of ageism in social work practice. She suggests that the social work role lies in:

- combatting ageism;
- communication, including sensitive listening and awareness of non-verbal communication;
- generating and organising resources;
- helping the helpers, including carers and colleagues;
- practical help;
- supporting people whose lives are constrained by illness and disability;
- supporting people with managing crises that arise through loss and change – e.g. bereavement, changing physical and mental health;
- taking time to assess needs, starting where the older person is;
- working with other professionals.

Another strategy to address ageism in social work is for social workers to ensure that there is sufficient understanding of the older person's relationship with their family when designing services to meet their needs.

A study by Ridgway (2019) examined the perceptions of ageing in the UK, drawing on data from a purposive sample of 20 social work students studying for a Master's degree in social work. The study used Kogan's attitudes towards older people scale (KATOPS), and the results identified that from the beginning of their studies most students had neutral to positive attitudes towards older people, which improved during the next stage to all positive attitudes.

Beresford and Davis (2008) acknowledge that although older people make up the largest section of social care service users, they are offered very few opportunities to share and voice their concerns or contribute to matters affecting them. They argue that involving older people is significantly more than requiring them to complete surveys, be part of research or attend meetings. Disrupting age-related discrimination has the potential to prevent disease in older adults and improve mental health and well-being (Jackson et al., 2019). Consequently, social workers will need to approach this by raising public awareness about what ageism is and its effects on the well-being of older adults, as well as providing older adults with the tools and strategies to navigate and cope with ageism when it does occur. These will go some way to minimise the impact of ageism on older people. Age is also related to socioeconomic and other life chances globally and in the UK. For example, it has been found that cuts to social care and financial support to elderly pensioners as result of the austerity measures have contributed to the rise in mortality among those aged 85 years and over (Stuckler et al., 2017).

According to the Joseph Rowntree Foundation (2016), 26 per cent fewer older people receive help due to consecutive years of cuts to local authority budgets and funding. This has resulted in the social care system struggling to meet the needs of older people. Recognising that anti-ageism work is an aspect of social justice and represents anti-oppressive practice principles is important in the lives and experiences of older people. Any assessment of need should consider the impact of ageism on the lives of older people without straying into stereotypical expectations. According to Dominelli (2004, p137), *the negative image of the older person as dependent and in need of care portrays an ageist construction that treats every older person the same by ignoring the specific needs of older individuals and the contribution that older people as a group have made and continue to make to society.*

Thompson (2001, pp107–110) identifies a number of areas that make for effective anti-ageist social work practice. These include:

- counterbalancing negative stereotypes by preserving dignity and self-esteem;
- ensuring holistic assessment while ensuring that needs are matched with the appropriate services;
- ensuring that social workers challenge ageist assumptions and myths such as old means dependent, while maintaining sensitivity to the language used to describe older people;
- understanding and acknowledging intersectionality, which involves the recognition of other characteristics of the older person's identity – for example, their race, ethnicity, gender, sexuality and disability;
- ensuring that anti-ageist practice is not tokenistic and does not stand alone, but rather that it should be seen from a wider perspective as contributing towards a wider emancipatory and anti-oppressive discourse;
- ensuring that protection against harm as well as the assessment of risk is not at the expense of rights.

In order to work effectively with older people, social workers should consider using the biographical approach, which, according to Crawford and Walker (2004), utilises storytelling, reminiscence and review of life. Social workers must acknowledge that old age in itself is not a problem and should not be pathologised. The need of older people for a service due to ill health or any other need is what should be of paramount concern to social workers who wish to work in an anti-oppressive way with older people.

Activity 7.2

Reflect on the following questions:

- What were some of your views about older people and ageing previously?
- How have these views changed?
- What can you describe as the critical incident(s) leading to your change of views?

Age discrimination with children and young people

Earlier in this chapter, I made the point that the literature on age discrimination tends to focus on older people. It is important, however, to examine how discrimination based on age impacts on children and young people. As a social worker, you can facilitate and promote anti-oppressive practice with children and young people, for example, by doing what is suggested below by Bannister and Huntington:

Following, rather than always thinking we can or should lead; actively listening rather than always talking; engaging with children on their terms not just ours; being respectful of what they can do rather than largely focusing on what they cannot do (applying the deficit model of child development); or bringing our creativity and knowledge to the interactions we have with them, are all examples of routes to child-centred interactions.

(2002, p12)

There is a legal requirement for social workers to engage with the child and ensure that their voices and views are represented in matters that affect them (Lumsden, 2019). However, it is clear from some of the published serious case reviews in England that this has not always been the case (Laird and Tedam, 2019). For example, Khyra Ishaq, the 7-year-old girl from Birmingham who was never spoken to on her own is a case in point. Khyra eventually died of severe neglect, and emotional and physical abuse at the hands of her mother and step-father. Young children are disproportionately disadvantaged by age-discrimination within their own families and sometimes by social workers. According to Lumsden (2019), when professionals such as social workers make children invisible by not seeing them regularly or not listening to them, they become complicit in the lack of protection for such children. Our own constructions of age and maturity are important for recognising how much control, influence and authority children have (or not) over their own lives and circumstances.

Firmin (2020), writing about contextual safeguarding of children in England, found that young people who encountered harm experienced unequal treatment after reporting to the police or through other official channels. The young people were often met with disbelief, which discouraged them from reporting any future incidents, placing them at risk of further abuse outside the home. This, she argues, contrasts with people who made allegations of young people engaged in anti-social behaviour and crime. This group of people were more likely to be believed because they were adults. Firmin found that inequality is a cause and consequence of contextual harm to children. This research reminds us as social workers that when working with children and young people, we must also listen to them.

Taking a child's rights approach in our work as social workers improves our chances of working anti-oppressively with children and young people. The United Nations Convention on the Rights of the Child (UNCRC) recognises children's rights as falling into three main categories: protection (from harm, maltreatment and abuse), provision (food, clothing, shelter, affection) and participation (having their voices heard in matters that affect them). When working with children and young people, you will need to understand what these rights mean and how you can support the realisation of these rights. Munro (2011) argued that children are vulnerable by virtue of their dependency, vulnerability and age. You should therefore seek to extend your knowledge about children's rights so you can use a rights-informed approach when working with children and young people. Lumsden (2019) acknowledges that the role of social workers in combatting adversity is to consider structural inequalities and power imbalances in relation to children and their families. She proposes that to achieve greater visibility for children and young people, social workers need to *understand intergenerational consequences and the structural influences that perpetuate the need to protect them from violence and exploitation* (p116).

Chapter summary

The United Nations Principles for Older Persons (1991) statement 18 clearly articulates that *Older persons should be treated fairly regardless of age, gender, racial or ethnic background, disability or other status, and be valued independently of their economic contribution*. This, in addition to social work values, ethics and professionalism, requires students and practitioners to consider how older adults cope with the ageing process and how they might contribute towards a positive and meaningful experience of older people and social care services. There is also now the International Day of Older People established by the United Nations (1 October). These further evidence the value of older people and the need to ensure that social workers respect and value this day of celebration. This chapter has sought to examine the complexities of age-related oppression and discussions about the nature of social work intervention with people of different ages.

Further reading

Cox, C and Pardarsani, M (2017) Aging and human rights: a rights-based approach to social work with older adults. *Journal of Human Rights and Social Work*, 2: 98–106.

This interesting article proposes a rights-based approach to social work with older adults, and outlines the physical, mental and financial impact of ageing and retirement on people. They argue that social workers are uniquely placed to ensure that services are more responsive to older adults.

Jackson, SE, Hackett, RA and Steptoe, A (2019) Associations between age discrimination and health and wellbeing: cross-sectional and prospective analysis of the English Longitudinal Study of Ageing. *Lancet Public Health*, 4: 200–8.

This study was undertaken in England and explored the association between health status and age discrimination. The authors found that age discrimination negatively affected their overall health and well-being.

8

Race

Achieving a Social Work Degree

This chapter will help you develop the following capabilities from the Professional Capabilities Framework (2018):

2. Values and ethics
3. Diversity and equality
5. Knowledge
6. Critical reflection and analysis

See Appendix 1 for the Professional Capabilities Framework Fan and a description of the 9 domains.

(Continued)

(Continued)

It will also introduce you to the following standards as set by the Social Work Subject Benchmark Statement (2019):

5.3   Values and ethics
5.14   Intervention and evaluation
5.16   Build relationships and work effectively with others

See Appendix 2 for a detailed description of these standards.

Introduction

Race (and, of course, other biological and social factors) plays a significant role in determining where people live, the jobs they do, their socioeconomic status, education, overall well-being and life chances. There is a growing interest in racial disparities in many societies and across professions and services. In the area of social care in the UK and elsewhere, the disproportionate numbers of Asian, Black and minority people supported by youth justice, mental health and looked-after systems of care services remains concerning (Laird and Tedam, 2019).

In this chapter, we will be exploring some definitions of race and racism, and will spend some time discussing racism, forms of racism and the impact on people who deliver or receive social care services. Using critical race theory (CRT), we will see how this theoretical lens can assist social work students and practitioners to understand the experiences of Black minority ethnic people and enhance their provision of effective and non-oppressive supports and interventions. I have chosen to have separate chapters for 'race' and 'ethnicity' in order to examine the differences between the concepts and the ways in which these are considered in social work education and practice contexts.

Garner (2010, p1) has suggested that *a striking element of all scholarly attempts to understand what 'race' is seems to be the impossibility of providing a definition.* While I agree with this view, it is important for social workers to have a useful definition of race if they are to work effectively across racial and other differences. Sociologists have argued that race is a socially constructed term. For the purpose of this chapter, race is defined as a social construct that is determined largely by their human features such as shape of their nose, mouth, eyes, hair texture, skin colour and physical features. The argument in this chapter is that social workers need more than diversity and equality 'training', which effectively allows practitioners to tick a box and say they have 'done' or 'completed' required anti-racist training. The chapter will highlight the need for personal and systemic change, and the recognition that all assessment of clients requires an understanding of service users' experiences of racism. As helpful (and perhaps convenient) as it may seem to defer to colleagues who may have an understanding or experience of people from specific cultures, it is a counterproductive strategy in that it excuses social workers from trying to understand and work with racial diversity.

Racism

Activity 8.1

In this activity, you are required to identify a situation where you read about, heard of or witnessed racism. It could also be an example from your own experience of racism.

- What were the key messages in the case?
- How did you feel?
- What did you do about it?

Guidance

This activity is designed to get you thinking about recognising and responding to racism. Sometimes people make 'jokes' which are racist or they witness racism and do nothing to intervene or challenge racist attitudes and behaviour. It is useful to reflect on how you felt, what you did about it or what you would do on another occasion.

Before we look in detail at the topic of race and racism within the context of social work, it is important to look first at the wider demographic in England and Wales. For students reading this book from outside England, you will need to refer to demographic data pertaining to the country you are training and working in.

The Office of National Statistics (ONS) reported that in the 2011 census, the total population of England and Wales was 56.1 million, with the majority of the population (86 per cent) being White. People from Asian ethnic groups made up the second largest percentage of the population (at 7.5 per cent), followed by Black ethnic groups (at 3.3 per cent), Mixed/Multiple ethnic groups (at 2.2 per cent) and Other ethnic groups (at 1 per cent) (ONS, 2011). The percentage of the population from a Black African background doubled from 0.9 per cent in 2001 to 1.8 per cent in 2011.

What do we mean by 'institutional racism'?

On 22 April 1993, a young Black man, Stephen Lawrence, was murdered as he waited at a bus stop in London with his friend, Duwayne Brooks. While Stephen's death was widely spoken about and resulted in significant global and national media attention, the police were unable to bring Stephen's killers to justice at that time (Solomos, 1999). This resulted in Stephen's parents pushing for an inquiry into the police investigation of their son's murder. Sir William Macpherson was appointed to lead the inquiry, which subsequently found the Metropolitan Police force to have been institutionally racist. Institutional racism was defined in the report to be

The collective failure of an organisation to provide an appropriate and professional service to people because of their colour, culture, or ethnic origin. It can be seen or detected in processes, attitudes and behaviour which amount to discrimination through unwitting prejudice, ignorance, thoughtlessness and racist stereotyping which disadvantage minority ethnic people.

(Macpherson, 1999, Ch. 6)

The above definition is not new and has been adapted from the USA. It espouses several key ideas that are relevant for social workers if they are to work in an anti-oppressive and anti-racist way with each other and with users of social care services. Institutional racism, though, some have argued, removes responsibility from individual acts and omissions, and could impede critical self-awareness.

Young concluded that:

> *Macpherson's report raised the standard of racial debate in this country at a crucial moment, bringing both perception and understanding of race and discrimination more closely into line with the reality of the black British experience.*

(1999, p330)

The Macpherson Report was well received and strongly recommended that colour-blind policing should be outlawed and that the lived experiences of Black people in Britain needed to be understood. It is important at this juncture to introduce you to critical race theory, which promotes the use of narratives and challenges colour-blind approaches.

Critical Race Theory

I first read about Critical Race Theory (CRT) after the death of Victoria Climbié in 2002, when I was invited by one university in England to deliver a workshop to social workers about working effectively with Black and minority ethnic service users and their families. In researching for my presentation, I was drawn to CRT not only for its acknowledgement of racism as a daily experience for Black people, but also for its action-oriented approach. Developed in the 1970s by Derek Bell (2007), an African American civil rights lawyer, Critical Race Theory (CRT) challenges the experiences of White people as a *normative standard and grounds its conceptual framework in the distinctive experiences of people of colour* (Taylor, 1998, p122). CRT attempts to place the 'Black' voice and experience at the centre; it challenges discrimination, racism and oppression, and is underpinned by social justice. It is critical that you develop your understanding of the experiences of Black minority ethnic students and service users in the UK. Such knowledge places you in the position to address the role of racism in maintaining systems that perpetuate social problems and that result in the disproportionate impact on Black and Asian people in the UK. Critical race methodologies emphasise the importance of listening to stories and 'counter' narratives to make sense of the experiences of Black people. It has been suggested by Kolivoski et al. (2014, p269) that CRT provides an important framework that social workers can use to recognise, analyse and change power dynamics that maintain institutional racism and reinforce racial inequality. Although not all authors agree on the number of tenets for CRT, we will look at the following five, which I believe are key when examining how racism can be understood.

1. CRT sees *racism as endemic,* a daily occurrence for Black and minority ethnic groups and therefore not an abnormal experience. The argument being made here is that if racism is seen as being produced and reproduced in systems, organisations and processes, it often goes unnoticed by people who are racially privileged. As a daily occurrence, Black and minority ethnic group users of social care services in the UK will experience 'otherness' in

professional encounters with social workers who may unknowingly through stereotyping, prejudice and unfair oppressive assessments make situations worse.

2. Another tenet of CRT is that it *promotes and advances the voices of the otherwise voiceless and marginalised*. Marginalised people are better placed to 'tell their story' than dominant groups who have the tendency to recount these on their behalf. In seeking to be anti-oppressive, social workers should use intervention tools that support the sharing of narratives and experiences. Social workers should enable service users to discuss their experiences of racism and discrimination, and their fears and hopes regarding the intervention which is taking place. Bernard and Harris (2016) argue that it is crucial that social workers effectively engage families who are socially excluded, marginalised or disadvantaged.

3. A third dimension of CRT is that of *differential racialisation* in which dominant groups possess the power to decide which groups are deserving and undeserving – the 'in' group who benefit from resources, opportunities for success and other privileges, while the 'out' group lacks access to similar opportunities for success and associated privileges. I have been party to discussions in a social work team where parents/families of Nigerian heritage were spoken of in a negative light in comparison to families from other African backgrounds. This is an example of differential racialisation, because although Nigerians are also Africans, in this example they were spoken of more negatively than the service user from Sierra Leone, and the language used was stereotyping of 'people from Nigeria'.

4. *Interest convergence* is another dimension of CRT, which proposes that the 'majority' groups are only interested in the minority group when there are benefits of a material, psychological, political or other gains to be made. This tenet will assist social workers to understand that some employers are only committed to addressing racism and racist practice in their organisations if they stand to benefit directly from this in the form of positive publicity, awards for being an equal opportunities employer or minimising the racial disparities often present in service provision and interventions.

5. The final tenet of CRT is around what has been called the *intersectionality of identities*. While race is the main concern of CRT, it recognises the importance of social class, religion, sexuality, gender, disability and the implications for outcomes within social work education and practice. Intersectionality has been one of the threads throughout this book and is an important principle for anyone using CRT. See, for example, the illustration below which shows a woman 'ticking boxes' and she appears to have ticked all the boxes available. What this illustration does not tell us is which of these are fluid (can change) and how these categories explain who the service user is in a holistic way.

Figure 8.1   Intersectionality of identities

Activity 8.2

The importance of understanding the 'whole' person and their experiences cannot be overstated. Reflecting on the illustration above, consider how you might engage with the woman and her child.

- What do each of these categories mean to you?
- Are they fixed states?
- How might these categories intersect to uncover the uniqueness of this service user?

Overall, CRT stresses that the value placed on 'Whiteness' means that Black people are usually seen through a deficit and pathological (inadequate) lens. Being White provides open doors to many places and to various opportunities. Indeed, my own doctoral research into the social work practice learning experiences of Black African students in England (Tedam, 2015, unpublished) uncovered structural, overt and covert racism aimed at promoting Whiteness and devaluing people from other backgrounds within practice learning contexts. The often unchallenged and unearned privileges that go with being White were played out in various ways in the spaces of social work practice learning. An anti-oppressive environment would be one where all learners are accorded respect, and are empowered and supported to achieve their full potential. That the social work office is a busy one is well established. However, these offices serve as learning spaces for many social workers who have been sensitised to anti-discriminatory and anti-oppressive practice principles in the classroom.

Case Study

Boyston Dodds is a 16-year-old male of African Caribbean heritage. He has been living with his paternal grandmother since the divorce of his parents nearly two years ago. His father has remarried and has the care of Boyston's younger brother, Jamie, who is 10 years old. Boyston's mother returned to the Caribbean to look after her mother who is critically ill and continues to be in regular communication with Boyston. Boyston's grandmother, Faith, is well known and active in her community, having retired from youth work five years ago. Recently, Boyston has been getting into trouble at school and following an altercation which left another pupil injured. The school requests a meeting with Faith to discuss their concerns. Faith asks her grandson about the events leading to the altercation and he informs her that a group of 'White boys' were picking on him and calling him names. Boyston alleges that he mentioned this to a teacher a few times but nothing had been done about it. On the day of the altercation, the boys had apparently teased him because he lives with his grandmother.

Faith attends the meeting to find that four members of staff (three teachers and one behaviour support worker), as well as the parents of the injured child, were in attendance. Faith immediately expresses her concern about not being informed about the number of attendees and says that she would have brought someone with her for support.

You are a social work student on placement at the school and have been called in to support Faith and Boyston at this meeting. You take a quick look around the room and notice that Faith and Boyston are the only Black people in the meeting. The meeting starts with introductions and you are introduced as the student social worker who will be working with Boyston following the meeting.

Faith seeks clarification, saying that it feels as though the outcome has already been decided because of what has been said and how the social worker has been introduced. In her upset state, she gets up and leaves the room. Boyston goes after his grandmother. After initial hesitation, you follow them outside.

- What may be some of the thoughts going through your mind at this time?
- What will you say to Faith and to Boyston?
- What (if anything) will you report to people at the meeting?
- How does this set you up for a working relationship (or not) with Boyston and his grandmother?

Commentary

In the case study above, you are introduced to a Black African Caribbean family at a meeting and asked to support her and her grandson. You find yourself in a difficult and possibly uncomfortable situation, which results in Faith and her grandson leaving the meeting. On first reading, you may feel that this is a perfectly normal situation and the family's reaction is consistent with other families. It might be useful for you to consider the following:

- What is your understanding of unconscious bias?
- Do you think there was any racism towards Faith and/or Boyston either before or during the meeting. If not, why not, and if so, what were they?
- As a social worker, do you think you have a duty to share your views and feedback with the people at the meeting?

Once you have reflected on and answered these questions, continue to read the following definitions of racism and consider the questions again in the light of this new information.

Racism is a system of advantage based on race and has been defined by Harper (2012, p10) as:

Individual actions (both intentional and unconscious) that engender marginalisation and inflict varying degrees of harm on minoritised persons; structures that determine and cyclically remanufacture racial inequity; and institutional norms that sustain White privilege and permit the ongoing subordination of minoritised persons.

The Institute of Race Relations defines racism as:

the belief or ideology that 'races' have distinctive characteristics which gives some superiority over others. Also refers to discriminatory and abusive behaviour based on such a belief or ideology. In the UK, denying people access to good and services on the basis of their colour, nationality, ethnicity, religion etc is illegal and called racial discrimination.

These two definitions are interesting and afford you the opportunity to critically reflect on your own positions and understanding of racism. Racism may be overt (direct) or covert (indirect) in nature. Direct or overt racism appears to be in decline, with covert (indirect) racism being more rampant. In social work, racism includes negative attitudes towards the use of different languages, 'foreign' accents or the use of non-standard variations of a dominant community language. Demographic changes over the next two decades forecast that by 2026, the older Black and ethnic minority population in the UK will have risen tenfold from 175,000 to over 1.8 million (Age Concern, 2005).

It is no coincidence that:

- Black and minority ethnic people face more barriers to accessing mental health services (Memon et al., 2016).
- Black and minority ethnic young men are disproportionately represented in gang, knife and other criminal behaviour (Bennet and Holloway, 2004).
- Older people from Black and minority ethnic backgrounds are more likely to develop vascular dementia and early onset dementia, yet they face more barriers to access healthcare services than other groups (Osman and Carare, 2015).

Activity 8.3

Read the three points in the above paragraph again, write down some of your views about each of the points and share these with a colleague or reflect on your own.

- What can you do to try to address this in your own practice?

According to Bhattacharyya et al. (2020), racism is increasingly entangled with the economic and political situations in many countries and where *all manner of disputes and divisions can become racialised, sometimes with little warning* (p1). At the time of writing this book, the spread of the coronavirus has taken this trajectory, resulting in what has been called by some as the racialisation of the coronavirus. This, according to Devakumar and colleagues (2020), has been caused by social and political fractures within communities, resulting in discriminatory responses to fear, which unfortunately is disproportionately affecting minority and marginalised groups.

Activity 8.4

Of particular interest is the case of a female surgeon in Queensland, Dr Rhea Liang, who insisted that the 'misinformation' about the virus that began in Wuhan, China, has led to racially motivated remarks, one of which was made to her at work.
    Read the story titled 'Chinese-Australians face racism after coronavirus outbreak' via the link below:

https://au.news.yahoo.com/coronavirus-australia-racism-062343568.html

- What are your views on this experience from the perspectives of the patient and the doctor?

In the UK, there is growing concern about White minority groups such as the Gypsy, Roma or Traveller communities. According to Barany (2002), historically the Roma community is recognised as one of the most oppressed and excluded ethnic groups in Europe with poorer access to education, healthcare, employment and other social services. This group will be discussed in more detail in Chapter 9 where we examine ethnicity and ethnic diversity.

The language of race

Language, as will continuously be mentioned throughout this book, can create stereotypes, misinformation, confusion and perpetuate half-truths. There are many terms and phrases used to describe Black people all over the world, so it is important that social workers ask service users how they wish to be described. This, of course, does not change the ethnic categorisations suggested on the many forms and assessment templates often used by social workers. The terms Black Ethnic Minority, Black, Asian Minority Ethnic, and Black Minority Ethnic have been used as a collective title. In this book, I have chosen not to use acronyms and instead I will clarify which groups I am referring to where necessary. These categorisations are not homogeneous, do not exist for 'White' groups and are terminologies of convenience. Therefore, it is important that social workers are continuously aware of this when working with service users. Any strategies to work with service users arising from a 'one-size-fits-all' approach will be an oppressive one and will not reflect the diversity of this group.

Race and anti-racist social work practice

Thompson (2006, p82) argues that there is a danger that social work assessment will be based on dominant White norms without adequate attention being paid to cultural, ethnic and racial differences. Failure to take such differences into account will not only distort, and thereby invalidate the basis of the assessment, but will also serve to alienate clients by devaluing their culture. Dominelli's work in the area of race and social work is known for suggesting that race, racism and anti-racism are central to debates about ethnic minorities in Britain. She argues that social workers, and indeed some allied professions, treat Black families in a poor manner, often resulting from negative stereotypes, labelling and a lack of understanding (or refusal to understand) the needs of these families. Black, Asian, other minority ethnic service users' experiences of social work will guide their future engagement (Dominelli, 2008). In Chapter 4, we have outlined a few practical tools which you can use to unpick and understand the experiences of service users in relation to issues of race.

Social work education has gained some positive ground in ensuring that issues of race are discussed and addressed in qualifying training, and many practising social workers will engage in continuous professional development to update and extend specific knowledge areas. Issues of cultural diversity and race equality have been high on the social work training agenda since the late 1970s, according to Williams and Parott (2013). However, there appears to be concern about how students and practitioners evidence this in their written work and in practice. Surprisingly, research by Williams and Parrott (2013) found that in at least one social work programme in Wales, *a student could complete their degree without having to consider issues of race equality, seemingly relating this to lack of exposure to service users from Black minority ethnic backgrounds* (p1216).

In a report by HMSO (2019), out of 31,720 child and family social workers employed by local authorities, 71.7 per cent were White British, 11.1 per cent were Black (including people from Black Caribbean, Black African and Other Black backgrounds), with approximately 1,270 social workers who self-defined as Black African. These figures provide a context about the diversity of the children and families' workforce and suggest that anti-racist practice should not be the responsibility of these few Black minority ethnic social workers. If anti-racism is concerned with identifying, challenging and changing the values, structures and behaviours that perpetuate systemic racism, then it is crucial that *all* social workers show commitment and are involved in this process. In the long term, managing racism may be as harmful to health as exposure to racism, so it is an important anti-oppressive strategy to ensure that racism in all its forms is disrupted. Font (2013), writing about the USA, found that racial demographics of child social workers compared to their clients have a profound impact on services and that social workers' decision making was often reliant on the race of the child. In addition, newly qualified social workers were more likely to report and act upon child abuse allegations involving a Black child (Ashton, 2004).

Activity 8.5

In this activity, you are presented with door signs relating to various staff at the organisation where you are undertaking your placement.

With a colleague or on your own, reflect on and discuss what you see.

Towards the end of your placement, you are invited to share some feedback with the team and organisation.

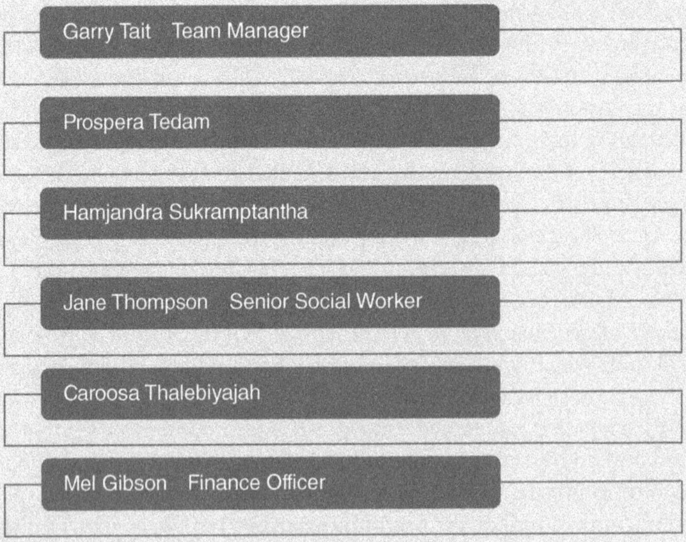

Garry Tait   Team Manager

Prospera Tedam

Hamjandra Sukramptantha

Jane Thompson   Senior Social Worker

Caroosa Thalebiyajah

Mel Gibson   Finance Officer

Figure 8.2 Door signs

Draft a letter explaining what your concerns are (if any) about the door signage and offer some recommendations for improved practice.

Guidance

Racism, according to Kohli and Solórzano (2012), can also manifest through affiliated factors such as immigration status, language or culture. In the preceding activity, there are two sets of names – the names that sound 'Western' versus the 'other' names. Research by Dion (2013) suggests that there is a relationship between a person's name and their sense of identity. There is also research about foreign-sounding names being disadvantageous in many recruitment processes, hence the idea of renaming oneself to 'fit' in with the majority is widely practised (Kohli and Solórzano, 2012). Useful questions to reflect on would be:

- Who instructed the signwriter to produce the signs?
- Who put up the signs?
- Who has been walking past those signs on a daily basis and said nothing?
- If people have commented or complained about this previously, whom have they complained to and what did they do when their concerns were not addressed?
- What message is this relaying to visitors and new members of staff?

It is a clear demonstration of racist practice that has been condoned until you, as the social work student, arrives on placement.

Black feminist perspectives

There was some discussion in Chapter 6 around Black feminist thought. However, it is useful to revisit these ideas in this chapter to help aid understanding. Black feminism, according to Allen (1996), is a political–social movement that arose from Black women feeling discontent with both the civil rights movement and the feminist movement of the 1960s and 1970s. It constitutes ideas produced by Black women that clarify a standpoint of and for Black women, but recognises that there is not a homogeneous Black women's experience, and that differences in age, social class, sexuality or ethnicity affect Black women's experiences variably. Black women's experiences are often overlooked or combined with Black men or all women (Collins, 1990) and has some synergies with CRT. The profession's historical links with disenfranchised groups makes it easy for Black feminist perspectives to thrive in this field, but to thrive means that social work educators must encourage students to engage with such perspectives. It is important that you understand that the levels of resilience shown by Black mothers, wives and sisters within families is a positive coping strategy. You should view this as an important anti-oppressive strategy – a strength and not a limitation.

Chapter summary

Social workers are uniquely positioned to both prevent and mitigate the consequences of racism as they work within a profession that proactively challenges and questions issues of privilege, discrimination and oppression. This chapter has sought to examine the area of race and its intersections with other elements of identity. I have provided a summary of CRT and identified how it may be useful for social work students in education and practice settings. It is incumbent upon social work educators to adopt anti-racist approaches that include active engagement with social workers and service users while also challenging any White privilege that appears to be automatic or unconscious. Reflexivity is an important vehicle through which anti-oppressive practice can be achieved. This is articulated well by Dominelli (2002, p9) who suggests that:

> Challenging inequality and transforming social relations is an integral part of anti-oppressive practice. Knowing oneself better equips an individual for undertaking this task. Self-knowledge is a central component of the repertoire of skills held by a reflective practitioner.... Moreover, reflexivity and social change form the bedrock upon which anti-oppressive practitioners build their interventions.

Further reading

Kolivoski, KM, Weaver, A and Constance-Huggins, M (2014) Critical Race Theory: opportunities for application in social work practice and policy. *Families in Society: The Journal of Contemporary Social Services*, 95(4): 269–76.

This article explains Critical Race Theory (CRT) and argues that despite its alignment with social works professional mission, the profession has not yet fully embraced its potential.

Macpherson, W (1999) The Stephen Lawrence Inquiry. London: HMSO.

Although there have been many developments since this inquiry, it is an important contribution to the discussion of race and race relations in Britain. Over 300 pages long, the report outlined 70 recommendations as a way of showing zero tolerance for racism in Britain.

9

Ethnicity

Achieving a Social Work Degree

This chapter will help you develop the following capabilities from the Professional Capabilities Framework (2018):

2. Values and ethics
4. Rights, justice and economic well-being
5. Knowledge
6. Critical reflection and analysis

See Appendix 1 for the Professional Capabilities Framework Fan and a description of the 9 domains.

(Continued)

(Continued)

It will also introduce you to the following standards as set by the Social Work Subject Benchmark Statement (2019):

5.3   Values and ethics
5.6   Communication skills
5.14 Intervention and evaluation
5.16 Build relationships and work effectively with others

See Appendix 2 for a detailed description of these standards.

Introduction

As the UK becomes more ethnically diverse, there is a growing need for social workers who can work in an ethnically sensitive manner with service users from many different ethnic backgrounds. Understanding ethnicity and the ways in which it can influence perceptions of events and circumstances, and how people approach problem solving is an important area of knowledge for social workers. Ethnicity is a complex concept and its complexity is evident in the multiple definitions that have developed over the years. Ethnic groups are bound by culture and customs that are shared (Cox and Ephross, 1997). Ethnicity and race are not the same, although they are often used interchangeably. This chapter will provide a definition for ethnicity and share UK statistics about the various ethnic groups. We will specifically examine Traveller communities and other more recent migrants from Eastern Europe, and propose ways of working anti-oppressively with these groups. Using a case study and number of activities, this chapter will assist you to understand how ethnic sensitivity is central to anti-oppressive social work practice and how specific minority ethnic groups experience social care services differently from the majority in the UK.

Essentialism

Essentialist thinking refers to the conviction that category membership is constant, unchangeable and permanent. Such thinking in relation to ethnicity can be dangerous because it promotes stereotypes and stereotypical thinking. Culture as a term is not fixed; it is fluid and changes over time. It is therefore important that social workers acknowledge the changing nature of culture and cultural practices to ensure that changes and adaptations to their responses to service users from Black minority ethnic communities. According to Cox and Ephross (1997), ethnicity has subjective and objective attributes which are an important consideration for social workers. For example, language, traditions and religion are objective attributes, while solidarity, belonging and having a sense of identity are more subjective attributes. People belonging to an ethnic group will usually adopt the norms, values and culture of the group.

Recognising and acknowledging ethnicity and ethnic differences is a core requirement of anti-oppressive social work practice. The case has already been made about why the chapters on race and ethnicity have been separated in this book, particularly to ensure that you understand the importance of the separation for your own practice. Read the example below.

Activity 9.1

Your supervisor/manager informs you that she is busy and asks you to go and meet with a service user who has been invited to the office to discuss her situation. The only information she has is that the service user is South African. You turn up and realise the service user is White.

- Would it be important for you to ask her ethnicity?
- If yes, why? If no, why not?

Reflect on this and make some notes.

Guidance

Asking the service user about her ethnicity is important because, as you will read shortly, race is usually more visible than ethnicity, and it may be that this service user requires interpreting services. In most cases and from experience, we begin to form a picture in our minds about service users even before we have met them. This might occur after a phone call or after reading a referral or related paperwork. In this activity, it would be good practice to ask the service user about their ethnicity – hopefully, not solely for the purpose of ticking that box on your form, but to enable you to consider carefully the implications for assessment and intervention.

According to Bhavnani et al. (2005, p130), ethnicity is defined as *a process of group identification . . . a sense of cultural and historical identity based on belonging by birth to a distinctive cultural group*. This definition is one that speaks to my own understanding of ethnicity because it straddles 'group identification' and 'belonging', which in my view are central to understanding ethnicity in contemporary practice.

Cox and Ephross (1997) provide a useful distinction between race and ethnicity, which is that 'race' can be visible and that ethnicity is reliant on people demonstrating links to particular cultures, languages, norms and values. Many ethnic groups can be subsumed under a particular 'race'. In the UK, for example, the category 'Black' is then followed by options such as 'Black British', 'Black African' and 'Black other'.

Social workers should ensure that policies meet the needs of people from different ethnic backgrounds and that any barriers are disrupted to ensure that service provision across ethnic groups is fair and adequate.

Ethnicity refers to group membership in which the defining feature is the characteristic of shared unique cultural traditions and a heritage that spans across generations. Membership in an ethnic group provides the cultural identity and lens through which the developing child comes to understand and act upon prescribed values, norms and social behaviour.

(Brookins, 1993, p1057)

This definition emphasises the shared cultural traditions as being important in understanding ethnicity. For example, in terms of race, you might see a person from Nigeria and a person from Barbados as Black; however, they will be from different ethnic groups which confer on to them specific values and norms from childhood.

Case Study

Telicia is a 14-year-old girl of dual heritage who is in the care of the local authority. She has had three foster home moves in the last 12 months and appears to be doing well with her current carers. Recently, her foster carers informed Gayle, the social worker, that Telicia is displaying sexualised behaviour. Telicia does not know her father but has been told he is White Irish. Telicia's mother who is African Caribbean and from Jamaica is currently in prison for drug offences and violence. All the foster carers she has lived with have been White British and Telicia has often told social workers that her foster carers do not understand her and that even though they make the effort to assist her, and to understand and appreciate her identity, she has not found it helpful because the focus has been on hair and skin care. Telicia also says that her social worker often seeks advice from an African colleague in the office who, according to Telicia, 'does not know a thing about Jamaican culture'.

Gayle meets with Telicia to address what has been reported as her sexualised behaviour. Telicia becomes upset, saying that all she does is a little twerking to music, a very popular dance routine among 'Black' girls.

- How might you respond if you were in Gayle's position?
- What advice might you give to the foster carers?
- How might you address this with Telicia?

Commentary

The above case study highlights issues that need to be considered by the social worker when working with the foster carers who are supporting Telicia. For example, the focus on hair and skin care is not viewed by Telicia as useful. Also, the foster carers' concern about sexualised behaviour arising from what Telicia refers to as 'twerking' is another area for discussion. To do this, the social worker needs to understand how this may be part of Telicia's identity.

Gayle's line manager has a role to play in preparing her and the other social workers to better understand the customs and beliefs of their service users, and to ensure ethnic sensitive practice. The duty to meet Telicia's cultural needs are enshrined in the Children Act 1989 (section 22 (5) (c)) and Gayle will need to reflect on whether her practice is sensitive to the ethnic and racial identity of Telicia. In addition, Gayle should encourage open and honest discussions with the foster carers about their concerns and support them to be creative in their approach to Telicia.

Ethnicity is also used to connote 'otherness' and has implications for the ways in which people from ethnic minority groups are treated and supported. Othering Telicia comes in the form of considering her to be non-mainstream or in the 'out' group. Otherness has been examined in depth in Chapter 1. It is this 'otherness' in relation to ethnicity and race that often results in various forms of discrimination and racism.

Institutional racism thrives where conversations about race, ethnicity and culture are avoided within the workplace and among social workers.

Ethnicity in contemporary Britain

According to Garner (2010), the ethnic categorisations used in the UK have grown since their first use in 1981. In 2001, the ethnic groups were White, Mixed, Asian, Black, Chinese, Other, Minority. By 2011, the census categories increased to include subcategories. So, for example, the White category is further divided into White British, White Irish, White Gypsy/Traveller, White Other and the Asian category now includes Bangladeshi, Chinese, Indian, Pakistani, Asian Other. The next census, which is scheduled to take place in 2021, is predicted to show significant increases in ethnic minority groups such as Black African and White Other, for example (ONS, online 2020).

The census used a process of self-definition in terms of ethnicity (ONS, 2011). Ethnic diversity has continued to grow in Britain over the last 20 years, resulting in the existence of many different ethnicities. Many ethnic groups can belong to a particular race – for example, Black African-Caribbean and Black African will all be classed as Black.

Ethnicity has been found to be a contributing factor to poor health outcomes in countries such as the USA, Australia, Canada and the UK. Individuals from Black and minority ethnic groups have been found to be more likely to report poor general health than the White British population, and this was found to be true also of the ageing Black and minority ethnic community. A study by Evandrou et al. (2016) found that Pakistani and Bangladeshi elders, both among men and women, experience a clear disadvantage compared with other ethnic groups.

In the area of social care services, this pattern of inequality and unequal access persists. According to Mantovani (2016), behaviours such as 'avoidance' and 'silencing' among Black minority ethnic communities in the UK resulted in people with mental illnesses being left without the appropriate intervention and services for adults. Research by Lai (2000) indicates that people from Black and minority ethnic backgrounds are over-represented in psychiatric hospitals, yet in all other areas their take-up of health services is low.

For minority children, ethnic identity was found to be an enabler and correlated positively with self-esteem – hence the need for social workers to bear this in mind when working with children (Baumann and Sunier, 2004).

It is important that we recognise the rich history of ethnic minorities across the UK who, according to Laird (2010), have been a part of British society from as far back as the sixteenth century, beginning with the slave trade and later with employment as seamen. People of African descent started to settle and form small communities in the port areas of Liverpool, London, Cardiff and Bristol.

Traveller communities

In the 2011 census for England and Wales, 58,000 respondents identified themselves as Gypsy or Irish Traveller. However, other sources estimate that the population size of Gypsies and Travellers could be anywhere between 82,000 and 300,000 people, and are the largest ethnic minority group in Europe (Sweeney and Matthews, 2017). Gypsies and Travellers have faced racism and persecution in many forms. It is suggested that suspicion and lack of understanding of their nomadic way of life has meant that Gypsy and Traveller groups have often found themselves being moved from place to place and feeling unwelcome in many areas.

According to Sweeney and Mathews (2017), children from Gypsy and Traveller communities face a myriad of unequal treatment in the UK. For example, they are three times more likely to be taken into care than other children. Writing about the rights of Traveller children in Ireland, Murray (2019) argues that Traveller children are a minority within a minority, and that a lack of understanding about their cultural practices has meant that they are continually being marginalised and oppressed. In the area of education, Traveller children perform less well than non-Traveller children. She argues that while 92 per cent of non-Traveller children complete secondary school, only 13 per cent of them achieve this, in part due to the lower expectations of teachers, reduced timetables by school systems and bullying by peers.

In the area of education, the 2011 census of England and Wales found that 60 per cent had no formal qualifications, which is three times higher than the national average. Despite being a minority group, Gypsy and Traveller people have higher prisoner rates when compared to other groups. One in twenty prisoners identified themselves as Gypsy, Roma or Traveller persons, despite representing only 0.1 per cent of the population.

In relation to health, the life expectancy of Gypsies and Travellers is said to be ten years shorter than the national average. This calls for an understanding of health inequalities and the implications for minority groups.

Sweeney and Matthews (2017) propose a series of strategies which they suggest should be adopted by social workers when working with Gypsy, Roma or other Traveller individuals and families. In the area of child care and child protection, they propose that social workers who receive referrals about children from any of these communities should consider carefully the cultural competence of the person making the referral. As a social worker, you will need to determine whether the referral reflects a lack of understanding of Traveller cultures or whether it is about a child or children at risk. They suggest that if the referral indicates a lack of understanding of Gypsy culture or reflects stereotypical negative views, then the social worker should attempt to visit the referrer for additional information. Of course, this is only possible if the referrer is named and wishes to be known. Where the referrer is a member of the public-seeking anonymity, then this needs to be considered within the context of the initial contact and subsequent assessment if required. Assessing routines and timekeeping is an area in which you will need to work with cultural sensitivity to avoid oppressive practice. Sweeney and Mathews (2017) suggest that Gypsy, Roma and Traveller parents tend to respond to their children's needs and not necessarily follow a routine. This sort of practice should not be undermined or disregarded by social workers, but rather used to ensure that the assessment is both fair and thorough. The presence and role of the extended family is another area that social workers need to be aware of when engaging within Traveller communities because it is common for people to live in extended family contexts and not in nuclear families. Consider this point when going through Activity 9.1 below.

Activity 9.2

You are a social worker who has received a referral regarding children potentially at risk of harm. When you arrive at the address given, you realise that it is a caravan site and begin to ask for the family you have come to speak to. Three people you ask say they do not know the family you are referring to. Disappointed and frustrated, you return to the office to seek advice.

- What could you have done prior to attempting the home visit?
- How might you go about trying to locate the right family to further your enquiries?

Guidance

It is always good practice to seek advice and guidance from social workers who have experience of working with Traveller families. In the absence of anyone with this experience within your immediate professional network, it is advisable that you read about this minority group. If you had done that prior to attempting the home visit, you would have found out that due to a mistrust of authorities and government officials, people would be hesitant to point out the family you were looking for. Importantly, by asking three different people, you have compromised the family's confidentiality and perhaps unknowingly engaged in oppressive practice. Going forward, you would need to collaborate with professionals who are already trusted by the community, because research suggests that this is a viable strategy. Social workers are used to working with settled communities and can find the nomadic lifestyles of Traveller families difficult to navigate. However, it is important to learn about these communities and access resources about best practice.

There are some recorded examples of good practice when working with Gypsy, Roma and Traveller communities which Davis (2010) has commented upon. In Haringey, for example, the Community Social Work Model appears to be successful in engaging children and families from these communities. The model emphasises a culture of development, while purposefully moving away from a culture of deprivation and poverty. By culture of development, this model seeks to work with Traveller communities as partners in their own growth and development through initiating projects, designing, implementing and evaluation. This model can be said to be non-oppressive in that it empowers through development and builds on strengths, thereby minimising stigma, discrimination and marginalisation.

When Gelfand (2003) suggests that ethnicity is shaped by structure and agency, he means that White people can exercise their agency by choosing to belong to an ethnic group, while Black people are limited by immigration laws and discrimination.

It has been reported that 3.6 million EU-born people now live in the UK in 2018, constituting 5.5 per cent of the UK population (Vargas-Silva and Fernandez-Reino, 2019). The highest numbers came from Poland followed by Romania, Ireland, Germany and Italy. Polish and Romanian people have been exposed to and are frequent victims of discrimination, bullying, harassment and xenophobia, according to Fox (2013). When working with younger people and children from Poland and Romania, as a social worker you will need to ask them about their experiences of racism as part of any anti-oppressive strategy. There is the assumption that because these communities are 'White', they do not experience discrimination and oppression. It is important for social workers not to make assumptions about families from these backgrounds, particularly assumptions arising from stereotyping.

Ethnicity in social work

Ethnicity, like race, should always be taken seriously in all social work specialisms. Oppression takes place in everyday practice and relationships, and the manner in which people are oppressed in contemporary society is increasing. What concerns us in this chapter is the way in which ethnicity and ethnic grouping result in hostility and growing inequalities. It is widely acknowledged that children of mixed heritage in the UK are disproportionately placed in the looked-after systems of care (Bernard and Gupta, 2008).

Ethnicity in the area of ageing is one that is significant for social work practice with older adults and the elderly in the UK. The continuum of care must consider older people's views about where they wish to live and how they wish to be supported. For example, at the time of writing in the current climate of the COVID-19 pandemic, it is important that social workers continue to work anti-oppressively by accessing information about and analysing whether or not certain ethnic groups are disproportionately represented in COVID-19 related deaths. While you are undertaking your social work training and after you qualify, you are required to critically reflect on your decisions leading to your intervention and to be continuously aware of the ways in which your value preferences influence and shape your practice.

Ethnic group membership

Ethnic group membership usually means a common approach for understanding and solving problems, which is important for social workers to know. Research by Valenti (2017) looked into the use of Family Group Conferences (FGC) with Black minority ethnic families in Scotland and found that overall, the benefits of using FGC worked well because Black minority ethnic families felt this served as a useful space for negotiations, led by the family, and moderated and supported by social workers and other professionals to make decisions about children's welfare.

FGCs were first used in New Zealand in the 1980s as a response to the over-representation of Maori children in the care of the state. The committee which was set up to investigate this concluded that the Maori population felt powerless and frustrated with the system that was in place (Frost et al., 2012). The research in New Zealand identified the need for the use of empowering interventions that positively valued the role of the extended family. FGCs are by the family and bring friends, professionals and relatives involved with a case to a meeting where any decisions about the child's welfare are discussed and made. This process minimises the chances of Black minority ethnic families being at the receiving end of oppressive or racist practices and interventions.

The stated success of this model led to its introduction into UK social work, and Valenti (2017) reported that FGCs can be used effectively with people from different cultures and backgrounds.

There are concerns, however, that Black minority ethnic families appear not to utilise or be referred for FGC as much as families from the White Scottish majority. The essence of the FGC approach, therefore, is one that offers Black minority ethnic families safe spaces within which to discuss and reach decisions about the care and well-being of children at risk of significant harm. As social workers, you should ask about FGCs in your organisation or agency, and understand whether these have proved useful to families in a way that is non-oppressive.

Ethnicity and anti-oppressive practice

Social workers should be mindful of the effect of ethnic group membership on the problems that service users experience. Ethnic Sensitive Practice is one strategy which you could use to minimise oppressive practice in social work. Ethnic sensitive practice supports the view that social workers should be respectful of service users' ethnicities and how these influence their world views and perspectives. To ensure ethnic sensitive practice, you should seek to know the ethnic backgrounds of the people you are working with. Tools such the cultural web (Tedam, 2013), discussed in Chapter 12, should assist you to uncover the ways in which anti-oppressive practice can be achieved and ethnic penalties minimised.

Ethnic penalties

In order to practise anti-oppressively in social work, you also need to be aware of what is referred to as 'ethnic penalties' (Heath and Cheung, 2007). The use of the term 'ethnic penalty' has extended to include the many areas where ethnic minority people experience overwhelming and disproportionate discrimination, thereby facing penalties that are otherwise not experienced by majority groups. The concept of ethnic penalties argues that penalties are the cause of the poor occupational success of ethnic minorities throughout the job-seeking process. This has resulted in Black ethnic minorities possessing lower incomes and higher unemployment than White minority groups as well as a general difficulty in appointments to occupations and job roles that reflect their high educational attainments. Understanding ethnic penalties will to some extent assist social workers when they are assessing circumstances, employment and socioeconomic situations which may be impacting on families. For example, one of the Es in the Social GGRRAAACCEEESSS framework (Burnham, 2012) discussed in Chapter 4 stands for 'Employment'. This provides a useful opportunity for you to discuss the family's financial situation, during which you could assess their employment status in line with what you know about ethnic penalties in employment.

Gilligan and Akhtar (2005), writing about child sexual abuse in Bradford, UK, acknowledged the low take-up of services by Asian communities because they did not always know where to go for support and help, compounded by a feeling of distrust of

White social workers in powerful organisations. They also found that information booklets translated into various languages (Punjabi, Urdu, Bengali and Gujarati) were considered useful in sharing information about child sexual abuse and services available. The practice of making important material and information available in different languages is another anti-oppressive strategy which supports inclusion.

Chapter summary

This chapter has highlighted how you might work non-oppressively with families from the Traveller community. We have also examined the concept of ethnicity and explained the ways in which ethnic penalties can and do undermine the lived experiences of Asian, Black, and minority ethnic individuals and families in the UK. Proposing ethnic sensitive approaches, I have highlighted the benefits of adopting this approach as part of an overall anti-oppressive practice strategy for social workers.

Further reading

Bhavnani, R, Mirza, HS and Meetoo, V (2005) *Tackling the Roots of Racism: Lessons for Success.* Bristol: Policy Press.

This book discusses topics of importance to this chapter and the book more widely. The authors examine the causes of racism and anti-racist interventions, and it is useful for students to see how they outline education as a tool to prevent racism.

Sweeney, S and Matthews, Z (2017) Friends, families and Travellers: a guide for professionals working with Gypsies, Roma and Travellers in Children's Service. Available online at: www. gypsy-traveller.org/wp-content/uploads/2017/03/A-guide-for-professionals-working-with-Gypsies-and-Travellers-in-the-public-care-system.pdf (accessed 10 March 2020).

This useful report outlines the experiences of Gypsy and Traveller communities in the UK and offers useful insight into how social workers and other professionals can work effectively with this group.

10

Disability

(Continued)

This chapter will also introduce you to the following standards as set out in the Social Work Subject Benchmark Statement (2019):

5.2   Social work theory
5.4   Service users and carers

See Appendix 2 for a detailed description of these standards.

Introduction

According to Meekosha and Dowse (2007), social workers are part of a 'disabling' as well as an 'enabling' profession, and this is seen in the many roles they occupy in contemporary education and practice arenas.

Traditionally, social workers employed in disability services have engaged in the assessment of people along psychological, educational, biological and psychosocial dimensions. In undertaking these assessments, social workers are often placed in the position of gatekeepers as they reach decisions about eligibility for services and financial support. This situation has seen a further decline due to austerity, which, according to Grootegoed and Smith (2018), has been brought about by governments reducing spending on welfare and care. In this chapter, we will examine a definition of disability, summarise Critical Disability Theory (CDT) and suggest ways in which it can be applied in social work practice. Models of disability will be discussed and provide critiques of each model. Using case studies and reflective exercises, this chapter will draw out the intersectional nature of disability and provide service user experiences.

Research Summary

Research by the Equality and Human Rights Commission (2017) found that in the UK:

1.   Disabled people are more likely to report less satisfaction with health services and processes, as well as experience health inequalities in comparison to non-disabled people. They also found that persons with disabilities were more likely to die younger than other people.
2.   Pupils with disabilities in England, Wales and Scotland were significantly more likely to be permanently or temporarily excluded from school, had a lower attainment rate and were more likely to be bullied than non-disabled pupils.
3.   More disabled people than non-disabled are living in poverty or are materially deprived and are more likely to experience difficulties in getting accessible housing.

The research highlighted above points to the existence of oppressive and discriminatory practice in the lives of persons with disabilities.

Defining disability

Disability, according to Meekosha (2006), is increasingly understood as a social relationship, not a characteristic of individuals with impairments. Consequently, disability is experienced at different sites of individual, group and societal interaction.

The United Nations (UN, 2008, p2) defined disability as

an evolving concept and that disability results from the interaction between persons with impairments and attitudinal and environmental barriers that hinders their full and effective participation in society on an equal basis with others.

The World Health Organization (WHO, 2011, p7), on the other hand, defined disability as

An umbrella term for impairments, activity limitations, and participation restrictions. Disability refers to the negative aspects of the interaction between individuals with a health condition (such as cerebral palsy, Down syndrome, mental health issues [such as depression, anxiety, panic attacks]) and personal and environmental factors (such as negative attitudes, inaccessible transportation and public buildings, and limited social supports.

In both definitions there is reference to interactions between the person and the environment and/or attitudes, which suggests that societal views and attitudes contribute to the experience of disability for disabled people. Social workers must avoid assessments and interventions which do not take into account the disabled person's self-definition and experiences, as these are very much central to their engagement with social care services. Disability is not an individual trait; it is not flaw or an individual tragedy (Slee, 2018).

Activity 10.1

Reflect on the two definitions of disability provided by the United Nations and the World Health Organization.

* What might you add to or change in the definition and why?

A word on intersectionality

People with disabilities can and do have other social and physical characteristics that provide them with unique identities. A person with a disability may also be female, male, LGBTQI, Black, White, young, old, rich, poor, educated, uneducated and a host of other characteristics. This intersectionality of identities requires social workers to engage with people on an individual level, avoiding stereotyping or relegating them to groups.

Recognising this will enable social workers to explore discrimination, vulnerability and difference, and how these occur within service users' unique contexts.

According to Meekosha (2006), disability is a gendered concept exposed when women with disabilities are questioned about their fertility, sexuality and reproductive rights. Similarly, men with disabilities are interrogated about their loss of masculinity and sexual behaviour. This misrecognition contributes to the stigma and discrimination faced by people with disabilities and, as social workers, we should work with service users to avoid social distress and disrupt all oppressive practices.

Like any other field of practice, social workers have much to contribute to the area of disabilities, primarily by providing appropriate services to meet the whole life needs of people with disabilities. Social work professionals must be able to identify the general needs of their service users, offer and provide a range of communication and intervention options to ensure that quality services are delivered. In doing this, social workers need to be aware of the impact of disablist and oppressive language.

Disablist language

In this section, an outline of how language influences the concept of disability and the status of disabled people will be undertaken. This often involves the images used to depict disabled people, as well as words used to describe disability.

It has been argued that some metaphors denoting a deficit or malfunction are oppressive and at odds with disability rights. A few of these examples are:

- blind to the truth;
- handicapped by a lack of knowledge;
- crippled with anxiety.

Although these terms in themselves are no longer used in the UK, there are many countries where language used to describe various forms of disability are questionable and offensive. The words and pictures used when referring to people with disabilities have a direct impact on social attitudes towards them.

Research by Heenan (2005) found that social work students often expressed stereotypes about people with disabilities claiming state benefits and support. The view that the majority of claimants were deliberate in their choices to receive disability benefits was articulated by students in one class in the following ways. One social work student remarked:

Some of them get the cars and then rent them out to taxi companies. Some of them can't even drive; it's just a racket.

(Heenan, 2005, p499)

While another claimed that:

Basically they are a pack of spongers. I see them with their new cars and buying rings round them, their children have the best of everything. Who do you think is paying for it all? It's us the mugs who have worked hard for every penny we have.

(Heenan, 2005, p499)

> **Activity 10.2**
>
> Think about the preceding statements made by two social work students in Northern Ireland and consider the following questions.
>
> * How might you address their comments with them?
> * How might you encourage a non-oppressive approach to class discussions about people with disabilities?

It is also known that in some non-English speaking communities, terminology representing various types and forms of disabilities have not changed and discussions with some people from these communities may reflect the lack of movement in this regard. As a social worker, you should be able to advise on appropriate language to be used by parents, carers or other family members about a person with disabilities. In addition, Tedam and Adjoa (2017) identified that among some Black minority ethnic communities, certain disabilities and conditions such as epilepsy and albinism were perceived as being linked to witchcraft and spirit possession. Consequently, the response or intervention tended to be one of abuse and neglect. In the 1950s, Rattray found that children born with an extra finger in Ghana were killed at birth. Today, a person with albinism in Tanzania is sought after for their body parts which are considered useful for spiritual purposes (Brocco, 2015). Such beliefs have exacerbated the plight of people with albinism and has resulted in many murders and machete attacks. It is important to be aware of and understand examples such as these because of attitudes to disability by some UK residents and citizens who may be affiliated to these and other countries where disability is poorly understood and supported. Social workers will need to be aware of contemporary research relating to these topics so that they can advise appropriately, especially in relation to safeguarding children where return to some of these countries may be a possibility.

Critical Disability Theory

Critical Disability Theory (CDT) emerged from Critical Theory created by the Frankfurt School. It is a framework that centralises disability and challenges the ableist assumptions that shape societal views and behaviours. Ableism is considered the most dominant disability narrative in Western societies. Campbell (2009) defines ableism as a set of beliefs that produces disability as a counter-image to able-bodiedness and, hence, as deviant or an unwanted difference. Critical Race Theory (CRT discussed in Chapter 8) focuses on the experiences of Black people in terms of racism and racial discrimination. Along similar lines, CDT offers you, as a social worker, the opportunity to challenge dominant discourses that support and promote ableism and oppress people with disabilities. In acknowledging the core beliefs of CDT, you will also be working to the various domains of the Professional Capabilities Framework (PCF) – for example, PCF 4: Rights, justice and economic well-being; PCF 5: Knowledge; PCF 7: Skills and intervention. Critical disability theorists direct their work towards activism and recognise the importance of intersectional approaches to understanding the lived experience of disability. Supporters of CDT utilise a social justice approach where the disruption of oppression towards disabled people is promoted and supported. As social justice, dignity and the worth of individuals and support for self-determination are key values of social work, practitioners who draw upon principles of CDT in their work will also be working to anti-oppressive paradigms.

Models of disability

There are four main models of disability which have made major contributions to the understanding of disability: the religious/charitable/social welfare model; the medical model; the social model; the affirmative model.

According to Harris and Enfield (2003), the *religious, charitable/social welfare model* is applied with a traditional or religious interpretation and is thought of as an impairment viewed as a punishment from God for some sin committed. As a result, having a disabled relative could be perceived as a source of shame, often for the whole family.

The *medical model* uses a clinical means of describing disability and focuses on the lack of physical, sensory or mental functioning. In this model, the focus tends to be on what the disabled person cannot do, such as the inability to walk, speak or dress themselves. By so doing, the disabled person is viewed as someone who needs to be fixed, repaired or improved. They are patients in need of medication and medical attention, with the medical personnel posing as the experts trying to identify and recommend a cure. Where there is no cure, the situation is then viewed as tragic, and professionals take on the care and rehabilitation of disabled people. According to Shakespeare (2006), this model has been criticised because of the way in which it views people with disabilities as unable to play a full role in society.

The *social model* of disability was coined by Michael Oliver in 1983. This model viewed disabled people not as individual victims of tragedy, but as collective victims of an oppressive society. Environmental barriers such as narrow doors, poor lighting and the absence of lifts limit mobility and can create difficulties for people, which eventually results in their exclusion from society. The model therefore often focuses on changes required in society such as, for example, improving physical structures, using accessible formats to share information and, of course, ensuring that this framework brings disabled people together to challenge inequality and discrimination.

The *affirmative model*, according to Swain and French (2000, p269), is a model of disability which they suggest is a

> non-tragic view of disability and impairment which encompasses positive social identities, both individual and collective, for disabled people grounded in the benefits of lifestyle and life experience of being impaired and disabled.

The model challenges any presumptions of tragedy, dependency or abnormality, and values disabled individuals' contributions to shaping their own identity and lifestyles.

Critique of the models

It is acknowledged that social workers are not confined to choosing between and among models of disability in their work. However, it is it necessary that social workers approach work with all people from a perspective of respect and non-oppression. In this section, we examine some of the critiques of the models and propose ways of working that may minimise discrimination and oppressive practice. Owens (2014) argues that the UK social model of disability can be critiqued for the idea that all disabled people experience oppression in the same way and to the same extent. She argues that people with disabilities may form a united front against discrimination and oppression, but that there is little room for recognising the individual body or individual experiences of oppression. In its current form, the UK social model of disability presumes that all disabled people experience oppression and ignores the variety of lived experiences of impairment. By exploring their experiences, the differences between disabled people will become recognised – for example, differences between people with learning difficulties and physically impaired people, reinforcing the individual (medical) model. More complexity then arises because disability is diverse and there has been a lack of appreciation of the mechanisms producing disability.

Another criticism of the social model of disability is that it could be perceived as suggesting that disability would be eradicated if society and societal attitudes changed in the appropriate ways. This could be misleading in that it does not acknowledge that pain, for example, cannot be removed by societal attitudes and barriers.

It is important to acknowledge that there are growing numbers of people with disabilities who are themselves training to become social workers or are already practising in the UK and elsewhere. Research by Bernard et al. (2013) found that students with disabilities fared less well on social work programmes in England and that reasonable adjustments as required by the Equality Act 2010 were not always provided. In addition to this, Sin and Fong (2009) argued that the regulatory fitness requirements of disabled people undergoing social work training was more stringent than for qualified and practising social workers. For example, some mental health conditions may affect students in various ways, such as the ability to work under pressure, in groups or to meet deadlines.

Medical models of disability can be oppressive in the sense that it often refers to something that is 'wrong' with a person's body or mind. The model suggests that the illness, injury or genetics are defective and may be cured or treated through the use of drugs, surgery or other interventions. I am not undermining the importance of medication and medical intervention for some disabilities. However, I am suggesting a more holistic appreciation of the role of society in further disabling people. The medical model is disablist because it views things from an ableist perspective and relegates people to labels that are further oppressive and discriminatory. For example, if a person using a wheelchair cannot access a building due to steps, the medical model would view this as a result of the wheelchair rather than the presence of steps and no lifts.

Activity 10.3

- Having read about the four models of disability, which of these models can you relate to and why?

Write down your thoughts or discuss these with a colleague.

Learning difficulties

People with learning difficulties can be found in all countries, communities and regions of the world. Williams (2009, p7) defines a person with learning difficulties as:

Someone whom society identifies as having an impairment in cognitive functioning but whose needs and interests are not well catered for by societal structures or by interactions of other people; he or she is a survivor of struggles to overcome this disadvantage and may need help to continue to do so.

Learning difficulties are said to be mild, moderate or severe, and involve the way a person understands information and how they communicate. In the UK, around 1.5 million people are said to have a learning disability, which impacts on the way they understand new or complex information and can impact on their ability to cope independently. Some learning disabilities such as Down's syndrome are diagnosed from birth, while others may be diagnosed as the child grows and develops. Children with learning difficulties are likely to require support in schools and this may be monitored through social care services.

People with disabilities often experience exclusion from many physical and cognitive spaces, and also within families and communities. In the UK, there are certain groups of people who are at risk of poverty and social exclusion. These include people who are unemployed, the elderly and disabled people. In 2013, the Department for Work and Pensions stated that there are 11.5 million people in the UK (19 per cent of the population) who were covered by the disability provisions set out in the Equality Act 2010. By 2017, this number rose to 13.9 million (SCOPE, 2019).

Case Study

Jamil Quentaar is a 30-year-old male with a physical disability which requires him to use a wheelchair and the services of a personal assistant as a scribe. As part of your module on Professional Practice, you are asked to write a letter inviting Mr Quentaar to your university as part of an assessment. This is all the information you have; however, you decide you require a bit more information.

On your own or with a colleague, consider the following:

- What additional information would you require?
- How might you use this additional information?
- Produce a draft of the letter inviting Mr Quentaar to your university.

Commentary

It is good practice to contact Mr Quentaar in advance, introduce yourself to him and explain the task you are undertaking for your social work course. You may wish to ask what adjustments he might need (these could be ramps, designated parking, etc.). You may feel that an initial phone call would be useful, but you may not have access to his phone number. Discuss these dilemmas with your colleague, particularly around how you might construct your letter to Mr Quentaar.

Anti-oppressive practice with persons with disabilities

Social workers practise in different settings such as child and family services, women's shelters, healthcare, schools, refuges, residential and rehabilitation facilities, prisons, young offenders' institutes, private and voluntary sectors, to mention a few. In all these practice settings, there will be service users, family members and carers, and professionals who are living with some form of disability.

Although understanding group dynamics and experiences is important to gauge the collective experiences of people with disabilities, it is equally important for social workers not to lose sight of the individuality of people with disabilities whom they might be working with. Social workers will encounter persons with disabilities during their work and they will be differentiated by age, gender, sexuality, race, ethnicity and social class. There is growing recognition of the importance of hearing and responding to views and perspectives of disabled people, with particular focus on their needs in different settings and situations. Children with disabilities, for example, may live at home with family or away from home in out-of-home care and it is important that these patterns of care reflect childcare arrangements more generally.

Research has found that parents of disabled children, particularly mothers, tend to experience higher levels of stress and burnout than the general population of parents. With this in mind, social workers need to ensure that all relevant information is provided to parents about the support and services available in their area for their child or children with disabilities. In addition, support and services available directly to parents should be sourced to avoid heightened stress and further burnout, which would have consequences for their ongoing parenting of their child.

Adolescents with disabilities are another group who have been found to be dissatisfied with services to meet their needs. The transition from childhood to adolescence poses new challenges for all, often because of poor coordination of services and the transition from adolescent into adult services is no different. In households where there might be a parent with a disability, social workers need to be aware of the ways in which oppressive practice might be played out in those spaces. For example, Gordon and Perrone (2004) on spousal care-giving found that additional demands on energy, time and resources related to having a partner with a chronic illness may exacerbate caregiver burden and affect elements of family roles and responsibilities. This also has implications for child–parent relations where perhaps some children may be in 'caring' roles.

Thiara et al.'s (2011) study found that unless disabled women made explicit disclosures of abuse, social workers and other professionals were not likely to recognise signs of partner abuse because they tended to focus on the impairment. This suggests that there is more work to be done by practitioners about unconscious bias and the role this plays in their interaction with, for example, disabled women who may experience domestic abuse and forms of sexual violence.

Social workers can use models of advocacy to mitigate the effects of oppression and to promote anti-oppressive practice. Broadly speaking, advocacy involves exerting influence for the benefit of an individual, group or organisation. Advocacy can be used as a means to achieve improvements and changes in practice, support and interventions for people with disabilities. It is not the responsibility of disabled people to champion their own cause and seek change; rather, it should be every social worker's responsibility to call out oppression and discriminatory practices which exploit, ignore and malign people with disabilities further.

Chapple (2019) argues, for example, that social work with D/deaf individuals has received limited attention in the USA as there are few social workers who specialise in working with D/deaf individuals. From an anti-oppressive perspective, such a situation calls for increased numbers of social workers trained in communication using sign language to minimise the cultural and linguistic challenges they are faced with when trying to access social care services.

Activity 10.4

Think about someone you know who has a disability (this could be a friend, family member or service user).

- Have they shared with you their experiences of being disabled in their homes, places of work or communities?

Reflect on this or discuss with a colleague.

Chapter summary

The United Nations Convention on the Rights of Persons with Disabilities (CRPD) states that people with disabilities have an equal right to protection from harm, discrimination and unfair treatment. Social workers advocate on behalf of and offer assessment, interventions and support to people with disabilities in order that they can reach their potential. Social work educators cannot teach anti-disablist practice using traditional methods of didactic delivery. Teaching methods and styles must include practical role play, debates and critical analyses supported by links to social work values, which take human dignity into account by respecting a client's autonomy and be aware of discriminatory patterns that often affect a client's well-being and welfare. Service users from this group must be recruited and be involved in recruiting, teaching and assessing students who are undertaking social work. Social workers should continuously reflect on their practice and must seek to avoid ableism which, according to Bolt (2015, p3), is a term that *renders people who are not disabled as supreme*. If social workers are to work anti-oppressively with service users, families and carers, they need to ensure that they listen to the needs of disabled people, involve them in decision making in matters that affect them and ensure that they are not encountering systemic and institutional barriers that non-disabled families are not experiencing. For example, failure to assign a social worker to a family where there is a disabled person should be duly challenged. As part of the duty to safeguard and promote the welfare of all children, social workers should be available to provide advice and interventions based on a comprehensive assessment of need. An anti-oppressive approach is an empowering respectful approach.

Further reading

Chapple, **RL** (2019) Culturally responsive social work practice with D/deaf clients. *Social Work Education*, 38(5): 576–81.

This article proposes best practice ideas for social workers providing culturally responsive social work when working with D/deaf clients.

Heenan, D (2005) Challenging stereotypes surrounding disability and promoting anti-oppressive practice: some reflections on teaching social work students in Northern Ireland. *Social Work Education*, 24(5): 495–510.

This article reports on a teaching strategy used with first-year Social Work students to enable them to recognise and reflect upon stereotypes about persons with disabilities.

11

Faith, belief, religion and spirituality

(Continued)

It will also introduce you to the following standards as set out in the social work subject Benchmark Statement (2019):

5.4   Service users and carers
5.15   Communication skills
5.16   Graduates in Social Work are able to build relationships and work effectively with others

See Appendix 2 for a detailed description of these standards.

Introduction

Social workers, in order to do their job in a culture in which religion is growing in intensity and diversity, have to engage in some form of religious dialogue.

(Knitter, 2010, p257)

This chapter will explore anti-oppressive practice around faith, religion, spirituality and beliefs, beginning with an outline of what these terms mean. We will then look at some of the ways in which beliefs can be detrimental to well-being when used to oppress, discriminate or cause harm to individuals. On the other hand, we will consider the protective features that can be beneficial to service users and their families. Case studies and activities designed to challenge you to carefully consider the ways in which social workers can practise in ways that are respectful of the service users' faith and beliefs, but also in line with the legal rules and frameworks. Drawing on some of my previous work, the chapter will encourage awareness of the complexities of beliefs, some of which result in harm to children and other vulnerable people. Finally, we will look at Islamophobia and the implications for social work practice.

Increasingly, the profession of social work is being challenged to acknowledge and reflect on the role of spirituality and religion in education and practice to represent the growing spiritual diversity of service users and to promote anti-oppressive practice. Not only is this important for the service user, but the social worker may also have their own faith or religious beliefs which they are encouraged to manage and not allow these to get in the way of fair, open and honest practice. The opening quotation from Knitter (2010) is a useful reminder that contemporary social work must engage with the *whole* client (my emphasis), even if as a starting point to the interaction. For this to occur in a way that enhances anti-oppressive practice, it is crucial that as a social worker, you demonstrate humility, trust in the common humanity, commitment, empathy and openness to change. Importantly, social workers must engage with service users fairly, not stating faith preferences or religious beliefs, but working with the beliefs of the service user. There are some third/voluntary/independent sector agencies in the UK and globally that may function as an affiliation to a specific faith or religion. An example of this is Catholic Care, which employs social workers and states on its website that *at Catholic Care we provide services to people of all faiths and none and also employ people of all faiths and none* (www.catholic-care.org.uk/about-us/history/). Such a disclaimer is a reminder that the agency is an equal opportunity employer and that service users and social workers from all faiths and none are welcome to apply for jobs and to seek services and support.

Definitions

In the following discussion, I will explain the key concepts of faith, belief, religion and spirituality to aid your understanding of how social workers might work anti-oppressively with service users who may hold beliefs and values linked to their religious persuasions.

Faith

Quite simply, faith is the trust and confidence we place in something or someone. When used in the relation to religion, it implies having the confidence in a superior being or entity to meet our needs.

Belief

A belief is accepting something as true and a belief system is a set of principles that affect our daily lives, usually structured around relying on the understanding that supernatural beings exist and can hurt or help human beings.

Religion

Religion is not easy to define and there is no attempt here to offer a universally agreed definition as one does not exist. Instead, I will propose a number of definitions, including one that reflects my own interpretation. Durkheim (1912) defined religion as *a unified system of beliefs and practices relative to sacred things, that is to say, things set apart and forbidden, beliefs and practices which unite into one single community called a church, all those who adhere to them.*

According to Benson et al. (2016, p1373) religion refers to *organised spiritually oriented beliefs, rituals and practices shared by a community.*

These have been found to be the six main 'world religions': Judaism, Christianity, Islam, usually known as the Semitic, and Hinduism, Buddhism and Sikhism which developed in an Indian context. There is no consensus about these because of what some are describing as newer religions and variations of these six religions. As social workers will work with people from various religious and faith backgrounds, it is important that they have some understanding of the different values and practices associated with the religion or faith that service users relate to. In an attempt to understand the extent to which social workers recognise the importance of faith and religion in service users' lives, Furman et al. (2005) undertook research with members of the British Association of Social Workers (BASW) in 2000 regarding their beliefs, views and practice tools. Their findings are relevant for contemporary social work practice in the UK in that, of the 789 responses included in the study, 41 per cent reported that private religious and spiritual practices played a role in their own lives. This is an important area for self-reflection for social workers in order that they are continuously aware of their values in order to avoid dissonance in the helping relationship.

Spirituality

According to Swinton (2001, p12) spirituality is a *slippery concept* as no one definition fully captures its essence. However, for the purposes of this chapter, I will draw upon the definition of spirituality by Rapp and Goscha (2011) who view it as *any set of beliefs and/or practices that give a person a sense of hope, comfort, meaning, purpose in their life, or a connection to a greater universe.* This definition provides a foundation upon which effective anti-oppressive practice can be achieved. Social workers can adopt a positive and optimistic outlook while believing in the possibility of change for their service users.

There was some evidence to suggest that social workers preferred 'non-sectarian' spirituality over religion, especially when applying them to practice situations with service users. The research further identified that 76 per cent felt that they did not receive content on religion or spirituality in their training to become social workers, a view that is supported by Oxhandler and Pargament (2014) in the USA context. This is most likely the reason why 57 per cent of respondents felt that social workers in general did not possess the skills to address religious or spiritual issues when working with service users. Furthermore, 57 per cent thought that social workers should increase their knowledge of spirituality.

Gilligan and Furness (2006, p634) conclude that

> many practitioners continue to equate a 'religion-blind' and 'spirituality blind' approach with what they see as 'anti-oppressive practice'. As a result, they frequently risk imposing culturally incompetent 'secular' and 'rationalist' interventions on service users, who may have very different actual needs and wishes.

Anti-oppressive practice requires social workers to be respectful of the role that spirituality, faith and religion have in the lives of service users.

Religion and spirituality are often discussed interchangeably, particularly within ethnic minority communities. It is important for social workers to seek clarity about the place of spirituality and/or religion in relation to service users' self-identity. I have argued in many of the chapters in this book about the need to recognise the intersectional nature of service users' lives and acknowledging the diversity within a single religion. For example, a service user who identifies as Christian will further relate to a specific Christian denomination. Someone who is a practising Catholic may express their faith differently from someone from a Baptist faith, for example. Similarly, there is diversity of practice among the various Islamic groups.

> **Activity 11.1**
>
> Reflecting on what you have read so far in this chapter, discuss whether (in your opinion) your Social Work programme covers sufficient content in the area of religion and spirituality.
>
> - What are some of the debates such content has generated?
> - What have you learnt (if anything) about the importance of religion and spirituality in social work practice?

Religious affiliation in the UK

The census in 2011 in the UK found that Christianity was the largest religion, with 33.2 million people (59.3 per cent of the population). The second largest religious group were Muslims, with 2.7 million people (4.8 per cent of the population) (ONS, 2018). In England and Wales, 14.1 million people reported they have no religion in 2011.

The Office of National Statistics (ONS, 2020) in a study of inequalities from 2016–18 in England and Wales found that people with 'no stated religion' were more likely than others to be smokers and that Sikhs were significantly less likely to smoke than Christians, Muslims and Buddhists.

In the area of mental ill health, those identifying as Sikh were significantly less likely to have mental ill-health difficulties (11.5 per cent) than those who identified as Christian (18.2 per cent), with no religion (18.9 per cent) or with 'any other religion' (32.5 per cent).

Islamophobia

According to Abbas (2011, p54), *Islamophobia did not emerge from thin air.* Ashencaen Crabtree et al. (2017) state that many Western countries have seen a rise in Islamophobia in the context of increased fear of terrorism and religious fundamentalism due to the events of 9/11 in the USA and 7/7 in the UK. In the UK, we have witnessed growing surveillance and marginalisation of Muslim communities and groups (Latham, 2016), with many Muslims who live in minority contexts being fearful of discrimination by children's social care services. According to Guru (2012), the fact that social work cannot be taken out of its political context means that service users with whom it works are connected to the political spheres, as well as the other environmental circumstances that surround them. This, it is argued, impacts on their readiness to engage with social workers and further creates a difficult environment for interaction and the provision of services (Ashencaen Crabtree et al., 2017).

As McKendrick and Finch (2017, p314) argue:

> *traditional social work parameters . . . emphasise a thorough examination of the internal and external factors in the lives of the individual, their families and their community . . . locating the issue purely within individuals is reductive, and fosters a culture of individual responsibility that could increase rather than decrease the possibilities for radicalisation.*

Oppressive and discriminatory practices towards Muslim service users and their families mean that tools for practice are needed. Hutchinson et al. (2015) recommended a few practitioner tools that child protection agencies might use in their engagement with Muslim communities. For example, working alongside Muslim leaders such as imams and sheikhs who are viewed as having a role in community education and social protection is one strategy. Another recommended strategy is supporting extended family, including grandparents, to protect children from abuse and to investigate any claims of abuse.

Rotabi and colleagues (2017, p22) suggest that *supporting religious traditions and mores where applicable is central to our role as social workers and to the successful integration and identity development to our clients*. Given that the person is at the heart of the helping process, intervention that is spiritually sensitive is recommended for social workers in the UK and beyond.

Spiritually sensitive social work practice

It has been suggested by Canda (2008) that religious and spiritual orientations of individuals and communities can support resilience and recovery or can exacerbate despair and crisis. For this reason, they are important considerations for social workers to think about when working with individuals, families, communities and groups. A working definition is offered by Canda (2008, ppx–xi) who states that spiritually sensitive practice

seeks to nurture persons' full potentials through relationships based on respectful, empathic, knowledgeable, and skillful regard for their spiritual perspectives, whether religious or nonreligious.

Mathews (2009) suggests that spirituality is an important element of humanity which should not be disregarded in social work practice. He further proposes that this is even more relevant in social work with people with disabilities, older people and people experiencing mental distress. He argues that *spiritual capital* (p85) which is generated through affirming the value and worth of each human being is an important consideration. Such a perspective is consistent with social work values and operationalises anti-oppressive practice.

Case Study

Sameera is a 32-year-old Muslim woman living in London with her husband, Abdul who is 35, and her two daughters, Huda and Mariam. The family is originally from Iran and speak Persian and limited English. The children have reported violence between the parents and social workers are concerned that this appears to be escalating and not improving. Sameera continues to assert that she can keep the children safe. However, she often adds *Insha'allah*, which means 'by the will of Allah'. As the social worker, you seek further clarification about these comments and you become aware that Sameera's responses could result in her not proactively seeking to keep the children from experiencing significant harm through witnessing violence within the home.

- How might you speak to Sameera and/or Abdul?
- How might you frame your questions about what you perceive as 'fatalistic' to ensure you understand her perspective of the situation?

Commentary

The case study above requires social workers to deal with these religious *roadblocks* (Knitter, 2010, p266) by engaging with Sameera and challenging her in a dialogical, compassionate manner (p266). The belief that everything is predetermined by an omnipotent power can lead people to 'tolerate the intolerable'. Similarly, the issue of karma, which is used to refer to what people have done in a previous life, can be a barrier to proactive engagement and can often prohibit taking responsibility. In undertaking an initial assessment with Sameera and her family, social workers need to understand that spirituality and religion are influenced by and influences the help-seeking behaviours and functioning of service users. The sociocultural context is therefore an important variable in illuminating the ways in which matters relating to faith and religion can impact on what service users view as important, concerning or requiring support and intervention. An anti-oppressive assessment would be cautious of language used and, while stating that the family practises the Islamic faith, it is critical that the focus of the assessment is not on their religion, but rather on the issue or concern at hand. For example, when exploring what their faith means to them, it is important to use empowering language, not accusatory or demeaning language. Social workers must consider the family's religion as part of their identity and build that into the assessment process, the recommendations and intervention as appropriate.

Sherwood (1998) argues that when social workers deliberately avoid discussions about service users' spirituality and religion, this is tantamount to professional incompetence, which in this context refers to the inability to draw upon skills, knowledge and values required to work effectively with service users. Research suggests that religion can contribute to the well-being of young adults (Cotton et al., 2006) and that in terms of spirituality, the *human spirit is nourished by and flourishes on hope* (Mackinlay, 2004, p82). Hopeful social work practice, as discussed in Chapter 4, *provides people with a vehicle to envisage the future and strengths to deal with frustration, despair, trauma and adversity in the present* (Boddy et al., 2018, p588).

Spiritually sensitive practice is anti-oppressive by nature because it operates from the position of being respectful and sensitive to service users' spiritual or religious needs and approaches. It requires social workers to adjust their analyses to include wider societal, community and national structures which privilege some and oppress others because of their religious and faith affiliations. As social work assessments are fluid and dynamic, it is imperative that questions of faith and religion are continuously asked since life circumstances continually change too. Where service users experience a loss of security which damages trust, they may question their spiritual or religious commitment. Conversely, where service users find that religious values have helped, they may continue or strengthen their faith. This can be a useful starting point for a spiritually sensitive professional dialogue and relationship to develop.

Case Study

You are the social work for Milly, an 8-year-old girl in the care of the local authority. Milly and her birth family are Jehovah's Witnesses and have made it clear that Milly is not to celebrate her own or others children's birthdays. Milly's foster carer rings you to say that she wants to reward Milly with a birthday party this year because of consistently good behaviour. The foster carer adds that Milly always appears to want to participate in parties that have previously been organised for other children in that home. You have arranged to visit Milly and her foster carer.

    With a colleague or on your own, outline what you intend to discuss with

1.   Milly;
2.   her foster carer.

Commentary

This kind of practice dilemma has often left even the most confident social worker unsure. For you as a student, I would encourage you to do some background reading before this meeting. This will help you contextualise the situation at hand. Meet and speak with Milly to confirm whether she really does wish to have a birthday party of her own, as this may have been a misinterpretation on the part of the foster carer. If the foster carer is right and Milly requests a birthday party, then it is important to discuss this with Milly's parents where possible. In the situation where Milly's parents disagree, as the social worker you should respect that and propose alternative ways that the foster carer can reward Milly for her good behaviour. Gilligan (2009, p94) suggests that some social workers are able to practise in a 'religion-blind' and 'belief-blind' way because they are not appropriately challenged by their organisations. It is therefore important that you, as the social worker, ensure anti-oppressive practice by engaging with service users' beliefs and appropriately challenging them should you need to for the purpose of safeguarding.

Religious beliefs and abusive practices

In this final section, I would like to explore the idea that some religious beliefs lead to practices and behaviours that are harmful in nature and that some religious beliefs meant ultimately that perpetrators were protected. We will examine the idea of faith-based abuse (Briggs and Whittataker, 2018), including child abuse linked to faith or belief (CALFB) (Oakley et al., 2019), or witchcraft labelling (Tedam and Adjoa, 2017). These terms have often been used interchangeably, but are quite different. The commonality in these definitions is around the abuse, maltreatment or harm towards children (or other vulnerable people) linked to faith or belief. This is not confined to any one faith, religion, nationality or ethnic community. In the UK, these have occurred among Christians, Muslims, Hindus and Pagans (Oakley et al., 2019) to mention a few. For the purposes of this book, I will use the term 'faith-based abuse' as an all-encompassing term, unless there is the need for specificity within the discussion. According to Briggs and Whittaker (2018), *faith-based abuse relating to the practice of witchcraft and spirit possession is a controversial, under-researched and poorly understood form of child abuse* (p2158). Doyle and Timms (2014, p158) state that *religions do not fare well* in discussions about child abuse as there is a growing recognition that while belief, faith and spirituality can enhance children's resilience, they can be spaces where children and vulnerable adults can be abused, exploited and oppressed. Children in Need census (online, 2017) showed that there were 1,460 cases of Child Abuse Linked to Faith or Belief for the year ending 31 March 2017. This has seen an increase to 1,630 in the year ending 2018.

Activity 11.2

* From your reading, research or practice experience, how would you appraise the view by Doyle and Timms (2014, p158) that in discussions about child abuse 'religions do not fare well'?

In the area of child safeguarding, Tedam and Adjoa (2017) concluded that witchcraft labelling, which is growing but underreported in the UK, was one example of how beliefs in the presence of spirit possession contributed to the abuse of particular children. The authors were keen to emphasise that beliefs in themselves are not being challenged, but rather the ways in which such beliefs make people act. In agreement with Gilligan (2009), Tedam and Adjoa (2017) caution social workers to take a holistic, non-oppressive but proactive position when working with children who may be labelled witches or viewed as possessed. As a social worker, you should seek to understand the context and drivers for such labelling and work with families to ensure children's safety in such homes. Further, faith leaders should be part of any discussions around witchcraft labelling involving children because of the position of power and respect they hold in their communities (Tedam and Adjoa, 2017).

In adult safeguarding contexts, vulnerable adults who may have disabilities or who may be unwell are also susceptible to accusations of witchcraft. In Nigeria, for example, Eboiyehi (2017, p248) argues that *witchcraft accusations are a critical factor in the violation of elderly women's rights. They also generate wider problems in families and communities.*

A study by Oakley et al. (2019) found that of the 91 social workers who responded to a survey about child abuse linked to faith and belief (CALFB), 93 per cent (n = 58) of social workers had heard of the term CALFB, 85 per cent (n = 50) were confident in their knowledge of what the term meant, 59 per cent (n = 37) were confident in identifying the indicators and 72 per cent (n = 45) felt confident in responding professionally.

The second area of examination are the ways in which some religious groups protect perpetrators. Goodley and Fowler (2006), writing from an American context, examined the relationship between domestic violence and spiritual abuse, and found that *many survivors of domestic violence turn to their faith-based communities for support, guidance, and safety* (p282) and that often, victims were advised to stay in the abusive relationship, usually with justifications from their interpretations of the Bible. They argue that social work education needs to respond to the limited curriculum content and provide students with specific strategies for assessment and intervention cognizant of the intersections between domestic abuse and spirituality.

Chapter summary

This chapter has sought to unpick some of the challenges and benefits of working across religious diversity. It has outlined the challenges that social workers can face when working with service users whose religious beliefs can result in harmful behaviours and practices. We have also examined through a case study and reflective activities how this is an ever-growing and changing area of practice. Social work practice is based upon relationships and in building these relationships, account must be taken of the diversity and intersectional nature of service users' experiences. The need for a framework that will assist social workers to identify, assess and intervene in the lives and circumstances of service users when belief, spirituality and religion are significant cannot be overstated. Social workers who are concerned that their own faith or religious beliefs might impact on their interventions should engage with the values matrix (Akhtar, 2013), which is designed to address law and policy, anti-discriminatory practice, reflective practice and professional codes of practice, and offer additional areas of discussion to support professional development. This chapter has also tried to highlight the importance of faith literacy training for social workers.

Further reading

Ashencaen Crabtree, S, Husain, F and Spalek, B (2008) *Islam and Social Work Debating Values, Transforming Practice*. Bristol: Policy Press.

This book examines spiritually and culturally sensitive practice with Muslims and outlines how an understanding of Islamic principles can support social workers.

Tedam, P and Adjoa, A (2017) *The W Word: Witchcraft Labelling and Child Safeguarding in Social Work Practice*. St Albans: Critical Publishing.

This book presents a first-hand narrative from a now adult survivor of witchcraft labelling. The authors propose a definition of witchcraft labelling and recommend an assessment tool to assist social workers in their assessment and intervention.

12

Refugees and people seeking asylum

(Continued)

The chapter will also introduce you to the following standards as set out in the Social Work Subject Benchmark Statement (2019):

5.3   Values and ethics
5.5   The nature of social work practice in the UK and more widely
5.11   Managing problem solving activities

See Appendix 2 for a detailed description of these standards.

Introduction

According to Alvaro Gil-Robles, Commissioner for Human Rights of the Council of Europe, in 2004:

A society that loses its sensitivity to the suffering of foreigners, simply because they are foreigners, has lost something very precious indeed . . . . A number of recent reforms have placed the effective enjoyment of human rights and the entitlement to refugee protection in some peril.

(The Independent, 2005)

In this chapter we will confront the scope of oppressions which a marginalised group such as refugees and asylum seekers are subjected to in their host countries and in some cases on their journeys towards their host destination. We will examine the ways in which social workers can mitigate these oppressive practices through working in partnership with refugees and people seeking asylum. We will argue that this is not a homogeneous group and that refugees, people seeking asylum and migrants are differentiated by age, gender, sexuality, disability, ethnicity, nationality, class, faith, and a host of other biological and social differences. This differentiation means that different but fair approaches and methods have to be used when working with people referred to as refugees and asylum seekers.

Refugees and people seeking asylum

Holscher and Bozalek (2012) suggest that social work with people seeking asylum and refugees is one of the profession's more recent specialisations and, as such, there are many areas of this specialism requiring training and further development which align with the research emerging from this area.

Research suggests that while Europe has always been a destination for people fleeing war and economic hardship, the year 2015 saw an unprecedented number of people entering the EU, often through illegal and dangerous channels, risking their lives and that of their children to reach places of safety. Yet the media was not kind in its coverage of what they termed the 'refugee crisis' and contributed to the discriminatory and oppressive responses by citizens of these destination countries.

According to Robinson (2014), refugees and people seeking asylum come from countries experiencing political persecution, war and famine. These include Iraq, Afghanistan, China, Iran, Zimbabwe, Sudan, Vietnam, Burma, West Papua and countries of the former Soviet Union. People fleeing these kinds of circumstances have the right to seek safety and security for themselves and their families. Hayes and Humphreys (2004) have argued that social workers are often conflicted when working with refugees and people seeking asylum, including unaccompanied minors, due to their professional responsibilities and duties.

You may already be familiar with the situation faced by people seeking asylum and refugees, and may be empathic towards their plight. Indeed, in 2015, the lifeless body of young Alan Kurdi washed onto Turkish shores sparked public outcry and concern about the levels of risk taken by families with children fleeing unsafe conditions in countries such as Syria. According to Ibrahim (2018), images such as that of the lifeless 3-year-old reminded the public that he could have been *anyone's child* (p3) contributed to the German Chancellor Angela Merkel and British Prime Minister David Cameron agreeing to take in large numbers of refugees from Syria. While these bold steps have been useful, it is important for us to understand how this particular group of refugees are experiencing life in their new homes and the extent to which social work and social care services are working with them. That *it took a dead toddler to re-awaken the West from its deep moral coma* (Ibrahim, 2018, p3) is in stark contradiction to the values and ethics of the social work profession.

In October 2019, 39 Chinese people died in the back of a lorry heading for England, believed to have travelled from Belgium. These 31 men and 8 women are thought to be victims of trafficking and modern slavery, and while this chapter does not focus on this group, it is important to state here that they are a group who are vulnerable to exploitation, discrimination and oppression. The reasons for their attempt to enter the UK are unclear at this time. However, given previous research, an assumption can be made that they were being trafficked to engage in hidden work with the traffickers having minimal regard for their safety and well-being.

Trafficking in all its forms is a concern for contemporary social work practice. Some of the media reporting of this tragedy has been almost heartless, while others such as Kelly (2019) draw your attention to the thin line drawn between being an illegal worker (criminal) and being a modern slave (victim). She argues that because the boundary is not clearly defined, often their immigration status precedes their experience of exploitation. This is important for you to note because public perceptions which often lead to moral panic can have detrimental effects on interventions with this group of people. According to Welch and Schuster (2005), moral panic theory can be understood to be *negative societal reaction aimed at people who are easy to identify and easy to dislike* (p397).

Activity 12.1

- Which agencies or organisations do you know that offer services to refugees and people seeking asylum?

(Continued)

(Continued)

Make a list of the agencies you know and undertake an internet search for others.

● What services do they offer and what are their sources of funding?

Guidance

The Refugee Council, established in 1951, champions the rights of refugees and asylum seekers of all ages in the area of resettlement, mental health, employment and general well-being. We have already considered oppressive practice as also resulting from the social workers' lack of knowledge of existing services. The list you make can be used throughout your studies and well into qualified practice. You can read more on the Refugee Council and its work at: www.refugeecouncil.org.uk

What are marginalised groups?

According to Schiffer (2008), people are said to be marginalised when they are *populations outside of mainstream society*. Such people or groups are on the fringes of society, often ill-treated, discriminated against and with few channels to express their views and frustrations. In this chapter, I have highlighted refugees and people seeking asylum for discussion, and have further examined this group with respect to children and young people, women and LGBTQI people.

Refugees and people seeking asylum are groups who fall into the broad category of being marginalised both globally and in the UK. Their well-being, welfare and needs often come second to citizens and UK nationals. They are often perceived as having left their countries of origin and many have been targeted while they try to settle into their new home. This makes them easy targets for various forms of discrimination, unfair treatment and oppression. According to Masocha and Simpson (2011), articulating the needs of people seeking asylum separately from refugees is important when writing about marginalised groups. One reason is, of course, the very distinct nature of these two groups and the fact that marginalisation is considered a dynamic process where people can move in and out.

Who is a person seeking asylum?

In line with the sentiments of this book and in solidarity with the UK Refugee Council, this chapter adopts the term 'person seeking asylum', defined as *someone who has left their country of origin and formally applied for asylum in another country but whose application has not yet been concluded* (Refugee Council online). Putting the person before the label is one way to minimise oppression and avoids the stereotype that subsequently shapes our view of the person or group we are working with. Labels can dehumanise and silence the background story of those who we, as social workers, wish to protect and work with.

Who is a refugee?

A refugee is defined by the United Nations (1951) as a person

who owing to a well-founded fear of being persecuted for reasons of race, religion, national-ity, membership of a particular social group or political opinion is outside of the country of his nationality and is unable to or owing to such fear, unwilling to avail himself of the protec-tion of that country.

For example, families caught up in war or conflict in their countries and who are at risk of losing their lives can seek refugee status in a safer country.

Research Summary

The UK is home to approximately 1 per cent of the 25.9 million refugees who have been forcibly displaced across the world (Refugee Council, online). 'Illegal' or 'bogus' asylum seekers do not exist under international law. Anyone has the right to apply for asylum in any country that has signed the 1951 Convention and to remain there until the authorities have assessed their claim (Refugee Council, online).

In the year ending June 2019, the UK gave protection – in the form of grants of asylum, humanitarian protection, alternative forms of leave and resettlement – to 18,519 people (up 29 per cent compared with the previous year), 40 per cent of whom (or 7,351) were children (Home Office, online).

Children and young people

In this section, we will critically examine the experiences of children and young asylum seekers and refugees in the UK, and highlight the ways in which their experiences in education and access to health and social care can be improved. Rigby (2011) asserts that unaccompanied asylum-seeking children are one of the most vulnerable groups, and there is concern about a growing proportion of them who are trafficked and who pose new challenges for child protection professionals as they have additional needs.

In the UK, an unaccompanied asylum-seeking child (UASC) is defined as someone under the age of 18 who arrives in the UK to seek asylum without a parent or guardian (Devenney, 2020). According to Wade (2019), children and young people who seek asy-lum on their own must first present themselves to a local authority Children's Social Care Team for protection and care under the provision of the Children Act 1989, section 17, as a 'child in need'. Children will then be assessed to determine their age should this be in dispute. Age assessments, according to Walker (2011), are challenging in themselves, both in terms of evolving practice guidelines and the availability of time. Social workers have often bemoaned time constraints and the implications for the quality of the age and other assessments of need for children and young people seeking asylum. Children and young people who have gone through traumatic and torturous experiences may present very differently from that of their peers. It is important, therefore, that social workers carefully commit to understanding the lived experiences of such children, as well as the impact of trauma on their transitions.

Private fostering arrangements

There has been concern that many unaccompanied asylum-seeking children in the UK may be vulnerable to private fostering arrangements that provide opportunities for exploitation, abuse, maltreatment and discrimination. According to Connolly (2015), 'private foster care', which is often conflated with kinship care, is open to interpretation because of how it is understood and practised by social workers in the different local authority areas. Section 66 of the Children Act (1989) defines private foster care as an arrangement that is made privately, without the involvement of the local authority, for the care of a child under the age of 16 (under 18 if disabled), by someone other than a parent or close relative, and as an arrangement that endures beyond 28 days (DCSF, 2005). Within the Act (section 105), close relatives are defined as parents, step-parents, siblings, brothers or sisters of a parent, grandparents, and aunts and uncles (whether full-blood, half-blood, by marriage or civil partnership). This means that if a child is in the care of anyone who is not any of these designations, and if the placement persists beyond 28 days, then the arrangement is, by legal definition, one of private foster care (Connolly, 2015). By definition, an unaccompanied child seeking asylum is unlikely to have the 'close relatives' defined in section 105 of the Children Act 1989 and is therefore more likely to be at risk of various types and forms of harm.

The study by Connolly (2015) analysed the experiences of 29 children and young people and found that the *average age at arrival for private foster care children was 11 years compared to 14 for those who had entered the country without any pre-given arrangement* (p338). The study also found that a number of these children were accompanied by 'aunts', 'uncles' and 'church pastors', and a few reported being held in domestic servitude and sexual exploitative circumstances. The study also concluded that children and young people *wanted more stringent checks to be made on them and accompanying adults at ports of entry* as many of them had entered using false passports and identity documentation. This recommendation further highlights the need for fair practice that ensures safety for *all* children in the UK, and for scrutiny through the immigration and children's social care processes.

Activity 12.2

Think about some of the news articles or headlines you have read in the papers or heard on the radio about refugees and asylum seekers.

- What have been the messages you took away from the media representation of asylum-seeking people and refugees?
- How do these messages help or hinder support given to these vulnerable groups?

Write down your thoughts.

Education, health and social care

Schools have been found to offer children seeking asylum and refugee children a space to form new friendships and identify new learning opportunities. Education also contributes to healing and recovery from the trauma that many such children would have experienced both on their journeys to and on arrival in the UK.

In school, they may also become accustomed to differential treatment in classrooms, playgrounds, trains and buses, or have little faith in the capacity of schools and authority figures to resolve the situation. Hamilton and Moore (2004) have referred to education institutions as places where *classification and labelling* (p7) occur. Children and young people will experience varying degrees of pre- and post-migratory trauma, which may be exacerbated by the nature and type of education setting they are placed in. Second or additional language, displaced anger, depression and emotional difficulties are additional challenges experienced by children seeking asylum or refugee children. Services to support such children should be available, and eligibility criteria must be fair and equitable. Social workers who may be involved with children who separated from their parents before, during or on arrival in the UK are particularly vulnerable as a result of separation and loss.

Writing about refugee access to healthcare services in Australia, Lloyd (2014) explains that language and literacy barriers can be at play and often determine the frequency of access to health services. Such situations would call for health and social care professionals to utilise interpreting services to facilitate communication and avoid assumptions being made in relation to the health needs of asylum-seeking people and refugees.

Anti-oppressive practice with refugees and people seeking asylum

Immigration issues have become a pervasive concern in many parts of the world and also in the UK. It has been suggested that migrant populations often require social care services; however, their legal status affects their eligibility for goods and services. Masocha and Simpson (2011) propose that serious consideration be given to the difficulties that arise as a result of refugees and asylum seekers living in societies and communities where racism and discrimination exist, which impacts on their overall well-being.

Martinez-Brawley and Zorita (2011) propose that Social Work academic programmes should provide an 'immigration friendly' module or course with the view to teaching students the various ways in which social workers might interact with immigrant populations and create less oppressive and hostile environments for them to live in. They propose the use of four discourses:

- Psychological.
- Socioeconomic.
- Advocacy/empowerment.
- Legal.

I have adapted what Martinez-Brawley and Zorita (2011) refer to as 'discourses' and instead present them as approaches to assist social workers to minimise oppressive practice towards refugees and asylum seekers.

Psychological approach

This approach involves social workers being able to understand the individual and collective group narratives of people seeking asylum and refugees. Much has been written about the psychological difficulties faced by these groups pre-migration, during migration and post-migration (Masocha and Simpson, 2011). These stages result in different forms of trauma and various levels of resilience which can impact on this group of people. You will need to listen to the stories and narratives, recommend interventions to assist refugees and people seeking asylum to overcome these difficulties. It is important that, as a social worker, you do not rush your interventions or expect quick fixes. People will heal at their own pace and any pressure to expedite this process is oppressive.

Socioeconomic approach

This approach encourages social workers to become aware of the economic disadvantage in most refugee and asylum-seeking households on arrival in the host country. Socioeconomic disadvantage affects options, life chances and general outcomes for both children and adults. Class and health disparities mean that refugees and people seeking asylum may face additional barriers to accessing health and social care in the host country. In the current Covid-19 pandemic, for example, health inequalities have been laid bare. Access to social care services in the UK has been used as an immigration control strategy to manage immigration with the intention of deterring asylum seekers from coming to Britain in the first place. For those already in the country, enforced destitution has been a policy tool to attempt to drive these groups of people out of the UK through discourses that label them as 'underserving'. According to Butler (2007), people seeking asylum and refugees are a group that experience disproportionate social exclusion and hostility induced by the media. Activity 12.2 will assist with understanding this phenomenon.

Moving away from the UK and speaking from a global perspective, refugee women are additionally vulnerable to various forms of sexual and gender-based violence. With the UNHCR approximating about 20 per cent refugee women arriving in the European Union (UNHCR, 2016), it has become even more urgent for social workers and other humanitarian agencies to provide support for women victims of SGBV and become sensitive to interventions. Pile (1997, p3) states that many refugees *were successful professionals in their own countries* who are *highly motivated to work*, and it is imperative that social workers should attempt to support such ambitions where possible.

Advocacy/empowerment approach

Given social work's commitment to anti-oppressive practice, advocacy can be used to inspire the type of actions that social workers take when working with refugees and asylum seekers. At an individual level, according to Masocha and Simpson (2011), advocacy might involve support with housing needs and may play an active role in attempting to change the image of asylum seekers within the community. Empowerment has become increasingly associated with refugee participation and self-help, and this can be achieved through active campaigning for policy changes at the local authority and central government levels. This increased participation approach can contribute to reducing the effects of social inequality.

Legal approach

According to Braye and Preston-Shoot (2006), *the strength of the relationship between law and social work practice varies . . . from one national jurisdiction to another* (p376). For this reason, it is important for social workers based in England, Northern Ireland, Wales and Scotland to know and understand the legal rules governing their interaction with refugee and asylum-seeking service users in their nation. It is also important that social workers understand the legal contexts from which people have arrived in the UK. For example, research by Freedman (2016) into refugee women's experiences of sexual and gender-based violence found that their transitions had not always been positive, and that often there were no guidelines, policies or laws to deal with the violence that women had experienced. Social workers are often put in the position of being border guards or police when dealing with people seeking asylum and refugees. Lavalette (2007) has suggested that social workers dealing with refugees and asylum seekers have to navigate the concepts of *care* and *control*. Financial constraints mean that more control has to be exerted over refugees and asylum seekers in place of meeting their social justice obligations of care and support.

In a study into the experiences of front-line social work with refugees and asylum seekers in the UK and Australia, Robinson (2014) found that coming face-to-face with migrants' stories was distressing and frustrating, and that social work programmes needed to better prepare students for working with asylum-seeking people and refugees. As a social work student, you can prepare yourself for work with refugees and asylum seekers by developing your resilience and coping skills, listening and observation skills and empathy. It is also important that you have experience of working through interpreters and have an awareness of the resources and services available to this service user group. Importantly, you should begin from a position of believing their narratives and not leave service users feeling that you disbelieve their stories and experiences.

Activity 12.3

On your own or with a colleague, consider this example from June 2015. *The Guardian* ran the headline, 'Refugees: this is the human tide the West doesn't want'.

- Draft a letter in response to the author of this article from the perspective of a social work student.

Guidance

Given that you are responding as a social work student, it would be helpful to include elements of the international definition of social work and highlight what our professional values are. You can also comment on the impact of the language used and make a case for anti-oppressive, anti-racist writing in future.

The cultural web

Figure 12.1 The cultural web (adapted by Tedam, 2013)

The cultural web, adapted from the Culturagram by Congress (1997) is a practical tool by Tedam (2013) recommended to assist social workers in understanding and assessing the *unique, complex and often ignored cultural and spiritual positions and perspectives* (p54) of service users who may be seeking asylum, may already have their refugee status, and who may require ongoing support and psychosocial interventions. In using the cultural web with people seeking asylum and refugees, it is important that social workers give sufficient time to fully explore the various components of the web to ensure that their current and historical circumstances are documented, understood and fairly assessed. In the following section, we will identify through case studies how and where the components of the cultural web can be applied to work with women and LGBTQI refugees and people seeking asylum and enable social workers to *reclaim their profession* (Dyke, 2019) through the use of their skills in relationship building, communication, anti-oppressive and evidence-informed practice.

Women asylum seekers and refugees

Chapter 6 was devoted to the discussion of gender within the context of anti-oppressive practice. However, the experiences of female asylum seekers and refugees has prompted specific consideration of women in this chapter on refugees and people seeking asylum. Research by Girma et al. (2014) into the experiences of female asylum seekers and refugees detained in the UK found that of the 46 women in detention,

- 40 said they had been guarded by male staff and 70 per cent of those said this made them feel uncomfortable;
- 50 per cent said that a member of staff had verbally abused them;
- 22 per cent said that staff had been racist towards them;
- 3 women said they had been physically assaulted and 1 said she was sexually assaulted.

This experience in detention is in addition to other forms of trauma experienced in their countries of origin and during their travel to the destination country. It is well documented that the journey to safe countries and destinations is fraught with a host of traumatic and dangerous experiences such as sexual, emotional and physical violence kidnapping, separation from family and the death of family members, all of which have short- and long-term effects on refugees and people seeking asylum.

For Muslim women seeking asylum, Spicer (2008) describes how a mother was house-bound due to experiences of racism and hostility whenever she went outside the house. Her own negative experiences coupled with that of her children resulted in her developing depression. In another example, a woman experienced difficulties and discrimination arising from being the main carer for her disabled husband and not understanding fully the services available to her, exacerbated by the lack of translation and language interpretation services. We will now turn our attention to another case study which helps us to understand the issues discussed above.

Case Study

Ruhia is a 31-year-old female seeking asylum in the UK. She arrived from Syria, having taken months to travel through a number of different countries. She arrived with her younger male cousin, Saif, who is about 15 years old and with a speech impairment. Ruhia is quiet and able to speak some English, having been educated in Syria and previously employed as a nurse. Ruhia is not married, having gone through a divorce when she was 28 years old due to domestic and financial abuse. On the journey to the UK, Ruhia disclosed that she was a trained nurse and so was asked to take care of a number of children who eventually died of pneumonia and other infectious diseases as a result of overcrowding in the refugee camps. Ruhia has mentioned that throughout her journey she experienced verbal and physical violence for travelling without a husband. Ruhia is responsible for Saif and has little idea about how to proceed with her situation.

Ruhia has been referred to you as the social worker for an assessment and you decide to use the cultural web to assist your understanding of her circumstances in order to provide appropriate intervention.

- Which elements of the web would you use and why?
- Which elements would be least useful to you in this case and why?

Commentary

There will be many domains of the cultural web to apply to this case, but I will examine two of these to highlight its applicability.

- *Family rules, expectations, power and gender* It would be useful for the social worker to examine the nature of family rules in terms of Ruhia's responsibility for her cousin Saif. How might gender play a role in the interaction between Ruhia and Saif? Who holds the power? Making any assumptions that Ruhia is older and holds the power or that Saif's speech impairment equates to powerlessness would be oppressive and detrimental to the intervention.
- *Experience of discrimination, oppression and racism* The social worker should give some attention to this element of Ruhia's experience as it is likely to impact on her current well-being. It is well documented that racism, sexism and other forms of discrimination have lasting negative impact on health and well-being. For Ruhia, the intersectional nature of her experiences and cumulative disadvantage provide additional elements for investigation and understanding.

Continuing with the theme of intersectionality, in the next section we will see how this manifests in the experiences of LGBTQI refugees and people seeking asylum.

LGBTQI refugees and people seeking asylum

It is not the intention of this chapter to examine fully the experiences of LGBTQI people in relation to their status as refugees and people seeking asylum. However, it is important to understand the intersectional nature of their experience and the way in which their experiences of asylum and immigration in the UK system is oppressive and discriminatory. Spijkerboer (2013) argues that due to the intimate nature of sexuality, proving one's claim for asylum on the basis of being lesbian, gay, bisexual, queer or intersex often relies on adjudicators who themselves may be biased or unfamiliar with non-Western expressions and articulations of sexuality. It has been suggested that there are over 75 countries where homosexuality is illegal. However, according to the UK Lesbian and Gay Immigration Group, *only a tiny proportion will come to the UK to seek a haven and most come only as a last resort*. Claims for asylum and refugee status involves a process that assesses credibility, although this has been found to be both subjective and oppressive. For this reason, Jansen and Spijkerboer (2011) propose professional training that covers areas such as LGBT cultural competency, confronting homophobia, as well as communication skills when working with sexual minorities. These courses should be mandatory for interviewers, legal aid officials and adjudicators. Social workers may become involved with LGBTQI people (see Chapter 2) seeking asylum through the need for safeguarding and protection, for housing and accommodation needs, for reasons of disability, or for more generic welfare-related needs. It is important that as a social worker you are able to recognise and challenge negative perceptions, myths and stereotypes about sexual minorities. Here, the 4D2P framework described in Chapter 4 can assist practitioners to understand the experiences and expectations of LGBTQI people and to disrupt oppressive practices directed towards them.

The illustration below shows the multiple barriers that refugees and asylum-seeking people must navigate. At every stage of their journey, they experience hurdles and barriers, and it is important that you, as a social worker, understand what these barriers are.

Figure 12.2 Barriers facing refugees and asylum seekers

The role of language

A common theme running through this book is the role of language in either promoting oppression or disrupting it. Jones et al. (2015, p3) caution that confusion about the labels used often causes misunderstanding and can create tensions. They note:

> *Legal statuses that migrants can have is confusing, and for many people in the wider public, the distinctions between 'illegal' and 'legal', and between asylum seeker, refugee, student, worker, resident, and sometimes between migrants and ethnic minority British-born people is difficult to understand.*

In addition, previously Theresa May as Home Secretary publicly announced her intention to create a 'hostile environment' within the UK for those she considered 'illegal immigrants'. This type of language by a person in a position of power can result in ordinary citizens acting in accordance with such sentiments and utterances. The use of the word 'hostile' is not open to interpretation and, as a social worker, you should avoid any language that is disempowering, oppressive and discriminatory.

Devenney (2020) explored the relationship between young people seeking asylum and social care workers, and found that the young people described social workers as helping them achieve their goals and aspirations. The young people also relied on social workers to assist them in navigating the terrain of their experiences. For this reason, understanding social care professionals as 'co-navigators' contributes positively to the experiences of unaccompanied asylum-seeking young people. In the following activity, we will consider the term 'social navigator' in more detail.

Activity 12.4

Devenney (2020), drawing upon the work of Vigh (2009) on social navigation, refers to social workers as 'social navigators' who, working with unaccompanied young people (UYP), are 'not only able to act, but to imagine future goals'.

Consider how such a role can contribute to anti-oppressive practice with unaccompanied young people. Discuss this with a peer or reflect on your own.

Guidance

Social navigation used in social work would involve the assessment of the present circumstances of service users, as well as a consideration of the options and possibilities available to them. It would also involve you, as the social worker, alongside service users, to chart and plot routes towards possible change. The role of the social navigator would be to move through the socially immediate and the socially imagined (Vigh, 2009, p425).

Chapter summary

This chapter has explored the experiences of refugees, people seeking asylum and migrants as a key example of groups of people often marginalised and excluded in the UK. We have examined how existing social work education may inadvertently promote oppressive practice towards these groups, and have suggested ways in which social work students and qualified practitioners might engage with anti-oppressive principles and processes when working with this group. You have been introduced the cultural web (Tedam, 2013) as a useful anti-oppressive tool which social workers might use when working with people seeking asylum and refugees.

Further reading

Bartoli, A (ed.) (2016) *Anti-Racism in Social Work Practice*. St Albans: Critical Publishing.

This is an edited volume that addresses the effects of racism in social work programmes. Drawing on their experiences as social work educators, the authors use a critical lens to explore the subtle and overt ways that discrimination, oppression and privilege are played out in the learning environment. They argue that the commitment to fighting racism has been abandoned and advocates for the critical language of anti-racism.

Robinson, K (2014) Voices from the front line: social work with refugees and asylum seekers in Australia and the UK. *The British Journal of Social Work*, 44(6): 1602–20. doi.org/10.1093/bjsw/bct040

This article examines the experiences of social workers operating on the front line with refugees and asylum-seeking people in non-governmental organizations in the UK and Australia. Using a feminist and human rights perspective, this article identifies the demands facing social workers in this field, and highlights some useful recommendations regarding content for the social work curriculum (Critical Race Theory) and investing in supervision in practice.

Part Three

Developing anti-oppressive practice through learning

13

Anti-oppression in practice learning

Achieving a Social Work Degree

This chapter will help you develop the following capabilities from the Professional Capabilities Framework PCF (2018):

1. Professionalism
7. Skills and intervention
8. Contexts and organisations
9. Professional leadership

See Appendix 1 for the Professional Capabilities Framework Fan and a description of the 9 domains.

(Continued)

> (Continued)
>
> The chapter will also introduce you to the following standards as set out in the Social Work Subject Benchmark Statement (2019):
>
> 5.3   Values and ethics
> 5.5   The nature of social work practice in the UK and more widely
> 5.11   Managing problem-solving activities
>
> See Appendix 2 for a detailed description of these standards.

Introduction

In this chapter, we will be extending our understanding of anti-oppressive practice in the context of practice learning, also known as placements, field education or practicum. We will examine anti-oppressive practice at the various stages of the practice learning process and offer some guidance on how various stages of a student placement can work proactively to ensure that discrimination and oppressive practices are kept away from this area of the social workers' training and development. Drawing on evidence from my doctoral research, we will examine the ways in which practice learning settings can disadvantage specific minority groups. I will also highlight the ways in which some placement settings have introduced strategies to minimise exclusion and discrimination.

Social work education

Social work students must successfully complete a period of learning in practice because practice learning constitutes half of the social work degree in England (minimum of 200 days) and has been referred to as the *signature pedagogy* (Wayne et al., 2010) and is said to have a *more profound and lasting impact than classroom teaching* (Domakin, 2014, p718). Consequently, social work practice learning is an integral element of successfully gaining the Social Work degree at undergraduate or graduate levels in England, and learning achieved on placements directly influence their future functioning as social workers in their careers.

In 2011, Bernard and colleagues undertook a study into the progression rates among diverse students in England. They focused on Black and minority ethnic students, male students, young students, students with disabilities and LGBTQI students, and found that these groups of students faced varying levels and severity of discrimination and oppression during their placement periods.

Preston-Shoot (2007) was concerned about how practice educators and academics assessed students' anti-oppressive practice and concluded that this dilemma resulted in a mostly 'tick-box' style which was inadequate in determining exactly what had been achieved and how.

Writing about social work education in Scotland, Collins and Wilkie (2010) found that when oppressive language was used among social workers, some students were able to challenge such oppression in wider team meetings. Students in Scotland are required to identify and challenge oppressive practice and summarise the ways in which oppression impacts on students and service users. Anti-oppression in the field of practice learning involves being aware of the implications of age, faith and spirituality, class and socioeconomic status, etc. which constitute all the elements discussed in this book.

Maidment and Cooper (2002) concluded that social work practice educators spent very little time discussing oppression and discrimination in their supervisions with students. However, this appears to have changed to some extent with practice educators focusing on these areas in contemporary social work supervisory practice with students (Field et al., 2016).

Research Summary

In Social Work practice learning settings, it is important for practice educators to understand the subtle and direct ways in which oppression can infiltrate the spaces and places where social work learning is supposed to occur. In these settings, often characterised by power due to the hierarchical nature of the student–practice educator, the relevance of naming and respecting difference and diversity cannot be underestimated.

The practice educator is effectively also a mentor to the social work student and it is important that they understand that some of the pitfalls inherent in their role are 1) clearly understanding the narrow line between being enabling vs. controlling; 2) being helpful vs. being interfering; 3) being a supportive mentor vs. creating dependency (Gravells and Wallace, 2012).

Creating and sustaining an anti-oppressive practice learning environment

Social Work practice learning settings are complex spaces because they involve a myriad activities, a range of people amid ongoing assessment of students and meeting the needs of service users. According to Doel (2009), placements can be both daunting and exciting and, in this section, we will be highlighting the various events, activities and stages of placements which can make minority students vulnerable to discrimination and oppressive practice. At the very start of the process is the placement matching which often occurs in universities. However, many teaching partnerships have stated that this early part of the process is collaboratively undertaken by the partners involved in the partnership.

Placement matching

Placement matching involves a careful look at student placement application forms (PAF) alongside the available placements and making an initial judgement of the suitability of students to these available placements. In many cases, you will be clear about which specialisms or areas of practice you wish to pursue. However, there are always some students who are less clear about which service user groups to work with on placements. Practice educators (PEs) are advised to avoid practices that enable oppression and discrimination to occur at this stage of the process. These include using the students' uncertainty of specialism as an opportunity to belittle their understanding of social work or assume they are not committed to their studies and the profession.

Once the above process has been undertaken, the students' profiles/CVs are sent to potential PEs for further consideration and selection. Usually at this stage, PEs can apply selection criteria, which should be fair and transparent. This criterion should align closely with the organisation's needs – for example, many services for female victims of domestic abuse have a requirement that the social work student must be female. In such a situation, it is fair that male students are declined, and a full and transparent explanation provided to them about the reasons why they have not been provided a learning opportunity in such a placement. Where the gender is unclear, PEs are advised not to rely on the use of names to second-guess the gender of the student, as this is certainly a form of stereotyping.

The PE is expected to respond either directly to the student or via their student placement lead about whether they wish to offer the student a placement. At this point, they would offer a telephone or face-to-face meeting to discuss the students' needs and the placement learning opportunities further.

Where an initial meeting with the student (pre-placement) has been offered, the PE must undertake this with utmost caution and transparency. Participants in my doctoral research felt that some of these pre-placement meetings were used to justify the rejection of students for a placement. They referred to some students turning up for a 'chat', while other students turned up and were faced with a *full blown interview and a scoring sheet* (Tedam, 2015).

Other students only went as far as submitting their placement application forms and waited varying lengths of time to hear back from these placement providers. In one case, the student (who was of Black African ethnicity) waited for over one year for a placement, and it was only through the intervention of the vice chancellor that her situation progressed and she was allocated a placement. She describes this as arising from her *African-sounding name* and was of the view that universities should reconsider this approach and perhaps only provide student numbers as a way of minimising oppressive recruitment and placement-matching practices.

The placement planning meeting is usually held when the student has been accepted on to a placement and there is the need to define the contours and remit of the planned work. These meetings will normally be held with a range of stakeholders, and where the PE is training in the role, then a PE mentor is likely to be present. As has already been articulated, in arranging these meetings, practice educators should ensure that the process and content are fair and transparent. The objectives of the meeting should be clear and the language used should not convey a sense of superiority over the student, as this will not set an anti-oppressive tone for the remainder of the placement. On the contrary, the student may be left feeling inadequate or anxious.

A student's induction and first few days will involve a structured programme aimed at them getting to know the team, organisation and focus of their work. The first few days are crucial in getting students to feel welcome, accepted and comfortable in their new placement setting. According to Leese (2010), induction is not a one-off event, but rather a structured process that involves varied tasks and activities. Inductions should assist social work students to develop a sense of belonging and support them to understand the aims of their organisation and their role within that. Recognising that students will settle into their placements at different paces is an important element of respecting difference and being non-oppressive.

As the name implies, supervision and ongoing involvement requires that the Social Work practice educators ensure that students get adequate time and space for supervision, during which they ensure that students understand the purpose and value of supervision. According to Morrison (2005, p32), supervision is a

process by which one worker is given responsibility by the organisation to work with another worker in order to meet certain organisational, professional and personal objectives which together promote the best outcomes for service users.

The functions of supervision therefore are managerial, developmental, supportive and meditative. In delivering each of these functions, it is important that the PE remains mindful to avoid oppressive practices, and promotes inclusivity and respect for diversity and difference. For example, a Muslim student may be unable to participate in supervision on Friday afternoons and may prefer to use their lunch break for religious purposes. A request for this type of consideration should be openly discussed and built into a supervision agreement, which is a document setting out the frequency, duration, boundaries and venue for supervisions (Maclean, 2013). The discussion should be recorded and any areas of disagreement made transparent and negotiated. Again, PEs need to ensure that language used in these discussions are not oppressive, discriminatory or offensive in any way.

Activity 13.1

Your new student tells you that they belong to the Islamic faith and would like to use their lunchtime on Friday for prayers. You are the onsite practice educator.

* How would you respond to this student?
* Which policies and working regulations will you consult and why?

Guidance

In this activity, you are encouraged to think about the fact that lunchbreaks are not a gesture of good will, but rather a mandatory break from work. There will be health and safety regulations in relation to taking periodic breaks from your computer. If in doubt, refer to those regulations and policy guidelines in the first instance. It is good practice to ask the student what time on Friday they would like to pray, and work to ensure that you avoid giving them tasks or require them to be in a meeting at that time.

Direct observations

Direct observations of practice require the practice educator to observe the student social worker in direct interaction with their service user or colleague to evaluate the quality of their interactions mapped against the requirements of the Social Work programme. Direct observation of practice will involve a minimum of three people – the student, the PE and the service user, carer and, in some cases, another professional or colleague. Observations require careful planning between students and their PEs, and to ensure that they are not being oppressive to service users, students must inform them of the fact that there will be an additional person observing their practice and must gain permission to do so. Direct observations have multiple benefits for students, service users and for PEs. For students, this is an opportunity for them to demonstrate 'how' to work with service users. They should be able to transfer classroom learning to the placement setting and receive feedback from their PE about the quality of their intervention (Maclean, 2013). The PE benefits from being able to evaluate the students' abilities and identifies areas for development. In the area of anti-oppressive practice, practice educators must ensure that students are provided with opportunities to demonstrate effective integration of theory into practice. It is fair to conclude that opening out practice to scrutiny is not an easy task, even for more experienced practitioners, so it is crucial that PEs are fully aware of how they approach this with their students. For example, research by Stone (2018) found that social work students did not always know when their practice was being observed or assessed, and students who did not have good relationships with their PEs were more likely to describe this as surveillance, watching their every move to see *where they might slip up* (p983). Such a strategy, which may be helpful for a student in their final placement, could be construed as oppressive. Consequently, I support the view by Parker (2010) that students must be informed of what is being assessed and how it might be evaluated.

When PEs offer an overview of students' written work again, caution should be exercised to ensure that this is devoid of any manifestations of micro-aggression or oppressive practice. For any learner, receiving feedback on their practice and knowledge is an integral part of their learning and can be a daunting experience. Feedback, according to Maclean (2013), can be positive or negative, and in order to keep a student engaged, it is important that feedback (particularly negative feedback) is well timed, clear, facilitative and empathetic. Tedam (2014) described a situation where a PE continually disagreed with the use of a word by a student for whom English is an additional language. The student stated that she had 'written an email' to a service user. However, her PE disagreed and urged her to change it to 'typed an email'. This student reported to have felt belittled and eventually changed the language to end the disagreement.

Mid-way review

Mid-way reviews provide opportunities for students to revisit their initial contracts and gauge where progress has been made, and outline areas requiring further development and growth. Again at this stage, PEs need to be honest and transparent about what areas of the student's competence need to be developed. At this stage, students are told whether they are making sufficient progress or not and what needs to be done (if anything) to improve the outcome. PEs should be aware that at this stage students may be anxious if they are told of areas for improvement. It is therefore incumbent on the PE to also suggest strategies that may assist the student to improve their knowledge, skills and expertise. Where a student is deemed to be struggling or at risk of failing, caution must be exercised when working with such students to understand what the barriers to their learning might be. Research by Stones and Glazzard (2018) has highlighted the increasing numbers of students in UK universities with mental ill health. This and other considerations are important in the context of anti-oppressive practice within the practice learning setting.

Grade and outcome of placement usually occurs at the end of the placement after all the formal and informal assessments have occurred. The result or outcome should not come as a surprise to the student, as this should have been openly discussed at specific points of the process.

Final PE report

The practice educators' report will be an accumulation of what has been observed and delivered throughout the practice learning period. The PE report is a written record of conclusions drawn from evidence gathered to enable the formulation of an outcome for the student. In writing this report, PEs are required to be factual and use evidence to support their decisions. At this stage, PEs must understand fully the repercussions of oppressive or discriminatory language, and should endeavour to avoid being overly critical of cultural and other differences in this report. It is important to remember that the report may be kept for a long period of time and could be used in the future as evidence of oppressive and discriminatory practice. Where a PE is commenting on how a student has developed their reflective practice, it is a good idea to understand and comment on how a student's cultural and ethnic locations might underly their ability to self-reflect while on placements. According to Lawson (2018), a skilled PE will assist a student to contain their emotions and support them to feel comfortable and empowered. This should then be reflected in the final report in a way that enables a student to construct knowledge through what they have learnt on placement.

End of placement

By the end of the placement, students are expected to have been assessed and an outcome reached regarding fitness to practice. At this stage, students should be winding down to leave the placement, and it is at this time that PEs may organise events to mark the end of a successful practice learning experience.

Oppression is not as easy to detect as some people might make it out to be, and in the practice learning context, this can be even more complex and hidden. For example, the PE, who has various types of power, such as the *power to determine* (Maclean, 2013), may utilise this power in oppressive ways when in practice the profession requires the PE to utilise honesty, openness and evidence in relation to the *power to determine* the placement outcome.

The placement cycle, regardless of how many days a student will be training, is fraught with complexity, anxiety and concern on many levels. Often, until students' complete placements successfully, they will be concerned about the possibility of difficulties, termination or indeed failure. An anti-oppressive practice learning environment should be one that promotes anti-oppressive values from the outset. Nothing should be taken for granted and students could experience culture shock from their involvement with service users whose circumstances may be very different from their own.

Case Study

Jeanette is a second-year student undertaking her first placement in a community-based Family Centre. She is 19 and has previously volunteered in her church working with children. She has been asked to work with the Thompson family and goes to visit them at home, with the aim of introducing herself and building a rapport with the family. Jeanette arrives at the home and after about 10 minutes becomes visibly upset about the Thompsons' living circumstances. Realising that she is not able to stay longer, Jeanette apologises to Mrs Thompson and returns to the Family Centre where she bursts into tears. Mrs Thompson rings the Family Centre and tells them she would like a change of social worker because Jeanette is young, inexperienced and will not be able to assist her and her family.

The PE meets with Jeanette who explains that she had never seen this level of poverty and deprivation (house with bare flooring, nails sticking out at the edges, sparse furniture, children sitting on the bare floor), with hardly any food in the fridge or cupboards. The PE was concerned about Mrs Thompson's response and reaction to Jeanette's tears and asked her to reflect on why she was moved to tears. Jeanette wanted the discussion in supervision to be focused on how the Thompson situation had made her feel and was not happy when asked to reflect on how the family (mother) may have felt because of her tears. The PE offered some guidance about how Jeanette should respond in a similar situation in the future.

At the end of her placement, Jeanette approached Mrs Thompson for service user feedback as part of the requirements of her university and, to Jeanette's surprise, Mrs Thompson expressed her feelings about Jeanette's tears months ago. She referred to the tears as an indication of 'disrespect' for her and her circumstances and that, as a social worker, Jeanette should have been aware of the levels of deprivation in the local authority and indeed the neighbourhood she was working in. She stated that Jeanette was not prepared for the reality of working with diversity in the area of class and economic disadvantage.

Commentary

The case study above clearly demonstrates how you may knowingly or inadvertently discriminate against service users by your responses, reactions and interactions during placement. Jeanette's tears were not automatically considered as empathy, but rather as discriminatory, oppressive and offensive. Mrs Thompson said that Jeanette had confirmed through her tears that her circumstances were not desirable. Jeanette could have written to Mrs Thompson or made a phone call, apologised for her reaction and acknowledged her gaps in knowledge. In the background, Jeanette should be focusing on understanding that anti-oppressive practice is a process as well as an outcome, and that socioeconomic disadvantage is not a lifestyle choice that Mrs Thompson would choose.

Trevithick (2000) emphasised that social work is a complex area of work, mainly because practitioners work across class, race, gender, age, disability, religions and other differences. These differences affect the way in which problems are described, and how interventions and solutions are reached. Service users must navigate their thoughts and feelings of despair, humiliation, confusion or anger, and arrive at a place where they are able to work meaningfully with social workers or other professionals to improve their circumstances.

I have offered elsewhere (www.scopt.co.uk/archives/4350) some considerations for practice educators who wish to create and sustain anti-oppressive practice learning environments. In summary, these considerations are generally good practice and it is important that these are used as such, rather than approaching anti-oppressive practice as a fixed measurable entity that is self-sustaining once it is introduced into any organisation or workplace. These strategies include fairness in the recruitment process and subsequent allocation of work for students, clarity about the grievance procedure, clarity about roles, expectations and targets, and caution about the use of language, avoiding colour-blind approaches. These suggestions are aimed at supporting PEs in their role with social work students and providing opportunities for students to transform and grow into reflective and critical practitioners. These ideas will also support efforts to build a productive learning partnership, which may continue well after the practice learning period has ended.

According to Field et al. (2016), practice educators play multiple roles, including manager, facilitator, teacher, supervisor, planner, mediator and assessor. These are complex and extensive enough as stand-alone roles, even before we consider them within a broader all-encompassing context. This is certain to make the most experienced of students feel vulnerable and anxious. Thus, it is incumbent on the practice educator to be mindful of the ways in which oppressive practice might creep into any of these many roles. The PE role has been likened to that of an orchestra conductor (Maclean, 2013) because of the way they take charge and coordinate the many people involved in a given practice learning context. Collaborative working will be explored in more depth in the next chapter. However, in this context, the PE must ensure that individual agendas by stakeholders in the practice learning setting do not undermine the quality of the students' learning, and must safeguard the student from potentially oppressive interactions and behaviours from others. The learning environment is a vast physical and emotional space, so PEs must acknowledge this in their planning and preparation for students. You should be given opportunities to take control of your learning. However, PEs are advised to get the timing right.

Research Summary

My doctoral research investigated the social work practice learning experiences of Black African students (BAS) in England using Critical Race Theory (CRT). I was interested in finding out why Black African students, who were the second largest ethnic minority group enrolled on social work programmes in England (GSCC, 2007, 2009), appeared to

(Continued)

(Continued)

experience delayed progression and poorer attainment. Placements were found to be a site where various forms of discrimination and oppression resulted in Black African students either failing placements or facing barriers to progression. Other studies had examined broader categories of minority students (male students, younger students, students with disabilities, LGBTQI students), so I became interested in the experiences of Black African students. In addition, I undertook a pilot study to test out my research questions and methodology. The findings from this pilot study revealed the presence of stereotyping, oppression, micro-aggressions and racism in practice learning settings (Tedam, 2014).

At this stage, you are probably wondering why 'Black'? Quite simply, this was my area of interest and existing research in addition to my own experience of teaching social work had given me sufficient cause to be concerned about this group of students. The key finding arising from this study was that race was a significant contributory factor in the experiences of BAS on social work placements and that CRT, despite its limitations, was a useful theoretical framework for analysing and understanding the situated experiences which are bound in racism and discrimination.

I also identified the subtle and unsubtle ways in which racism manifested itself, and highlighted that unacknowledged privileges associated to being White contributed to the marginalisation, exclusion and isolation of BAS on placements. This exclusion was evident not only during placement, but also within the placement allocation and matching processes.

I referred to the fact that many of the placement agencies in this study can be said to be toxic and detrimental to the health and well-being of BAS as they failed to empower or liberate this group of students. The post-race and colour-blind approach adopted by some of the PEs demonstrated a lack of respect for diversity and viewed BAS as lacking in competence and being incapable of achieving success. It has been suggested that in social work, education practice learning is the component that students most remember (Doel and Shardlow, 2005). Therefore, it is imperative that BAS's memories of their placements are not limited to their experiences of discrimination and racism, but rather embrace and reflect the positive transformational potential that placements can have for all students.

My research concluded that social work practice education in England needs to interrogate its Whiteness and put in place structures that support BAS and accentuate positives rather than reinforcing prejudice, outsider or othered status. I argued that it is possible to identify and address coherently factors that contribute to poor placement experiences for BAS. However, this requires respectful dialogue and a change in many institutionalised processes that currently work to make BAS invisible. I also reported the possibility of understanding the grounded experiences of BAS in order to develop proactive strategies that are bound in anti-racism and value-based praxis to challenge the double standards and unfairness experienced by BAS, which continues to be reflected in the poorer attainment and slower progression rates (Tedam, 2015).

Since completing this research, I have been seeking models and strategies that make assessment while on placement more transparent. To this end, I highlight recommend the Transparency in Assessment in Practice Education (TAPE) model. It is a useful tool offered by Stone (2018, p989) as a means to *engage students, tutors and practice educators in dialogue before and during placements to stimulate discussion about assessment so that all parties are clear about the nature and form of assessment.*

It is my view that this model can also serve to minimise the potential for oppressive assessment practice for students on social work placements because it illuminates the power dynamics involved in the roles of all stakeholders in a student's practice placement by robustly answering the where, why, who, when, way and what (the six Ws), which enable the student to talk about their experiences of being assessed so that any issues that may exist can be addressed at an early stage in the placement.

Activity 13.2

On your own or with a colleague, consider the ways in which oppression in practice learning settings might impact on:

1. the learner (you);
2. the practice educator;
3. the team;
4. the organisation or agency.

Guidance

Throughout this book, we have made the case that oppression and oppressive practice are neither welcome nor desirable in social work and that at all times, we must ensure that we are not colluding with oppressive practice or being the oppressors. Your learning will be stifled and hampered by an oppressive PE or oppressive systems. Therefore, you should be proactive in ensuring that the environment and learning culture should enable learning. Any PE will be ineffective when working within an oppressive environment as there will be few examples of good, ethical practice for the PE to refer the student to. In relation to the team and wider organisation, it is important for you to consider their professional responsibilities and accountability in relation to codes of ethics. Ramsundarsingh and Shier (2017) highlight that it is important for organisational practice and policy to value service users and staff, and it is important to align anti-oppressive principles with organisational goals and targets.

Chapter summary

In this chapter, we have highlighted the ways in which practice learning settings might create and perpetuate discrimination and oppression, and how this might disadvantage students and others undertaking practice learning. We have examined strategies to avoid oppression and discrimination in practice learning settings, and ways to promote a fair, equitable and non-oppressive setting in which students can be nurtured and supported in their learning. Using the main stages of a practice placement cycle, we have outlined areas for consideration and critical reflection.

Further reading

Stone, C (2018) Transparency of assessment in practice education: the TAPE model. *Social Work Education,* 378(8): 977–94.

This article discusses how the use of the six Ws in assessing you as a student will reduce ambiguity, discrimination and mistrust. Students are empowered to take more control of their own learning and assessment, thus minimising the opportunity for oppressive practice.

Tedam, P (2014) When failing doesn't matter: a narrative inquiry into the social work practice learning experiences of Black African students in England. *International Journal of Higher Education,* 3(1): 136–45.

This article reports the findings from a case study involving two Black African students studying social work in England. It is useful for students to understand the experiences of minority students in universities and on placements.

14

Multi-agency and interprofessional practice

> (Continued)
>
> The chapter will also introduce you to the following standards as set out in the Social Work Subject Benchmark Statement (2019):
>
> 5.3   Values and ethics
> 5.5   The nature of social work practice in the UK and more widely
> 5.11   Managing problem solving activities
>
> See Appendix 2 for a detailed description of these standards.

Introduction

From its very beginning, social work has aligned itself to a number of different disciplines and has drawn from these areas to form its own unique knowledge and practice base. For this reason, it would appear that working with others is a unique hallmark of the profession. The aim of this chapter is to outline the various definitions of interprofessional practice and to identify where oppression might occur in these working arrangements. The importance of professional identity will be a key consideration in this chapter.

Multi-agency working

Social workers engage with other professionals on a daily basis during the course of their work and as such have to ensure that they not only understand the value of other professional involvement, but also ensure that they work in collaboration with these professionals to provide a good quality service delivery and outcomes for service users. It has been suggested that there is no agreed definition for multi-agency working (MAW) or interprofessional practice (IPP), and that while these two concepts can be interchangeable, there are subtle differences and unique facets that need to be highlighted.

Following the death of Victoria Climbié in 2000 and the subsequent Laming Inquiry, multi-agency working was viewed as a necessary part of professional practice because, according to the Department for Education and Skills (DfES, 2004, p18),

Multi-agency working is about different services, agencies and teams of professionals and other staff working together to provide the services that fully meet the needs of children, young people and their parents or carers. To work successfully on a multi-agency basis you need to be clear about your own role and aware of the roles of other professionals; you need to be confident about your own standards and targets and respectful of those that apply to other services, actively seeking and respecting the knowledge and input others can make to delivering best outcomes for children and young people.

This definition is clear and straightforward about the importance of working together, and goes on to suggest that clarity of role as well as an understanding of the role of other professionals is key to effective working. In addition, there is the caution contained in the definition about being respectful of the contributions made by others in the collaboration. This issue of respect is an important one and contributes to a non-oppressive work environment. Drawing upon Tuckman's stages of team development (forming, storming, norming, performing and adjourning – see below), this chapter will examine how anti-oppressive practice principles can be embedded in each of these stages in order to enhance MAW.

The aim of interprofessional practice is to have a number of professionals in the health and social care sector working towards the same goal and with the view of safeguarding vulnerable children and their families. As you will see in the case study about David and his family, interprofessional practice requires the renegotiation of power, control and authority across different professional boundaries due primarily to the fact that there is more than one agency involved. Roles and responsibilities will need to be negotiated and renegotiated to create an environment that meets the needs of service users.

In this chapter we will use the terms 'multi-agency' and 'interprofessional working' interchangeably to refer to the collaborative partnership formed to safeguard and protect children and other vulnerable people. In the following case study, you are presented with a situation that involves a range of professionals working in the best interests of David and his family.

Case Study

Judy is a senior social worker in a Family Support team. Following organisational restructuring, the new team has been constituted and Judy is the team manager of ten staff comprising herself, three children and families social workers, one mental health social worker, one education psychologist, a learning disability nurse, an education support worker, a domestic abuse worker and one youth offending social worker.

David is a 29-year-old a single father and his two sons have been referred to the team for support. The father is the victim of an abusive same-sex relationship and the youngest son, 7-year-old Sean, has Down's syndrome and the older son, Gareth who is 11, has behavioural difficulties which the school have notified the team about.

- Given that the team has only recently been formed, what do you think should be Judy's primary focus in terms of working with the whole team to understand and address some of the current difficulties facing the family?
- Which professionals should be involved with this family?

Commentary

This case study can be understood from different perspectives of the organisational/team perspective and the needs of the family. The team manager should consider the source of the referrals and seek to involve the specialist workers who need to be involved immediately – for example, the education support worker, the learning disability nurse, child and family social worker, and the domestic abuse worker may be the ones to involve immediately, but bearing in mind that that the constitution of the team around this family may change in the future. Multi-agency working has many benefits and challenges, a few of which will be highlighted below.

Benefits of multi-agency working

Multi-agency working brings a myriad of benefits to all involved and in particular to people who use social care services.

1. MAW helps to improve understanding and raise awareness of broader issues, and also enables professionals to understand each other's practice remits and competence.
2. Specifically, in relation to social work with children and families, MAW can enhance and improve outcomes through a range of connected services, advice and support.
3. MAW relies upon practitioners merging their skills, expertise, experience and knowledge to achieve maximum results for their service users.
4. MAW has the benefit of increasing staff morale and minimising isolation and lone working.

Challenges of multi-agency working

1. Blurred professional boundaries and lack of clarity around roles is a main challenge for working with others in health and social care.
2. Conflicting values, work practices and knowledge is also another disadvantage of multi-agency working. This is linked to competing priorities, placing multiple demands and expectations on the team.
3. There is the danger of initiative overload, which means that the many team members wish to have their agendas and ideas prioritised. If they are not managed well, this will result in too many initiatives and unrealistic chances of undertaking them successfully.
4. Another challenge of multi-agency working is that when key staff members leave, delays in replacing them can impact on the effectiveness of partnerships.

Tuckman and anti-oppressive multi-agency team development

In 1965, Bruce Tuckman proposed four stages of team development, stating that this process was necessary for all teams to grow, problem solve, address challenges and work together in order to deliver positive results. These stages are forming, storming, norming and performing. In later years, Tuckman added a fifth stage, which he called adjourning. In the discussion to follow, I will examine how these stages can create oppressive situations and how they can be used as opportunities to promote anti-oppressive practice in multi-agency teams.

Forming

In the forming stage, members from a range of agencies begin to establish relationships and clarify roles. High on the agenda will be a discussion of the aims and goals of the team and the individual contributions towards the overall goal(s). In this first stage, the leader's skills and expertise are tested as members of the team try to identify the leader's weaknesses and strengths. Oppression could occur at this stage as members try to push their individual agendas into the team's goals and aims. Anti-oppressive practice can be maintained at this stage, especially by the leader who may be quite directive at this point with the aim of managing members of the new team. As people introduce themselves to each other, it is important to focus on the aims rather than, for example, dwell on educational levels and qualifications or other such detail that can leave some people feeling overwhelmed or inadequate.

Storming

This is the second stage of team development and here, team members are often found to be actively seeking positions of power and authority within the team. At this stage, cliques may form as members begin to identify themselves according to skillset and expertise, personal qualities, or along many other lines. This possible formation of factions enables oppression to creep into a multi-agency team – for example, a team comprising a mental health social worker, a children and families social worker, a paediatrician and a teacher may find that its members connect based on their professional affiliations, or from the perspective of gender, race or other factors. It is important that any conflicts and tensions are resolved early on at this stage. An example of oppression is in the form of bullying where the person being bullied is excluded from work activities or other related events. Bullying involves the abuse of power or perceived power and can manifest itself in the form of shouting or humiliating individuals. 'Jokes' about other professions should be avoided and, if this occurs, the leader/manager should disrupt it immediately.

Norming

The norming stage, according to Tuckman (1965), is generally where roles and responsibilities have become clear and have been accepted by members of the team. Decisions are made as a team and small working groups can be formed to undertake bespoke and smaller tasks. Team members are now committed to working towards the aims and goals of the group as team identity grows and solidifies. This is a stage where people may be keen to leave behind some of the difficulties and disagreements of the previous stage. However, some may still feel aggrieved that their ideas and contributions have not been taken forward, so there needs to be open and honest discussions about why and how the decision was reached to exclude particular ideas or suggestions.

Performing

At this stage, the multi-agency team has a shared vision and there is a high degree of autonomy and strategic awareness as individual team members become more effective and self-confident. They are confident in each other's abilities and skills, and are more productive. At this performing stage, care must be taken not to overstep the boundaries due to the autonomy available. For example, although managers and multi-agency team leaders do not have to be consulted about everything, it is important that all members of the team ensure that information is shared with team members so that they are aware of what is happening and the rationale behind specific decisions is understood. At this stage, anti-oppressive practice is likely to be at play where members of the multi-agency team praise and acknowledge each other's skills and expertise, and avoid overt or covert displays of undermining and disrespect.

Adjourning

In 1975, Tuckman added this fifth stage, which has also been referred to as 'mourning' or 'de-forming'. In this stage, the task would have been completed, the goals and objectives met and members would have moved on to other things. From an anti-oppressive point of view, it needs to be recognised that team members will experience this stage differently and some members may feel particularly vulnerable about having to move on or be apprehensive about change more generally.

Activity 14.1

Thinking about the storming stage of Tuckman's framework, make a note of how you might approach this stage.

• What are some of things you could do to go through this stage successfully?

Reflect on your own or discuss with a colleague.

Professional identity

According to Webb (2017), professional identity is not a stable concept. It is an ever-moving process and an important one for social workers to understand and practise. Social workers, as stated by Wiles (2013), have a growing awareness of professionalism arising from the profession gaining registration status. This is consistent with the view of Troman (2008), who suggests that the meaning of professional identity is influenced by changing academic and political contexts. The idea of professional identity is important in social work and should be regarded as more than registration, adhering to values and owning a knowledge base (Wiles, 2013). Slay and Smith (2011) suggest that a professional identity is an individual's image of who they are as a professional, which affects individual behaviour in the workplace. In the field of social work, professional values, norms and a knowledge base impact upon job attitudes and shape the behaviour of social workers. Consequently, social workers in multi-agency teams must demonstrate in-depth understanding of the knowledge and skills associated with the profession, and this is crucial to exhibit throughout Tuckman's stages discussed above. Compton and Galaway (1984) discuss four key traits of a profession which very much align with social work. They state that a profession:

- must have a distinctive body of knowledge;
- must have restrictions through qualifications and/or registration;
- must have a code of ethics;
- must possess recognised practice expertise.

In addition to the above, the PCF also clarifies the levels of professionalism it expects from people along the journey to becoming a social worker and beyond. The main requirement is to *identify and behave as a professional social worker, committed to professional development.*

Table 14.1 Professionalism pre- and post-qualification

For students who have just began their training	For qualified social workers
Demonstrate an initial understanding of the role of the social worker.	Am able to meet the requirements of the professional regulator.
Demonstrate motivation and commitment to become a social worker.	Actively promote the profession and its reputation in a growing range of contexts.
Identify my own potential strengths and challenges in relation to the role of social worker.	Understand that social work is an international profession with a global definition that supports my professional identity, ethics and practice with diverse communities in England.
Demonstrate an initial understanding of the importance of personal self-care, resilience and adaptability in social work.	Take responsibility for obtaining regular, effective supervision from a professional supervisor/manager to ensure effective practice, reflection, continuing professional development and career opportunities.
Demonstrate the ability to take responsibility for my own learning and development (BASW, 2019).	Maintain professionalism in more challenging circumstances.
	Manage workload more independently, seeking support and suggesting solutions for workload and demand management difficulties.
	Maintain appropriate personal/professional boundaries in more challenging circumstances.
	Make skilled use of self as part of my interventions.
	Maintain awareness of my own professional limitations and knowledge gaps, and seek to address these.
	Establish a network of internal and external colleagues from whom to seek advice and expertise.
	Routinely promote well-being at work and self-care for myself and others.
	Promote excellence in practice and raise and address issues of poor practice or inadequate working conditions for professional practice, internally through the organisation, and then independently if required.

The above, taken from BASW (2019, online) aims to show the clear difference between how professionalism is expected to be demonstrated at the start of one's training and when a person qualifies as a social worker. This distinction clearly supports the view by Webb (2017) who sees the development of professional identity as a process. It is also important to note that there are a few more stages in between these two which have not been discussed here. They are: *readiness for practice*; *end of first placement*; *end of last placement*; *newly qualified social worker (NQSW)*.

Activity 14.2

Reflect on the above requirements for professionalism as per the PCF and carefully consider your own circumstances.

- Which areas have been easiest to achieve and which ones have been (or could potentially) be challenging for you? Why?

Working relationships

Communication is key to developing positive working relationships with service users, peers and other professionals in social work. In multi-agency teams, effective communication is even more important as every effort is made to demonstrate respect, understanding and value for other professionals we may be working with. Effective communication, according to Koprowska (2014), involves being reliable at all times. If you promise to do something for other team members or for a service user, you should keep to your word. Honesty in communication is another key ingredient. Do not make up stories to please service users, but rather do what is right as per your professional social work ethics, values, organisational guidance and legislation. Be aware of the subtle and overt oppressive messages that non-verbal communication may convey. For example, standing over a colleague to complete a task may send the message that they are either not trusted or that they are not working fast enough. Respect is the cornerstone of good practice, a respectful approach is also a non-oppressive approach and should be encouraged at all times.

It has been suggested that service user involvement can be stifled in multi-agency teams, and it is my view that this stifling of service user involvement is in itself oppressive and discriminatory. Service users must be given ample opportunities to contribute to matters that affect them. In a multi-agency setting where there are many people involved, it may be that the service user voice is relegated to the background. This is unacceptable oppressive practice. Arnstein's (1969) ladder of participation is a useful tool to assist us to understand the oppressive nature of some service user participatory models. The ladder has eight rungs, of which rungs 1–5 provide tokenistic, non-participation for service users and social workers are urged to avoid these. However, rungs 6–8 provide greater participation and control for service users.

Activity 14.3

On your own or with a colleague, think about how you might support key practitioners from different agencies to ensure that service user participation is effective.

Guidance

This activity requires you to consider the ways in which social workers might collaborate for effective service user participation in terms of sound coordination, continuity and minimising duplication. Using the ladder of participation mentioned earlier, you may find that keeping a record of service user feedback on practice and other related issues, and actively seek feedback with the view to improving services. This strategy will contribute to empowering practice while minimising practice that is oppressive and discriminatory.

Anti-oppressive multi-agency and interprofessional collaboration

So far in this chapter, we have identified where oppressive practice could occur during and within multi-agency partners, and the following are a few ideas about how social workers might work anti-oppressively in these situations and settings.

- Valuing the knowledge, skills and expertise, each member brings to the multi-agency team.
- Acknowledging the organisational capital that each member brings to the collaboration.
- Ensuring the swift flow of information to all the members of the team. Knowledge is power, so by withholding information, we are making some members of the team powerless.
- Respectful engagement (through actions and communications) should be a hallmark of MAW.
- Reporting oppressive and discriminatory practices to appropriate managers and team leaders.

Case Study

Peter is the only social worker in a hospital-based mental health team in Littleborough. The team of five comprises one psychiatrist, two mental health nurses and one occupational therapist. Peter joined this team from a purely social work mental health support team and his work was underpinned by the social model. Peter is becoming increasingly concerned that there is little consideration for the social model in this team and that the medical model underpins work. Earlier this week, the psychiatrist made a comment about social workers being all 'nicey nicey and not doing real work'. Peter feels that the comment is offensive and oppressive, so he decides to approach the psychiatrist about this.

On your own or with a colleague, consider these questions.

(Continued)

(Continued)

- Do you think that Peter has grounds to confront the psychiatrist? What are the reasons for your answer?
- How might Peter address the wider issues that are contained within the case study?

Commentary

The case study draws out some of the challenges associated with the use of language and should enable you to consider the importance of abstaining from 'banter', which can cause offence to others. Peter will have to do this in a constructive manner, to avoid doing what he is accusing the psychiatrist of. Peter should spend some time discussing his role and the role of social work in the area of mental health with not just the psychiatrist, but with other members of the team if required.

Chapter summary

This chapter has sought to outline how MAW and interprofessional working can enable oppressive practice and has offered strategies about how social workers might enhance anti-oppressive practice in these settings. The multi-agency and interprofessional arena creates a context where each discipline's professional identity is scrutinised as they are expected to make unique contributions to enhance their collaboration. We have recognised the value of professional identity in an interprofessional practice context and identified best practice when working anti-oppressively in an interprofessional context.

Historically, social work has brought a range of professionals to the collaboration because of its interrelationship with other disciplines. These collaborations have not always been smooth and require you, as the social worker, to understand your role and the unique insights you can contribute to MAW.

Further reading

Koprowska, J (2014) *Communication and Interpersonal Skills in Social Work.* London: Learning Matters/Sage.

This book is a must read for all social work students seeking to understand communication in context and the importance of good interpersonal skills.

Wiles, F (2013) Not easily put into a box: constructing professional identity. *Social Work Education*, 32(7): 854–66.

This article provides useful insight into social work professional identity and outlines the dynamic nature of professional identity.

15

Anti-oppressive practice beyond qualification

> (Continued)
>
> It will also introduce you to the following standards as set out in the Social Work Subject Benchmark Statement (2019).
>
> 5.14 Intervention and evaluation
> 5.15 Communication skills
>
> See Appendix 2 for a detailed description of these standards.

Introduction

In this final chapter for Part Three of the book, I aim to provide you with strategies and information about how you might maintain and continue to develop your understanding of anti-oppressive practice well into qualified social work practice. As an example of good practice, I will share with you how I maintain my own continuous learning in my career as a social work academic and practitioner.

The chapter will begin with a discussion about the importance of continuous professional development (CPD) for social workers and will also highlight some strategies for maintaining currency of knowledge required for the ever-changing nature of social work practice in the UK and globally.

This chapter also highlights the need for you to practise in an ethically sound way, to use, not abuse your positions of power and to ensure that service users are enabled to contribute to decisions that affect them. Promoting their right to self-determination, being non-judgemental, treating service users as individuals, avoiding stereotypes and upholding confidentiality are all required during training as a social worker, but more so as a qualified practitioner who can be referred to fitness to practise panels and hearings for breaching these and other professional values.

Transitioning from student to social worker

Transitions are an inevitable experience for every human being and they affect people differently. There is evidence to suggest that when we are aware of the transition which is about to occur, we are more able to plan and adapt successfully, while a sudden unplanned transition may cause anxiety, distress and confusion as a result of feeling less prepared for the new role (Battaglia and Flynn, 2019). Inductions are a useful way to provide a structured and well-planned welcome into a new setting as a qualified social worker. Keen et al. (2009, p20) identify the key dimensions of social work induction as:

- Building relationships with those who support your practice.
- Building relationships with your team and supervisors.
- Clarify your specific role and responsibilities.
- Mobilise resources which can enhance your effectiveness.

In progressing, it is important to firmly embed anti-oppressive practice principles into all these above dimensions. For example, in building relationships with team members, supervisors and all who support your practice, it is important that you show eagerness to maintain anti-oppressive practice and promote social justice from the outset. To achieve this, there are some important considerations to bear in mind. Who are the members of your team? What is the diversity of the team – race, ethnicity, disability, gender, LGBTQI, nationality – and how might these influence power and relationship dynamics? How are colleagues with caring responsibilities, for example, spoken about in their absence? What are the subtle or overt messages that team members convey about each other?

What is your role and who are your service users? Again, colleagues need to ensure that they confront oppression and privilege embedded in their roles and in the policies and guidelines that underpin their work with service users.

Continuing professional development

Continuing professional development (CPD) is the ongoing process of developing, maintaining and documenting professional skills throughout your career and working life. You can develop these skills through courses, training events, conferences, personal and private study and research, or even through placements and internships.

According to Field et al. (2014), practitioners and their employers are responsible for ensuring that CPD for social workers is high on the agenda. Organisations and managers no longer have the luxury of blaming staff for not taking up learning opportunities post-qualification. Preston-Shoot (2007) suggests that it is in the best interest of organisations to provide learning and development opportunities for social workers, and also to enable them to attend these events with time off work, workload reduction and any other positive strategies. Research by Preston-Shoot (2007) found that social work practitioners' knowledge was out of date, particularly in the area of understanding changes to legal rules. This corroborates an earlier suggestion by Balloch et al. (1999) that the social care workforce is unable to reskill staff at a speed aligned with the pace of change. This assertion calls for a more flexible and considered approach to CPD.

The link between CPD and evidence-informed practice or evidence-based practice cannot be overstated, as CPD is a necessary component for the successful application of evidence informed practice. Social workers will know of researchers and academics who have expert knowledge in the area of anti-oppressive practice. Keeping abreast with research publications from known experts is important, as well as engaging oneself in broader reading to discover new authors, is the responsibility of the social worker. Social workers need to develop appropriate skills to find and use evidence to underpin their practice and, by so doing, demonstrate their effectiveness. This does not have to be solely literature from the UK and should include global perspectives wherever possible.

Where employers are responsible for nominating and funding their staff to undertake CPD, Channer and Doel (2009) highlight the disproportionately low numbers of Black minority ethnic social workers supported to undertake post-qualifying social work training courses. More recently, Mbarushimana and Robbins (2015) found that Black minority ethnic social workers in the UK experienced 'covert rejection' from their managers and racism from their colleagues. This often resulted in low motivation and self-confidence on the part of Black minority ethnic social workers. For the most part, Black minority ethnic social workers felt that they needed to work harder to prove themselves and their abilities. Such experiences undermine the push for anti-oppressive practice beyond qualification and requires urgent attention from employers. It is perhaps necessary to state here that the selection criteria for CPD opportunities should not disadvantage any one group of people over others, but should be fair, transparent and based on known and advertised criteria.

Activity 15.1

Think about something you recently read which provided new or different insight into your understanding of anti-oppressive practice.

* Why did you choose the text, book, article or paper?
* What did you learn?
* How will you use what you learnt?

My personal story

I left social work practice before Multi-Agency Safeguarding Hubs (MASH) came into being. I was conscious that this lack of experience of MASH was unhelpful to the students and to me as an academic. I made the decision that I needed to spend a few days shadowing a MASH team, so I sent a formal request through my contacts at a London borough and was able to observe the work of a MASH team for two days and I found the learning invaluable. I was proactive about this and made a list of questions to ask and practice I wanted to observe. Conversations within the team that day confirmed to me the importance of collaborative working and the benefits for service users. I was asked for feedback about my shadow experience, but I kept these to a minimum. What I observed was the way in which some members of the MASH team spoke about others. The comments had roots and histories. For example, a comment that James (not his real name) would take his 'sweet time' to get back to them with the required information was heard more than once during my two-day shadowing experience.

I concluded that James, for example, had perhaps unintentionally built a reputation for himself, leading others to comment about the lengths of time he took to share information with others. It may be important to consider here whether this inference could be that James was a worker who was thorough and therefore needed additional time to get the information to them or whether he was a slow worker. Whichever the situation, you are reminded about the use of language which could further oppress and undermine colleagues.

Strategies for keeping informed

There are many ways through which social workers can keep informed about anti-oppressive practice. In this section, I will highlight four strategies and invite you to add to this list.

CPD journal

Traditionally, social workers think of ongoing professional development being about training and if you ask to see social workers' CPD records they might well show a training record. However, training is only one small part of CPD. Practitioners need to think more widely than training, with the focus moving away from 'What training have you done?' to 'What have you learnt?'. For example, watching a television programme, listening to a podcast or reflecting on a home visit will all lead to learning and development. The CPD journal (Maclean, 2018) helps practitioners record every element of their CPD with spaces to record learning from supervision, feedback, training and wider activities. This journal will enable social workers to critically reflect not only on oppressive practice they may have witnessed, but also on how they may respond or react on another occasion to promote anti-oppressive practice.

Self-motivation

If we are to enhance our understanding of anti-oppressive practice when we are no longer students in the classroom, we need to be motivated to learn and grow in our chosen profession. Motivation can be intrinsic (internal factors) or extrinsic (external factors). Intrinsic factors are our personal internal motivations for CPD. These could be the desire to gain new understandings and increase our knowledge, while extrinsic factors are external to us – for example, work and role requirements, employee awards or promotion. Whatever the motivation, it is important that social workers pursue CPD and maintain commitment to improving their practice for the benefit of service users and the wider communities in which they work.

Social media

Social media has come to stay and is collectively defined as interactive web-based tools for communication and engagement. For social workers, the skilful use of IT and computer-based technology is a requirement for their role. Twitter is my personal favourite, and Hitchcock and Battista (2013) argue that it is a professionally relevant tool that *helps students develop knowledge and skills for social work as well as the digital literacies of metacognition, critical evaluation, and attention management demanded today* (p33).

Hitchcock et al. (2019) suggests that social workers can create a virtual learning and information platform with colleagues where information and updates about social work can be shared. This lifelong learning tool can be used to update learning and cultivate the skills that align with the competencies, imperatives and core values of the social work profession. Twitter debates in the area of social work often highlight issues of oppression and discrimination, and could signpost you to relevant research and resources.

Agency/organisational policies

Agency and organisations employing social workers have requirements not only for undertaking but evidencing the ongoing learning they have achieved. They will also have clear polices and guidelines for the successful completion of probation and towards promotion and other progression stages. This means that social workers will have to continuously review their career progression and provide evidence about how they continue to meet social work values, the PCF and other organisational priorities and targets.

Dominelli (2002, p151) cautions organisations against what she calls 'short-termism', which is the belief that once a practice or part of an organisation is changed, then the whole organisation will change. For anti-oppressive practice to be truly embedded into organisations, all the parts of the organisation will need to engage in change, otherwise the changes are unsustainable.

Anti-oppressive practice in assessments and interventions

According to Dominelli (2002), *unless social workers understand 'oppression' and the ways it is reproduced, their interventions can become 'oppressive' directly or indirectly*. In this section, I will examine how social work assessments and interventions can be sites that permit oppressive practice to exist and suggest ways in which social workers can avoid oppression in their assessments and engagement with service users.

As a commitment to social justice, anti-oppressive practice in social work assessments is complex and can be viewed through multiple lenses. All social work assessments must be based on an understanding of privilege, identity and power for the social worker and in relation to the service user. The social worker brings to the assessment elements of their own identity, beliefs, attitudes and values, and must take time to understand how these might impact on the assessment of the service user. Social divisions such as age, disability, gender, race and ethnicity already discussed in this book require social workers to consider the holistic needs of service users. Non-oppressive assessments take place when the social worker acknowledges the differential vulnerability embodied in the different groups. For example, a conservative Muslim family in receipt of social work services should be respected for their request not to hold meetings on a Friday, and also for requesting the services of a specific gender social worker or for other such considerations.

The person-centred approach is both inclusive and non-oppressive in that it usefully structures the relationship between the service user and the social worker, with the aim of empowering the service user, focusing on the process as well as on the outcome of the intervention. Person-centred approaches minimise hierarchical relationships in practice and embed the principles of empathy, respect, unconditional positive regard and genuineness, which are all paramount to working non-oppressively.

Case Study

Zane is a male social worker with the local Children in Need (CIN) team. He qualified as a social worker two years ago and is enjoying the work he does with children and their families. He describes himself as health conscious and uses the gym several times a week.

Kutoh is a 10-year-old boy who has recently been referred to children's social care due to his behavioural difficulties at school and suspected safeguarding concerns at home. Zane invites Kutoh's mother, Salama, to meet him in the office to undertake an initial assessment and notices that Kutoh appears to be overweight. Zane asks Salama what she feeds her son and proceeds to say Kutoh must have a very healthy appetite. Zane also recommends exercise, sporting activities and offers dietary advice to Salama.

Kutoh's mother speaks to the head teacher the following day and complains about the new social worker, Zane. The principal is concerned that this initial meeting may not have gone well and that the mother is unlikely to engage going forward. He decides to ring Zane to discuss Salama's concerns.

- What, if anything, might be inappropriate about Zane's approach?
- Do these equate to oppressive practice or not? Why?
- What is the principal likely to say to Zane?
- With your understanding of anti-oppressive practice, how should Zane salvage the situation?

Commentary

Social workers have a duty to be respectful and polite, yet truthful and honest with service users. With that in mind, it is easy to see little wrong with Zane's behaviour and conduct during the initial meeting with Kutoh and his mother, Salama. However, with a focus on anti-oppressive practice, the following considerations might be useful.

- Social workers must keep their knowledge about anti-oppressive practice up to date through CPD and other related activities.
- It is important for social workers to continually think about how they contribute to oppression and how they might proactively work to disrupt oppressive practice.
- There are growing forms of oppression which social workers need to familiarise themselves with such as 'body/image' shaming and 'period shaming'.

You are invited to further reflection on this case study.

Chapter summary

In this chapter, we have examined the importance of anti-oppressive practice beyond qualification, and have sought to offer some strategies about how social workers might avoid oppressive practice and disrupt all forms of discrimination through their work. As part of my own professional development, I recognised the need to enhance my understanding of social work in Islamic contexts for a variety of personal and professional reasons. I relocated to teach social work at the United Arab Emirates University as my opportunity to develop this area of knowledge and practice for the future. In the many roles I have undertaken (Chair of Fostering Panel, Safeguarding Advisor to the Minister for Immigration, UK Home Office, Chair of the Board of Trustees for Africans Unite Against Child Abuse (AFRUCA), I have found there to be the need for greater understanding of Muslim service users primarily because in child safeguarding matters – for example, *acting outside of the context in which a child lives could be detrimental to engaging and working with families* (O'Leary et al., 2019, p3). It could also leave open the opportunities for stereotyping, Islamophobia and other forms of oppressive and discriminatory practice. As a social work academic, I have never stopped wanting to learn and keep my practice current, particularly in the area of anti-oppressive practice and anti-discriminatory practice more generally. This has meant that in over 23 years since I qualified as a social worker, my practice continues to reflect the anti- oppressive principles of the profession.

Further reading

Keen, S, Gray, I, Parker, J, Galpin, D and Brown, K (2009) *Newly Qualified Social Workers: A Handbook for Practice.* Exeter: Learning Matters.

Although social work education and post-qualifying training have undergone changes since the publication of this book, it is still very relevant in that it outlines strategies for managing the transition from student to social worker, managing induction and probation, lifelong learning and continuous professional development.

Hitchcock, LI and Battista, A (2013) Social media for professional practice: integrating Twitter with social work pedagogy. *Journal of Baccalaureate Social Work*, 18: 33–45.

In this article, the authors argue that Twitter is a professionally relevant tool to help students enhance their knowledge and skills for social work education and practice. They outline the ways in which social media influences trends in information seeking.

Conclusion

I begin this concluding section by offering a few ideas based on my research and about my perspective on what it means to be an anti-oppressive social worker. It is my hope that if this book is to leave you with anything, it is pride about belonging to a profession that challenges oppression, inequality, discrimination and social injustice. If that is not the case, then you either need a further period of developing that consciousness or you are in the wrong profession.

The anti-oppressive social worker

I would like to address the question 'Who is an anti-oppressive social worker?'. It is my view that anti-oppressive practice is a way of life. You cannot claim to be anti-oppressive only in the workplace with other social workers and become oppressive in other situations.

The anti-oppressive social worker is one who uses strengths-based and person-centred approaches when working with service users. The anti-oppressive social worker seeks to achieve the liberating element of the profession's mandate by confronting and challenging labelling, micro-aggressions and inequalities on individual and structural levels. Drawing upon critical and empowerment theories, anti-oppressive social workers value and respect service user perspectives, while continually seeking opportunities to update and extend their knowledge of inequality, discrimination, exploitation and social injustice. The anti-oppressive practitioner is not defensive and should justify their practice using the law, policy and research evidence. Finally, the anti-oppressive social worker considers the intersectional nature of identities, can recognise their own privilege – not feel guilty about it – (Johnson et al., 2008), while being aware that these benefits grant them access to spaces and opportunities not always available to service users.

Being anti-oppressive requires social workers to be cognizant of the power of language and aware that we exclude service users when we use words, jargon and acronyms that they do not understand. That type of exclusion does not reflect a commitment to anti-oppressive practice. I am guilty of occasionally straying into acronyms. However, I am also a firm believer that words carry meaning, so in this book I have avoided using the acronym for anti-oppressive practice and have spelt it out in full. By spelling and naming it in full, I am owning it. Similarly, you need to name it to own it. The anti-oppressive social worker uses respectful and clear language, which is not judgemental, insulting, dehumanising, derogatory or demeaning. When engaging in research, the anti-oppressive social worker should ensure that their research does not further oppress people, but rather achieves real and sustained change.

Concluding thoughts

In 2017, a colleague and I were approached by a publisher with an invitation to write a book on anti-oppressive practice in social work. Without much hesitation, we accepted the invitation. However, days later, my colleague advised that she was no longer able to work on this project, so effectively I would be writing it on my own. It was at that point that I began to wonder what I had let myself into. It had all the ingredients for a disaster! Who did I think I was and who would want to read a book solely written by me? Each time I looked at the title, I was immediately reminded that this book might cause me to lose more 'friends', because over the years I have parted ways with friends who did not always act in ways consistent with my values of fairness and justice. Indeed, a few of these friends constantly reminded me that as a second-language speaker of English, putting my writing in the public domain was a bold step to take. Others reminded me that there were some 'high-flyers' researching and writing about oppression, discrimination and racism, and that my work would need to match existing work. There were people who referred to my other work as simplistic and easy, and then the colleagues who recommend my work to students but who do not engage with it themselves. In all of these experiences, I was acutely aware of being 'othered' and their preferred option would be for me to stay silent. These 'othered' experiences have given me unique insight into many of the areas discussed and hope towards changing the systems that oppress. Throughout this book I have referred to privilege and power, and how social workers must address their privilege and acknowledge the power they hold when working with people who use social work services. I frequently reflect on my privilege and recognise that I do have privilege in the job I do and the people I interact with and through my 'Dr' title. Yet this privilege quickly turns to disadvantage when the Dr is followed by my foreign-sounding name. In Ghana, the country of my birth, that same surname is recognised and respected, yet as a White male once told me a few years ago in England, this same name sounded to him like a piece of machinery. How interesting it is when we consider the contexts within which oppression and oppressive practices occur. My motivations for scholarly activity in this area will continue for as long as required to illuminate the value of diversity while creating further awareness about the need to disrupt and dismantle oppression.

The menu of topics discussed in this book will be challenged: some will seek to identify the gaps (and there will be many), while others will find it too crowded (there will be many), and perhaps a happy few will find it just right. It is impossible for a broad area like this to be covered adequately to everyone's approval in one textbook. In the end, I have considered what areas of learning are relevant for student social workers and have tried to balance the theoretical with the practical. Importantly, I have integrated a diverse range of research from across the world to further demonstrate the global reach of social work. This will assist you to evaluate your social and emotional growth and development as you progress your studies. The self-awareness, empathy, value for diversity and appreciation of the intersectional nature of our identities will help you to see how you connect to the profession, not just locally but also at the global level.

Had this book been completed earlier, I would not have been able to comment on the coronavirus pandemic, the related socioeconomic hardship, the cruel murders of Ahmaud Arbery, George Floyd and the subsequent #BlacklivesMatter protests in many countries. In all these events, social workers have been at the forefront of the fight against oppression and discrimination in all its forms in line with its history of activism.

The aim of this book has been to remind student social workers that they must have the theoretical understanding of oppression in order to intervene appropriately and sensitively with service users from a diversity of backgrounds and life experiences.

As I have sought to highlight throughout this book, anti-oppressive practice is central to sound social work practice and it is impossible to claim to be a social worker without understanding what oppression is and how it manifests in daily interactions with service users. It is important to remind readers that the book is structured in the way that it is to enable a discussion about many of the ways through which individuals, groups and communities experience oppression historically and more recently. The importance of understanding intersectional approaches in the context of oppression cannot be overemphasised. Dominelli (2008) suggests that while focusing on one aspect of oppression may be helpful to an individual at a point in time, it will not eradicate oppression completely or from groups of people.

This book has provided students of social work with the tools and knowledge required to practise in ethically appropriate ways with a range of stakeholders, service users and other professionals from diverse backgrounds.

Tools such as the Power Flower and cultural web are helpful practice tools to use in your practice. Frameworks and models such as the SHARP, SPEAR, MANDELA, SHARE and 4D2P can assist you to work anti-oppressively with service users. Theoretically, locating social justice within the broader anti-oppressive practice framework is useful, as are the discussions about power and powerlessness, othering, critical race theory and critical disability theory. The division of the book into chapters focusing on specific areas of difference is deliberate, with the aim of enabling a deeper exploration of issues. However, the need to have an intersectional lens when reading this book cannot be overstated. We have addressed the area of refugees and people seeking asylum, and identified the multiple layers of oppression they experience and how social workers can work effectively with them.

Finally, we move the discussion of oppression into the context of practice learning (placements) and provide an overview about how oppressive practices manifest in sites of learning and impact on professional development.

As social work practitioners, we have a moral, ethical and legal responsibility to challenge inequality and disadvantage regardless of where it comes from, thereby promoting social work. An anti-oppressive social worker, through strategies, tools, advocacy and activism helps people to breathe from under the burden and strain of oppression and oppressive systems.

Appendix 1

Professional capabilities framework

The 9 Domains

1. PROFESSIONALISM – Identify and behave as a professional social worker, committed to professional development
2. VALUES AND ETHICS – Apply social work ethical principles and value to guide professional practices
3. DIVERSITY AND EQUALITY – Recognise diversity and apply anti-discriminatory and anti-oppressive principles in practice

4. RIGHTS, JUSTICE AND ECONOMIC WELLBEING – Advance human rights and promote social justice and economic wellbeing

5. KNOWLEDGE – Develop and apply relevant knowledge from social work practice and research, social sciences, law, other professional and relevant fields, and from the experience of people who use services

6. CRITICAL REFLECTION AND ANALYSIS – Apply critical reflection and analysis to inform and provide a rationale for professional decision-making

7. SKILLS AND INTERVENTIONS – Use judgement, knowledge and authority to intervene with individuals, families and communities to promote independence, provide support, prevent harm and enable progress

8. CONTEXTS AND ORGANISATIONS – Engage with, inform, and adapt to changing organisational contexts, and the social and policy environments that shape practice. Operate effectively within and contribute to the development of organisations and services, including multi-agency and inter-professional settings.

9. PROFESSIONAL LEADERSHIP – Promote the profession and good social work practice. Take responsibility for the professional learning and development of others. Develop personal influence and be part of the collective leadership and impact of the profession.

Published with kind permission of BASW – www.basw.co.uk

Appendix 2

Subject benchmark for social work

5 Knowledge, understanding and skills

Subject knowledge and understanding

5.1 During their qualifying degree studies in social work, students acquire, critically evaluate, apply and integrate knowledge and understanding in the following five core areas of study.

5.2 Social work theory, which includes:

   i. critical explanations from social work theory and other subjects which contribute to the knowledge base of social work
   ii. an understanding of social work's rich and contested history from both a UK and comparative perspective
   iii. the relevance of sociological and applied psychological perspectives to understanding societal and structural influences on human behaviour at individual, group and community levels, and the relevance of sociological theorisation to a deeper understanding of adaptation and change
   iv. the relevance of psychological, physical and physiological perspectives to understanding human, personal and social development, well-being and risk
   v. social science theories explaining and exploring group and organisational behaviour
   vi. the range of theories and research-informed evidence that informs understanding of the child, adult, family or community and of the range of assessment and interventions which can be used
   vii. the theory, models and methods of assessment, factors underpinning the selection and testing of relevant information, knowledge and critical appraisal of relevant social science and other research and evaluation methodologies, and the evidence base for social work
   viii. the nature of analysis and professional judgement and the processes of risk assessment and decision-making, including the theory of risk-informed decisions and the balance of choice and control, rights and protection in decision-making
   ix. approaches, methods and theories of intervention in working with a diverse population within a wide range of settings, including factors guiding the choice and critical evaluation of these, and user-led perspectives.

5.3   Values and ethics, which include:

   i.   the nature, historical evolution, political context and application of professional social work values, informed by national and international definitions and ethical statements, and their relation to personal values, identities, influences and ideologies

   ii.   the ethical concepts of rights, responsibility, freedom, authority and power inherent in the practice of social workers as agents with statutory powers in different situations

   iii.   aspects of philosophical ethics relevant to the understanding and resolution of value dilemmas and conflicts in both interpersonal and professional context

   iv.   understanding of, and adherence to, the ethical foundations of empirical and conceptual research, as both consumers and producers of social science research

   v.   the relationship between human rights enshrined in law and the moral and ethical rights determined theoretically, philosophically and by contemporary society

   vi.   the complex relationships between justice, care and control in social welfare and the practical and ethical implications of these, including their expression in roles as statutory agents in diverse practice settings and in upholding the law in respect of challenging discrimination and inequalities

   vii.   the conceptual links between codes defining ethical practice and the regulation of professional conduct

   viii.   the professional and ethical management of potential conflicts generated by codes of practice held by different professional groups

   ix.   the ethical management of professional dilemmas and conflicts in balancing the perspectives of individuals who need care and support and professional decision-making at points of risk, care and protection

   x.   the constructive challenging of individuals and organisations where there may be conflicts with social work values, ethics and codes of practice

   xi.   the professional responsibility to be open and honest if things go wrong (the duty of candour about own practice) and to act on concerns about poor or unlawful practice by any person or organisation

   xii.   continuous professional development as a reflective, informed and skilled practitioner, including the constructive use of professional supervision

5.4   Service users and carers, which include:

   i.   the factors which contribute to the health and well-being of individuals, families and communities, including promoting dignity, choice and independence for people who need care and support

   ii.   the underpinning perspectives that determine explanations of the characteristics and circumstances of people who need care and support, with critical evaluation drawing on research, practice experience and the experience and expertise of people who use services

   iii.   the social and psychological processes associated with, for example, poverty, migration, unemployment, trauma, poor health, disability, lack of education and other sources of disadvantage and how they affect well-being, how they interact and may lead to marginalisation, isolation and exclusion, and demand for social work services

   iv.   explanations of the links between the factors contributing to social differences and identities (for example, social class, gender, ethnic differences, age, sexuality and religious belief) and the structural consequences of inequality and differential need faced by service users

   v.   the nature and function of social work in a diverse and increasingly global society (with particular reference to prejudice, interpersonal relations, discrimination, empowerment and anti-discriminatory practices)

5.5   The nature of social work practice, in the UK and more widely, which includes:

   i.   the place of theoretical perspectives and evidence from European and international research in assessment and decision-making processes

   ii.   the integration of theoretical perspectives and evidence from European and international research into the design and implementation of effective social work intervention with a wide range of service users, carers and communities

   iii.   the knowledge and skills which underpin effective practice, with a range of service users and in a variety of settings

   iv.   the processes that facilitate and support service user and citizen rights, choice, co-production, self-governance, well-being and independence

   v.   the importance of interventions that promote social justice, human rights, social cohesion, collective responsibility and respect for diversity and that tackle inequalities

   vi.   its delivery in a range of community-based and organisational settings spanning the statutory, voluntary and private sectors, and the changing nature of these service contexts

   vii.   the factors and processes that facilitate effective interdisciplinary, interprofessional and interagency collaboration and partnership across a plurality of settings and disciplines

   viii.   the importance of social work's contribution to intervention across service user groups, settings and levels in terms of the profession's focus on social justice, human rights, social cohesion, collective responsibility and respect for diversities

   ix.   the processes of reflection and reflexivity as well as approaches for evaluating service and welfare outcomes for vulnerable people, and their significance for the development of practice and the practitioner.

5.6   The leadership, organisation and delivery of social work services, which includes:

   i.   the location of contemporary social work within historical, comparative and global perspectives, including in the devolved nations of the UK and wider European and international contexts

   ii.   how the service delivery context is portrayed to service users, carers, families and communities

   iii.   the changing demography and cultures of communities, including European and international contexts, in which social workers practise

   iv.   the complex relationships between public, private, social and political philosophies, policies and priorities and the organisation and practice of social work, including the contested nature of these

   v.   the issues and trends in modern public and social policy and their relationship to contemporary practice, service delivery and leadership in social work

   vi.   the significance of legislative and legal frameworks and service delivery standards, including on core social work values and ethics in the delivery of services which support, enable and empower

   vii.   the current range and appropriateness of statutory, voluntary and private agencies providing services and the organisational systems inherent within these

   viii.   development of new ways of working and delivery, for example the development of social enterprises, integrated multi-professional teams and independent social work provision

   ix.   the significance of professional and organisational relationships with other related services, including housing, health, education, police, employment, fire, income maintenance and criminal justice

    x. the importance and complexities of the way agencies work together to provide care, the relationships between agency policies, legal requirements and professional boundaries in shaping the nature of services provided in integrated and interdisciplinary contexts

   xi. the contribution of different approaches to management and leadership within different settings, and the impact on professional practice and on quality of care management and leadership in public and human services

  xii. the development of person-centred services, personalised care, individual budgets and direct payments all focusing upon the human and legal rights of the service user for control, power and self-determination

 xiii. the implications of modern information and communications technology for both the provision and receipt of services, use of technologically enabled support and the use of social media as a process and forum for vulnerable people, families and communities, and communities of professional practice.

Subject-specific skills and other skills

5.7 The range of skills required by a qualified social worker reflects the complex and demanding context in which they work. Many of these skills may be of value in many situations, for example, analytical thinking, building relationships, working as a member of an organisation, intervention, evaluation, and reflection. What defines the specific nature of these skills as developed by social work students is:

    i. the context in which they are applied and assessed (for example, communication skills in practice with people with sensory impairments or assessment skills in an interprofessional setting)

   ii. the relative weighting given to such skills within social work practice (for example, the central importance of problem-solving skills within complex human situations)

  iii. the specific purpose of skill development (for example, the acquisition of research skills in order to build a repertoire of research-based practice)

  iv. a requirement to integrate a range of skills (that is, not simply to demonstrate these in an isolated and incremental manner).

5.8 All social work graduates demonstrate the ability to reflect on and learn from the exercise of their skills, in order to build their professional identity. They understand the significance of the concepts of continuing professional development and lifelong learning, and accept responsibility for their own continuing development.

5.9 Social work students acquire and integrate skills in the following five core areas.

Problem-solving skills

5.10 These are subdivided into four areas.

5.11 Managing problem-solving activities: graduates in social work are able to:

    i. think logically, systematically, creatively, critically and reflectively, in order to carry out a holistic assessment

   ii. apply ethical principles and practices critically in planning problem-solving activities

  iii. plan a sequence of actions to achieve specified objectives, making use of research, theory and other forms of evidence

  iv. manage processes of change, drawing on research, theory and other forms of evidence.

5.12   Gathering information: graduates in social work are able to:

    i.   demonstrate persistence in gathering information from a wide range of sources and using a variety of methods, for a range of purposes. These methods include electronic searches, reviews of relevant literature, policy and procedures, face-to-face interviews, and written and telephone contact with individuals and groups

    ii. take into account differences of viewpoint in gathering information and critically assess the reliability and relevance of the information gathered

   iii. assimilate and disseminate relevant information in reports and case records.

5.13   Analysis and synthesis: graduates in social work are able to analyse and synthesise knowledge gathered for problem-solving purposes, in order to:

    i.   assess human situations, taking into account a variety of factors (including the views of participants, theoretical concepts, research evidence, legislation and organisational policies and procedures)

    ii. analyse and synthesise information gathered, weighing competing evidence and modifying their viewpoint in the light of new information, then relate this information to a particular task, situation or problem

   iii. balance specific factors relevant to social work practice (such as risk, rights, cultural differences and language needs and preferences, responsibilities to protect vulnerable individuals and legal obligations)

   iv. assess the merits of contrasting theories, explanations, research, policies and procedures and use the information to develop and sustain reasoned arguments

    v. employ a critical understanding of factors that support or inhibit problem-solving, including societal, organisational and community issues as well as individual relationships

   vi. critically analyse and take account of the impact of inequality and discrimination in working with people who use social work services.

5.14   Intervention and evaluation: graduates in social work are able to use their knowledge of a range of interventions and evaluation processes creatively and selectively to:

    i.   build and sustain purposeful relationships with people and organisations in communities and interprofessional contexts

    ii. make decisions based on evidence, set goals and construct specific plans to achieve outcomes, taking into account relevant information, including ethical guidelines

   iii. negotiate goals and plans with others, analysing and addressing in a creative and flexible manner individual, cultural and structural impediments to change

   iv. implement plans through a variety of systematic processes that include working in partnership

    v. practice in a manner that promotes well-being, protects safety and resolves conflict

   vi. act as a navigator, advocate and support to assist people who need care and support to take decisions and access services

  vii. manage the complex dynamics of dependency and, in some settings, provide direct care and personal support to assist people in their everyday lives

 viii. meet deadlines and comply with external requirements of a task

   ix. plan, implement and critically monitor and review processes and outcomes

    x. bring work to an effective conclusion, taking into account the implications for all involved

   xi. use and evaluate methods of intervention critically and reflectively.

Communication skills

5.15   Graduates in social work are able to communicate clearly, sensitively and effectively (using appropriate methods which may include working with interpreters) with individuals and groups of different ages and abilities in a range of formal and informal situations, in order to:

   i.   engage individuals and organisations, who may be unwilling, by verbal, paper-based and electronic means to achieve a range of objectives, including changing behaviour
   ii.   use verbal and non-verbal cues to guide and inform conversations and interpretation of information
   iii.   negotiate and, where necessary, redefine the purpose of interactions with individuals and organisations and the boundaries of their involvement
   iv.   listen actively and empathetically to others, taking into account their specific needs and life experiences
   v.   engage appropriately with the life experiences of service users, to understand accurately their viewpoint, overcome personal prejudices and respond appropriately to a range of complex personal and interpersonal situations
   vi.   make evidence-informed arguments drawing from theory, research and practice wisdom, including the viewpoints of service users and/or others
   vii.   write accurately and clearly in styles adapted to the audience, purpose and context of the communication
   viii.   use advocacy skills to promote others' rights, interests and needs
   ix.   present conclusions verbally and on paper, in a structured form, appropriate to the audience for which these have been prepared
   x.   make effective preparation for, and lead, meetings in a productive way.

Skills in working with others

5.16   Graduates in social work are able to build relationships and work effectively with others, in order to:

   i.   involve users of social work services in ways that increase their resources, capacity and power to influence factors affecting their lives
   ii.   engage service users and carers and wider community networks in active consultation
   iii.   respect and manage differences such as organisational and professional boundaries and differences of identity and/or language
   iv.   develop effective helping relationships and partnerships that facilitate change for individuals, groups and organisations while maintaining appropriate personal and professional boundaries
   v.   demonstrate interpersonal skills and emotional intelligence that creates and develops relationships based on openness, transparency and empathy
   vi.   increase social justice by identifying and responding to prejudice, institutional discrimination and structural inequality
   vii.   operate within a framework of multiple accountability (for example, to agencies, the public, service users, carers and others)
   viii.   observe the limits of professional and organisational responsibility, using supervision appropriately and referring to others when required

ix.   provide reasoned, informed arguments to challenge others as necessary, in ways that are most likely to produce positive outcomes.

Skills in personal and professional development

5.17   Graduates in social work are able to:
   i.   work at all times in accordance with codes of professional conduct and ethics
   ii.   advance their own learning and understanding with a degree of independence and use supervision as a tool to aid professional development
   iii.   develop their professional identity, recognise their own professional limitations and accountability, and know how and when to seek advice from a range of sources, including professional supervision
   iv.   use support networks and professional supervision to manage uncertainty, change and stress in work situations while maintaining resilience in self and others
   v.   handle conflict between others and internally when personal views may conflict with a course of action necessitated by the social work role
   vi.   provide reasoned, informed arguments to challenge unacceptable practices in a responsible manner and raise concerns about wrongdoing in the workplace
   vii.   be open and honest with people if things go wrong
   viii.   understand the difference between theory, research, evidence and expertise and the role of professional judgement.

Use of technology and numerical skills

5.18   Graduates in social work are able to use information and communication technology effectively and appropriately for:
   i.   professional communication, data storage and retrieval and information searching
   ii.   accessing and assimilating information to inform working with people who use services
   iii.   data analysis to enable effective use of research in practice
   iv.   enhancing skills in problem-solving
   v.   applying numerical skills to financial and budgetary responsibilities
   vi.   understanding the social impact of technology, including the constraints of confidentiality and an awareness of the impact of the 'digital divide'.

© The Quality Assurance Agency for Higher Education, 2019 http://www.qaa.ac.uk/

References

Abbas, T (2011) *Islamophobia and the Politics of Young British Muslim Ethno-religious Identities: Youth Work and Islam*. Leiden: Brill.

Age Concern (2005) *Regions for All Ages: The English Regions and Demographic Agenda: Key Trends and Issues*. Conference Report. London: Age Concern.

Akhtar, F (2013) *Mastering Social Work Values and Ethics*. London: Jessica Kingsley.

Allen, BJ (1996) Feminism and organizational communication: a Black woman's (re)view of organizational socialization. *Communication Studies*, 47: 257–71.

Allport, GA (1954) *The Nature of Prejudice*. Reading, MA: Addison-Wesley.

Alvesson, M (1998) Gender relations and identity at work: a case study of masculinities and femininities in an advertising agency. *Human Relations*, 51(8): 969–1005.

Anderson, SK and Middleton, VA (eds) (2011) *Explorations in Diversity: Examining Privilege and Oppression in a Multicultural Society* (2nd edn). Belmont, CA: Brooks/Cole.

Arboleda-Florez, J and Stuart, H (2012) From sin to science: fighting the stigmatization of mental illnesses. *The Canadian Journal of Psychiatry*, 57(8): 457–63.

Arnold, R, Burke, B, James, C, Martin, D and Thomas, B (1991) *Educating for Change*. Doris Marshall Institute for Education and Action, Toronto.

Arnstein, S (1969) A ladder of community participation. *Journal of the American Institute of Planners*, 35: 216–24.

Asakura, K and Maurer, K (2018) Attending to social justice in clinical social work: supervision as a pedagogical space. *Clinical Social Work Journal*, 46: 289–97.

Ashencaen Crabtree, S, Husain, F and Spalek, B (2017) *Islam and Social Work: Culturally Sensitive Practice in a Diverse World* (2nd edn). Bristol: Policy Press.

Ashton, V (2004) The effect of personal characteristics on reporting child maltreatment. *Child Abuse and Neglect*, 28(9): 985–97.

Atchley, RC (1989) A continuity theory of normal aging. *The Gerontologist*, 29(2): 183–90.

Baines, D (2011) *Anti-oppressive Practice: Social Justice Social Work* (2nd edn). Manitoba: Fernwood Publishing.

Balloch, S, McLean, J and Fisher, M (1999) (eds) *Social Services: Working Under Pressure*. Bristol: The Policy Press.

Bannister, A and Huntington, A (2002) *Communicating with Children and Adolescents: Action for Change*. London and Philadelphia, PA: Jessica Kingsley.

Barany, Z (2002) *The East European Gypsies: Regime Change, Marginality, and Ethnopolitics*. Cambridge: Cambridge University Press.

Barker, RL (2003) *The Social Work Dictionary* (5th edn). Washington, DC: NASW Press.

Barnoff, L, George, P and Coleman, B (2006) Operating in survival mode: challenges to implementing anti-oppressive practice in feminist social service agencies in Toronto. Canadian Social Work Review/*Revue canadienne de service social*, pp 41–58.

Bar-On, A (2002) Restoring power to social work practice. *British Journal of Social Work*, 32: 997–1014. doi:10.1093/bjsw/32.8.997

Barretti, M (2001) Social work, women and feminism: a review of social work journals, 1988–1997. *Affilia: Journal of Women and Social Work*, 16(3): 266–94.

Bartoli, A, Kennedy, S and Tedam, P (2008) Practice learning: who is failing to adjust? Black African student experience of practice learning in a Social Work setting. *Journal of Practice Teaching and Learning*, 8(2): 75–90.

BASW (2019) *Code of Ethics*. Available online at: www.basw.co.uk/about-basw/code-ethics (accessed 20 July 2020).

Battaglia, LM and Flynn, CA (2019) A review of research about the transition from student social worker to practitioner: exploring diversity. *Journal of Social Work*, 46: 2016–32. doi. org10.1177/1468-173198852598

Baumann, G and Sunier, T (2004) The school as a place in its social space. In Shiffaur, W, Baumann, G, Kastoryano, R and Vertovec, S (eds), *Civil Enculturation: Nation-state, Schools and Ethnic Difference in Four European Countries*. Oxford: Berghahn Books, pp21–32.

Bell, LA (2007) Theoretical foundations for social justice education. In Adams, M, Bell, LA and Griffin, P (eds), *Teaching for Diversity and Social Justice*. New York: Routledge; Belmont, CA: Brooks/Cole.

Ben-Harush, A, Shiovitz-Ezra, S, Doron, I, Alon, S, Leibovitz, A, Golander, H and Ayalon, L (2016) Ageism among physicians, nurses, and social workers: findings from a qualitative study. *European Journal of Ageing*, 14(1): 39–48. doi:10.1007/s10433-016-0389-9

Bennet, TH and Holloway, K (2004) Gang membership, drugs and crime in the UK. *British Journal of Criminology*, 44(3): 305–23.

Benson, PW, Furman, LD, Canda, ER, Moss, B and Danbolt, T (2016) Spiritually sensitive social work with victims of natural disasters and terrorism. *The British Journal of Social Work*, 46(5): 1372–93. doi.org/10.1093/bjsw/bcv053

Beresford, P and Davis, R (2008) Users at the core. *Community Care*, 1718: 14-16, 17 April.

Bernard and Harris, P (eds) (2016) *Safeguarding Black Children: Good Practice in Child Protection*. London: Jessica Kingsley.

Bernard, C and Gupta, A (2008) Black African children and the child protection system. *The British Journal of Social Work*, 38(3): 476–792.

Bernard, C and Greenwood, T (2019) 'We're giving you the sack' – social workers' perspectives of intervening in affluent families when there are concerns about child neglect. *The British Journal of Social Work*, 49(8): 2266–82, December.

Bernard, C, Fairtlough, A, Fletcher, J and Ahmet, A (2011) *Diversity and Progression among Social Work Students in England*. Available online at: http://research.gold.ac.uk/6326/ (accessed 22 July 2020).

Bernard, C, Fairtlough, A, Fletcher, J and Ahmet, A (2013) A qualitative study of marginalised social work students' views of social work education and learning. *British Journal of Social Work*, 44(7): 1934–49.

Bhattacharyya, G, Virdee, S and Winter, A (2020) Revisiting histories of anti-racist thought and activism. *Identities*, 27(1): 1–19. doi: 10.1080/1070289X.2019.1647686

Bhavnani, R, Mirza, HS and Meetoot, V (2005) *Tackling the Roots of Racism: Lessons for Success*. Bristol: Policy Press.

Boddy, O'Leary, Tsui, Pak and Wong (2018) Inspiring hope through social work practice. *International Social Work*, 61(4): 587–99.

Bogo, M (2006) Field instruction in social work: a review of the research literature. *The Clinical Supervisor*, 24(1/2): 163–93.

Boler, M and Zembylas, M (2003) Discomforting truths: the emotional terrain of understanding difference. In Trifonas, P (ed.) *Pedagogies of Difference: Rethinking Education for Social Change*. New York: Routledge Falmer.

Bolt, D (2015) Enabling the classroom and the curriculum: higher education, literary studies and disability. *Journal of Further and Higher Education*, 41(4): 556–65.

Braye, S and Preston-Shoot, M (2003) *Empowering Practice in Social Care*. Maidenhead: Open University Press.

Braye, S and Preston-Shoot, M (2006) Broadening the vision: law teaching, social work and civil society. *International Social Work*, 49(3): 376–89.

Briggs, S and Whittaker, A (2018) Protecting children from faith-based abuse through accusations of witchcraft and spirit possession: understanding contexts and informing practice. *British Journal of Social Work*, 48(8): 2157–75.

Brocco, G (2015) Labeling albinism: language and discourse surrounding people with albinism in Tanzania. *Disability & Society*, 30(8): 1143–57. doi: 10.1080/09687599.2015.1075869

Brooke, J and Jackson, D (2020) Older people and COVID-19: isolation, risk and ageism. *Journal of Clinical Nursing*, 29(13–14): 2044–6.

Brookins, GK (1993) Culture, ethnicity and bicultural competence: implications for children with chronic illness and disability. *Pediatrics*, 1056–62.

Bundy-Fazioli, K, Quijano, LM and Bubar, R (2013) Graduate students' perceptions of professional power in social work practice. *Journal of Social Work Education*, 49(1): 108–21. doi: 10.1080/10437797.2013.755092

Burdge, B (2007) Bending gender, ending gender: theoretical foundations for social work practice with the transgender community. *Social Work*, 52(3): 243–50.

Burke, B and Harrison, P (2016) Exploring the political and ethical dimensions of social work practice with the 'other'. In Williams, C and Graham, MJ (eds), *Social Work in a Diverse Society: Transformatory Practice with Black and Minority Ethnic Minority Individuals and Communities*. Bristol: Policy Press.

Burke, P and Parker, J (2007) *Social Work and Disadvantage: Addressing the Roots of Stigma Through Association*. London: Jessica Kingsley.

Burnham, J (2012) Developments in social GGRRAAACCEEESSS: visible–invisible and voiced–unvoiced. In Krause, I-B (ed.) *Culture and Reflexivity in Systemic Psychotherapy: Mutual Perspectives*. London: Karnac.

Burnham, J, Alvis Palma, D and Whitehouse, L (2008) Learning as a context for differences and differences as a context for learning. *Journal of Family Therapy*, 30: 529–42.

Butler, RN (1980) Ageism: a foreword. *Journal of Social Issues*, 36(2): 8–11

Butler, V (2007) Students and refugees together: towards a model of practice learning as service provision. *Social Work Education: The International Journal*. 26(3): 233–46.

Campbell, F (2009) *The Contours of Ableism: The Production of Disability and Abledness*. London: Palgrave Macmillan.

Campinha-Bacote, J (2002) The process of cultural competence in the delivery of healthcare services: a model of care. *Journal of Transcultural Nursing*, 13: 181–4.

Canda, ER (2008) Foreword. In Bein, A (ed.) *The Zen of Helping: Spiritual Principles for Mindful and Open-hearted Practice*. Hoboken: John Wiley.

Carniol, B (2005) Analysis of social location and change: practice implications. In Hicks, S, Fook, J and Pozzuto, R (eds) *Social Work: A Critical Turn*. Toronto: Thompson Educational.

Chand, A, Clare, J and Dolton, R (2002) Teaching anti-oppressive practice on a diploma in social work course: lecturers' experiences, students' responses and ways forward. *Social Work Education*, 21(1): 7–22.

Channer, Y and Doel, M (2009) Beyond qualification: experiences of black social workers on a post-qualifying course. *Social Work Education: The International Journal*, 28(4): 396–412.

Chapple, RL (2019) Culturally responsive social work practice with D/deaf clients. *Social Work Education*, 38(5): 576–81. doi: 10.1080/02615479.2019.1595569

Charlton, JI (1998) *Nothing About Us Without Us: Disability Oppression and Empowerment*. Berkeley, CA: University of California Press.

Children in Need Census (2017) *Characteristics of Children in Need: 2017–2018*. Available online at: www.gov.uk/government/statistics/characteristics-of-children-in-need-2017-to-2018 (accessed 24 July 2020).

Chinook Fund (2010) The Four '1's of Oppression. Available online at: https://chinookfund.org/wp-content/uploads (accessed 22 August 2020).

Christie, A (ed.) (2001) *Men and Social Work: Theories and Practices*. Houndmills: Palgrave Macmillan.

Clarke, P and Smith, J (2011) Aging in a cultural context: cross-national differences in disability and the moderating role of personal control among older adults in the United States and England. *The Journals of Gerontology. Series B, Psychological Sciences and Social Sciences*, 66(4): 457–67. doi: 10.1093/geronb/gbr054

Coleman, M, Collings, M and McDonald, P (1999) Teaching anti-oppressive practice on the diploma in social work: integrating learning. *Social Work Education*, 18(3): 297–309.

Collins, P (1990) *Black Feminist Thought: Knowledge, Consciousness and the Politics of Empowerment*. Hove: Psychology Press.

Collins, S and Wilkie, L (2010) Anti-oppressive practice and social work students' portfolios in Scotland. *Social Work Education*, 29(7): 760–77. doi: 10.1080/02615471003605082

Compton, BR and Galaway, B (1984) *Social Work Processes*. Homewood, IL: Dorsey Press.

Congress, E (1997) Using the culturagram to assess and empower culturally diverse families. *Multicultural Perspectives in Working with Families*. New York: Springer Press, pp. 3–16.

Connolly, H (2015) Seeing the relationship between the UNCRC and the asylum system through the eyes of unaccompanied asylum seeking children and young people. *The International Journal of Human Rights*, 23(1): 52–77.

Cotton, S, Zebracki, K, Rosenthal, SL, Tsevat, J and Drotar, D (2006) Religion/spirituality and adolescent health outcomes: a review. *Journal of Adolescent Health*, 38(4): 472–80.

Coulshed, V (1991) *Social Work Practice: An Introduction* (2nd edn). Basingstoke: Macmillan.

Council on Social Work Education (2017) *Statistics on Social Work Education in the United States*. Online at https://www.cswe.org/Research-Statistics/Research-Briefs-and-Publications/CSWE_2017_annual_survey_report-FINAL.aspx (accessed 24 August 2020).

Cowie, A (2010) Anti-oppressive social work practice in child welfare: journeys of reconciliation. *Critical Social Work*, 11(1): 45–51.

Cox, CB (2007) *Dementia and Social Work Practice: Research and Intervention*. New York: Springer.

Cox, CB and Ephross, PH (1997) *Ethnicity and Social Work Practice*. Oxford: Oxford University Press.

Cox, C and Pardarsani, M (2017) Aging and human rights: a rights-based approach to social work with older adults. *Journal of Human Rights and Social Work*, 2: 98–106).

Coxshall, W (2020) Applying critical race theory in social work education in Britain: pedagogical reflections. *Social Work Education*. doi: 10.1080/02615479.2020.1716967

Crawford, K and Walker, J (2004) *Social Work with Older People*. Exeter: Learning Matters.

Crawford, R (2002) *What is Religion?* London: Routledge.

Cree, V (2001) Men and masculinities in social work education. In Christie, A (ed.), *Men and Social Work: Theories and Practices*. Houndmills: Palgrave Macmillan, pp. 147–63.

Crenshaw, K (1989) Demarginalizing the intersection of race and sex: a Black feminist critique of antidiscrimination doctrine, feminist theory and antiracist politics. Chicago: University of Chicago Legal Forum, pp139–67.

Cross, T, Bazron, B, Dennis, K and Isaacs, M (1989) *Towards a Culturally Competent System of Care* (Vol. 1). Washington, DC: Georgetown University Child Development Center; CASSP Technical Assistance Center.

Cumming, E and Henry, WE (1961) *Growing Old: The Process of Disengagement*. New York: Basic Books.

Cutcliffe, J and Happell, B (2009) Psychiatry, mental health nurses, and invisible power: exploring a perturbed relationship within contemporary mental health care. *International Journal of Mental Health Nursing*, 18(2): 116–25.

Dalrymple, J and Burke, B (2006) *Anti-Oppressive Practice: Social Care and the Law*. Buckingham: Open University Press.

Davis, R (2010) Specialist team earns trust of travellers. *Community Care*, pp20–1, 10 June.

DeGue, S, Fowlder, KA and Calkins, C (2016) Deaths due to use of lethal force by law enforcement: findings from the National Violent Death Reporting System 2009–2012. *American Journal of Preventative Medicine*, 51(5): 176–87.

Department for Children, Schools and Families (DCSF) (2005) *Research Into Private Fostering*. London: HMSO.

Department for Education and Skills (DfES) (2004) *Every Child Matters: Change for Children*. London: Her Majesty's Stationery Office.

Deutsch, M (2006) A framework for thinking about oppression and its change. *Social Justice Research*, 19(1): 7–41.

Devakumar, D, Shannon, G, Bhopal, SS and Abubakar, I (2020) Racism and discrimination in COVID-19 responses. *The Lancet*, 395(10231): 1194.

Devenney, K (2020) Social work with unaccompanied asylum-seeking young people: reframing social care professionals as 'co-navigators'. *The British Journal of Social Work*, 50(3): 926–43. doi. org/10.1093/bjsw/bcz071

Dion, KL (1983) Names, identity and self-names. *Names: A Journal of Onomastics*, 31(4): 245–57.

Doel, M (2009) *Social Work Placements: A Traveller's Guide*. London: Routledge.

Doel, M and Shardlow, S (2005) *Modern Social Work Practice: Teaching and Learning in Practice Settings* (3rd edn). London: Routledge.

Domakin, A (2014) Are we making the most of learning from the practice placement? *Social Work Education*, 33(6): 718–30.

Dominelli, L (1998) Anti-oppressive practice in context. In Adams, R, Dominelli, L and Payne, M (eds), *Social Work: Themes, Issues and Critical Debates*. Houndmills: Macmillan.

Dominelli, L (2002) *Anti-oppressive Social Work: Theory and Practice*. Houndmills: Palgrave Macmillan.

Dominelli, L (2004) *Social Work: Theory and Practice for a Changing Profession*. Cambridge: Polity

Dominelli, L (2008) Anti-oppressive practice as contested practice. In Barnard, A, Horner, N and Wild, J (eds), *Value Base of Social Work and Social Care: An Active Learning Handbook*. Maidenhead: Open University Press.

Doyle, C and Timms, C (2014) *Child Neglect and Emotional Abuse: Understanding, Assessment and Response*. London: Sage.

Durkheim, E (1912) *The Elementary Forms of the Religious Life*. New York: Dover Publications.

Dyke, C (2019) *Writing Analytical Assessments in Social Work* (2nd edn). St Albans: Critical Publishing.

Eboiyehi, FA (2017) Convicted without evidence: elderly women and witchcraft accusations in contemporary Nigeria. *Journal of International Women's Studies*, 18 (4): 247–65.

Edwards, KE (2006) Aspiring social justice ally identity development: a conceptual model. *NASPA Journal*, 43(4): 39–60.

Englebrecht, L (2006) Cultural friendliness as a foundation in the support function of the supervision of social work students in South Africa. *International Social Work*, 49(2): 256–66.

Equality and Human Rights Commission (2017) Being disabled in Britain: a journey less equal. Available online at: www.equalityhumanrights.com/sites/default/files/being-disabled-in-britain. pdf (accessed 13 January 2020).

Evandrou, M, Falkingham, J, Feng, Z (2016) Ethnic inequalities in limiting health and self-reported health in later life revisited. *Journal of Epidemiology Community Health*, 70: 653–62.

Ferguson, I and Lavalette, M (2017) Editorial. *Critical and Radical Social Work*, 5(3): 265–67. doi: 10.1332/204986017X15029695444987

Field, P, Jasper, C and Littler, L (2016) *Practice Education in Social Work: Achieving Professional Standards*. St Albans: Critical Publishing.

Finn, JL and Jacobson, M (2003) Just practice. *Journal of Social Work Education*, 39(1): 57–78. doi: 10.1080/10437797.2003.10779119

Firmin, C (2020) *Contextual Safeguarding and Child Protection: Rewriting the Rules*. Abingdon: Routledge.

Flynn, C (2012) Caring for the children of imprisoned mothers: exploring the role of fathers. *Child Abuse Review*, 21: 285–98.

Font, SA (2013) Service referral patterns among Black and White families involved with child protective services. *Journal of Public Child Welfare*, 7: 370–91.

Fook, J (2012) *Social Work: A Critical Approach to Practice*. London: Sage.

Foucault, M (1998) *The History of Sexuality*. Harmondsworth: Allen Lane.

Fox, JE (2013) The uses of racism: whitewashing new Europeans in the UK. *Ethnic and Racial Studies*, 36(11): 1871–89. doi: 10.1080/01419870.2012.692802

Freedman, J (2016) Sexual and gender-based violence against refugee women: a hidden aspect of the refugee 'crisis'. *Reproductive Health Matters*, 24(47): 18–26.

Freire, P (2000) *Pedagogy of the Oppressed* (30th anniversary edn). New York: Continuum.

French, J and Raven, B (1959) The bases of social power. In Cartwright, D and Zander, A (eds), *Group Dynamics: Research and Theory*. New York: Harper & Row, pp. 259–69.

Frost, N, Abram, F and Burgess, H (2012) Family group conferences: context, process and ways forward. *Child and Family Social Work*, 19: 480–90.

Furman, LD, Benson, PW, Canda, ER and Grimwood, C (2005) A comparative international analysis of religion and spirituality in social work: a survey of UK and US social workers. *Social Work Education*, 24(8): 813–39.

Furness, S and Gilligan, P (2014) 'It never came up': encouragements and discouragements to addressing religion and belief in professional practice – what do social work students have to say? *The British Journal of Social Work*, 44(3): 763–781. doi.org/10.1093/bjsw/bcs140

Gair, S, Miles, D, Savage, D and Zuchowski, I (2014) Racism unmasked: the experiences of Aboriginal and Torres Strait islander students in social work field placements. *Australian Social Work*. doi: 10.1080/0312407X.2014.928335 (accessed 19 July 2014).

Gale, T and Densmore, K (2000) *Just Schooling: Explorations in the Cultural Politics of Teaching*. London: Open University Press.

Gardner, A (2008) Beyond anti-oppressive practice in social work: best practice and the ethical use of power in adult care. In Jones, K, Cooper, B and Ferguson, H (eds), *Best Practice in Social Work: Critical Perspectives*. Basingstoke: Palgrave Macmillan.

Garner, S (2010) *Racisms: An Introduction*. London: Sage.

Garrett, PM (2000) Responding to Irish 'invisibility': anti-discriminatory social work practice and the placement of Irish children in Britain. *Adoption & Fostering*: 24(1): 23–33.

Gelfand, DE (2003) *Ageing and Ethnicity: Knowledge and Services*. New York: Springer.

Gellman, J (2006) Gender and sexuality in the Garden of Eden. *Theology and Sexuality*, 12(3): 319–35.

General Social Care Council (GSCC) (2007) Social work education in England: delivering quality, recognising success. *Social Work Education Quality Assurance Report*. London: GSCC.

General Social Care Council (GSCC) (2009) *Raising Standards in Social Work Education in England 2007–8*. London: GSCC.

Gibson, P (2014) Extending the ally model of social justice to social work pedagogy. *Journal of Teaching in Social Work*, 34(2): 199–214.

Gilligan, P (2009) Considering religion and beliefs in child protection and safeguarding work: is any consensus emerging? *Child Abuse Review*, 18: 94–110.

Gilligan, P and Akhtar, S (2005) Child sexual abuse among Asian communities: developing materials to raise awareness in Bradford. *Practice*, 17(4): 267–84. doi: 10.1080/09503150500426735

Gilligan, PA and Furness, SM (2006) The role of religion and spirituality in social work practice: views and experiences of social workers and students. *The British Journal of Social Work*, 36(4): 617–37.

Girma, M, Radice, S, Tsangarides, N and Walter, N (2014) Detained: women asylum seekers locked up in the UK. Available online at: www.refugeewomen.co.uk/wp-content/uploads/2019/01/women-for-refugee-women-reports-detained.pdf (accessed 10 October 2019).

Giroux, HA (2003) Spectacles of race and pedagogies of denial: anti-black racist pedagogy under the reign of neoliberalism. *Communication Education*, 52(3/4): 191–211.

Goodley, TB and Fowler, DN (2006) Spiritual and religious abuse expanding what is known about domestic violence. *Affilia: Journal of Women and Social Work*, 21(3): 282–95.

Gordon, P and Perrone, K (2004) When spouses become caregivers: counselling implications for younger couples. *The Journal of Rehabilitation*, 70: 27–32.

Graddol, D (2004) The future of language. *Science*, 27(303): 1329–331.

Gravells, J and Wallace, S (2012) *Dial M for Mentor: Critical Reflections on Mentoring for Coaches, Educators and Trainers*. St Albans. Critical Publishing.

Griffin, P (1997) Introductory module for the single issue course. In Adams, M, Bell, LA and Griffin, P (eds), *Teaching for Diversity and Social Justice: A Sourcebook*. New York: Routledge.

Grootegoed, E and Smith, M (2018) The emotional labour of austerity: how social workers reflect and work on their feelings towards reducing support to needy children and families. *British Journal of Social Work*, 48(7): 1929–47.

Guru, S (2012) Under siege: families of counter-terrorism. *The British Journal of Social Work*, 42(6): 1151–73. doi.org/10.1093/bjsw/bcs089

Hamilton and Moore (2004) *Educational Interventions for Refugee Children: Theoretical Perspectives and Implementing Best Practice*. London: Routledge.

Harper, S (2012) Race without racism: how higher education researchers minimise racist institutional norms. *Review of Higher Education*, 36(1): 9–29.

Harris, A and Enfield, S (2003) *Disability, Equality, and Human Rights: A Training Manual for Development and Humanitarian Organizations*. Oxford: Oxfam.

Harrison, G (2012) 'Oh, you've got such a strong accent': language identity intersecting with professional identity in the human services in Australia. *International Migration*, 51(5): 192–204.

Havighurst, RJ and Albrecht, RE (1953) *Older People*. New York: Longmans, Green.

Haworth, S (2019) A systematic review of research on social work practice with single fathers. *Practice*, 31(5): 329–47.

Hayes, D and Humphreys, B (2004) *Social Work, Immigration and Asylum: Debates, Dilemmas and Ethical Issues for Social Work and Social Care Practice*. London and New York: Jessica Kingsley.

Healy, K and Mulholland, (2007) *Writing Skills for Social Workers*. London: Sage.

Heath, A and Cheung, S (2007) *Unequal Chance: Ethnic Minorities in Western Labour Markets*. Oxford: Oxford University Press.

Heenan, D (2005) Challenging stereotypes surrounding disability and promoting anti-oppressive practice: some reflections on teaching social work students in Northern Ireland. *Social Work Education*, 24(5): 495–510.doi: 10.1080/02615470500132780

Heron, J (2001) *Helping the Client: A Creative Practical Guide*. London: Sage.

Hicks, S (2015) Social work and gender: an argument for practical accounts. *Qualitative Social Work*, 14(4): 471–87.

Higgs, P and Gilleard, C (2015) *Rethinking Old Age: Theorising the Fourth Age*. London: Palgrave Macmillan.

Hitchcock, LI and Battista, A (2013) Social media for professional practice: integrating Twitter with social work pedagogy. *Journal of Baccalaureate Social Work*, 18: 33–45.

Hitchcock, LI, Sage, M and Smyth, NJ (2019) *Teaching Social Work With Digital Technology*. Arlington, VA: CSWE Press.

HMSO (2019) Social workers for children and families. Available online at: www.ethnicity-facts-figures.service.gov.uk/workforce-and-business/workforce-diversity/social-workers-for-children-and-families/latest (accessed 10 February 2020).

Hodge, D (2013) Implicit spiritual assessment: an alternative approach for assessing client spirituality. *Social Work*: 58(3): 223–30.

Holden, KB, McGregor, BS, Starla, H, Blanks, SH and Mahaffey, C (2012) Psychosocial, socio-cultural, and environmental influences on mental health help-seeking among African-American men. Available online at: http://health-equity.lib.umd.edu/4068/1/Psychosocial,_socio_cultural,_environmental.pdf (accessed 28 June 2019).

Holmström, C (2012) Social work's new 'non-traditional' students? Learning from the experiences of our younger students. *Social Work Education*, 31(3): 269–86.

Hölscher, D and Bozalek, VG (2012) Encountering the other across the divides: re-grounding social justice as a guiding principle for social work with refugees and other vulnerable groups. *The British Journal of Social Work*, 42(6): 1093–112.

Home Office online. *Asylum statistics*. Available online at: https://researchbriefings.files.parliament.uk/documents/SN01403/SN01403.pdf (accessed 16 July 2020).

hooks, b (1996) *Killing Rage*. New York: Holt.

hooks, b (2000) *Feminism is for Everybody: Passionate Politics*. Cambridge, MA: South End Press.

Hutchinson, AJ, O'Leary, P and Hope, K (2015) Child protection in Islamic contexts: identifying cultural and religious appropriate mechanisms and processes using a roundtable methodology. *Child Abuse Review*, 24(6): 395–408.

Ibrahim, Y (2018) The unsacred and the spectacularized: Alan Kurdi and the migrant body. *Social Media + Society*, 1–9.

Independent, The (2005) Britain condemned for flouting human rights. Available on line at: www.independent.co.uk/news/uk/crime/britain-condemned-for-flouting-human-rights-493538.html (accessed 20 July 2020).

Institute of Race Relations. Available online at: www.irr.org.uk/research/statistics/definitions/ (accessed 24 July 2020).

International Federation of Social Workers (IFSW) (2014) International definition of social work. Available online at: www.ifsw.org/global-definition-of-social-work/ (accessed 17 June 2020).

Irizarry, C, Marlowe, JM, Hallahan, L, Bull, M (2016) Restoring connections: social workers' practice wisdom towards achieving social justice. *The British Journal of Social Work*, 46(7): 1855–71.

Jackson, SE, Hackett, RA and Steptoe, A (2019) Associations between age discrimination and health and wellbeing: cross-sectional and prospective analysis of the English Longitudinal Study of Ageing. *Lancet Public Health*, 4: 200–8.

Jansen, S and Spijkerboer, T (2011) Fleeing homophobia, asylum claims related to sexual orientation and gender identity in Europe. Available online at: www.refworld.org/docid/4ebba7852.html (accessed 19 July 2020).

Jeffery, D (2007) Radical problems and liberal selves: professional subjectivity in the anti-oppressive social work classroom. *Canadian Social Work Review*, 24(2): 125–39.

Jin, K (2010) Modern biological theories of aging. *Aging and Disease*, 1(2): 72–4.

Johnson, JR, Rich, M and Cargile, AC (2008) "Why are you shoving this stuff down our throats?": preparing intercultural educators to challenge performances of White racism. *Journal of International and Intercultural Communication*, 1(2): 113–35.

Johnsen, S, Fitzpatrick, S and Watts, B (2018) Homelessness and social control: a typology. *Housing Studies*, 33(7): 1106–26.

Jones, H, Bhattacharyya, G, Davies, W, Dhaliwal, S, Forkert, K, Gunaratnam, Y, Jackson, E and Saltus, R (2015) *Mapping the Unfolding Controversy of Home Office Immigration Campaigns. End of Project Conference: Findings Briefing June 2015*. Available online at: https://mappingimmigrationcontroversy.files.wordpress.com/2014/03/mic-findings-leaflet.pdf (accessed 24 July 2020).

Joseph Rowntree Foundation (2016) *Social Care for Older People: Home Truths*. Available online at: www.kingsfund.org.uk/sites/default/files/field/field_publication_file/Social_care_older_people_Kings_Fund_Sep_2016.pdf (accessed 2 July 2019).

Jupp, V (2005) Issues of power in social work practice in mental health services for people from Black and minority ethnic groups. *Critical Social Work*, 6(1).

Kadushin, A and Harkness, D (2014) *Supervision in Social Work* (5th edn). New York: Columbia University Press.

Keen, S, Gray, I, Parker, J, Galpin, D and Brown, K (2009) *Newly Qualified Social Workers: A Handbook for Practice*. Exeter: Learning Matters.

Kelly, A (2019) The 39 people who died in the lorry were victims: why does the law treat them as criminals? Available online at: www.theguardian.com/commentisfree/2019/oct/29/39-people-lorry-victims-law-criminals-immigration-slavery (accessed 29 October 2019).

Knitter, PF (2010) Social work and religious diversity: problems and possibilities. *Journal of Religion & Spirituality in Social Work: Social Thought,* 29(3): 256–70.

Kohli, R and Solórzano, DG (2012) Teachers, please learn our names!: racial microaggressions and the K-12 classroom. *Race Ethnicity and Education*, 15(4): 441–62. doi: 10.1080/13613324.2012.674026

Kolivoski, KM, Weaver, A and Constance-Huggins, M (2014) Critical race theory: opportunities for application in social work practice and policy: families in society. *The Journal of Contemporary Social Services*, 95(4): 269–76.

Koprowska, J (2014) *Communication and Interpersonal Skills in Social Work*. London: Sage.

Lai, C (2000) Reaching out to black ethnic minorities: a voluntary sector perspective on mental health. *Practice*, 12(1): 17–28. doi: 10.1080/09503150008415174

Laird, SE (2008) *Anti-Oppressive Social Work: A Guide for Developing Cultural Competence*. London: Sage.

Laird, S and Tedam, P (2019) *Cultural Diversity in Child Protection: Cultural Competence in Practice*. London: Red Globe Press.

Latham, S (2016) The global rise of Islamophobia: whose side is social work on? *Social Alternatives*, 35(4): 80–4.

Lavalette, M (2007) Social work today: a profession worth fighting for? In Mooney, G and Law, A (eds), *Hard Labour/New Labour*: Bristol: Policy Press.

Lawson, H (2018) The role of the field educator in helping students develop critical reflection. *Journal of Practice Teaching and Learning*, 15(2): 38–55.

Leese, M (2010) Bridging the gap: supporting student transitions into higher education. *Journal of Further and Higher Education*, 34(2): 239–51.

Lindemann, S (2002) Listening with an attitude: a model of native-speaker comprehension of non-native speakers in the United States. *Language in Society*, 31(3): 419–41.

Lister, R (2008) Recognition and voice: the challenge for social justice. In Craig, G, Burchardt, T and Gordon, D (eds) *Social Justice and Public Policy*. Bristol: The Policy Press.

Lloyd, A (2014) Building information resilience: how do resettling refugees connect with health information in regional landscapes – implications for health literacy. *Australian Academic & Research Libraries*, 45(1): 48–66.

Lorde, A (1984) *Sister Outsider: Essays and Speeches*. Trumansburg, NY: Crossing Press.

Lumsden, E (2019) The (in)visibility of infants and young children in child protection. In Murray, J, Swadener, BB and Smith, K (eds) *The Routledge International Handbook of Young Children's Rights*. London: Taylor & Francis.

Lupton, B (2000) Maintaining masculinity: men who do women's work. *British Journal of Management*, 11: 33–48.

Mackinlay, E (2004) The spiritual dimension of ageing. In Jewell, A (ed.), *Ageing, Spirituality and Well-being*. London: Jessica Kingsley.

Maclean, S (2013) *Developing Quality Practice Learning in Social Work: A Straightforward Guide for Practice Educators and Placement Supervisors* (2nd edn). Litchfied: Kirwin Maclean.

Maclean, S (2018) *My CPD Journal*. Litchfield: Kirwin Maclean.

Maclean, S, Finch, J and Tedam, P (2018) *SHARE: A New Model for Social Work*. Litchfield: Kirwin Maclean.

Macpherson, W (1999) *The Stephen Lawrence Inquiry*. London: HMSO

Maddox, GL (1965) Fact and artefact: evidence bearing on disengagement theory from the Dukes Geriatrics Project. *Human Development*, 8: 117–30.

Maidment, J and Cooper, L (2002) Acknowledgement of client diversity and oppression in social work student supervision. *Social Work Education*, 21(4): 399–407.

Mantovani, N, Pizzolati, M and Edge, D (2016) Exploring the relationship between stigma and help-seeking for mental illness in African-descended faith communities in the UK. *Health Expectations: An International Journal of Public Participation in Health Care and Health Policy*, 20(3): 373–84.

Marshall, M (1990) *Social Work with Old People*. London: Palgrave Macmillan.

Martinez-Brawley, EE and Zorita, PMB (2011) Immigration and social work: contrasting practice and education. *Social Work Education*, 30(1): 17–28.

Masocha, S and Simpson, MK (2011) Developing mental health social work for asylum seekers: a proposed model for practice. *Journal of Social Work*, 12(4): 423–43.

Mathews, I (2009) *Social Work and Spirituality*. Exeter: Learning Matters.

Mbarushimana, JP and Robbins, H (2015) "We have to work harder": testing assumptions about the challenges for black and minority ethnic social workers in a multicultural society. *Practice: Social Work in Action*, 27(2): 135–52.

McKendrick, D and Finch, J (2017) 'Under heavy manners'?: social work, radicalisation, troubled families and non-linear war. *British Journal of Social Work*, 43: 308–24.

McLaughlin, H (2012) *Understanding Social Work Research* (2nd edn). London: Sage.

Meekosha, H (2006) What the hell are you? An intercategorical analysis of race, ethnicity, gender and disability in the Australian body politic. *Scandinavian Journal of Disability Research*, 8(2): 161.

Meekosha, H and Dowse, L (2007) Integrating critical disability studies with social work education and practice: an Australian perspective. *Practice*, 19: 169–83.

Memon, A, Taylor, K, Mohebati, LM, Sundin, J, Cooper, M, Scanlon, T and de Visser, R (2016) Perceived barriers to accessing mental health services among black and minority ethnic (BME) communities: a qualitative study in Southeast England. *BMJ Open*, 6(11): e012337. doi:10.1136/bmjopen-2016-012337

Miller, D (1999) *Principles of Social Justice*. Cambridge, MA: Harvard University Press.

Moriarty, J and Murray, J (2007) Who wants to be a social worker?: Using routine published data to identify trends in the numbers of people applying for and completing social work programmes in England. *British Journal of Social Work*, 37(4): 715–33.

Morrison, T (2005) *Staff Supervision in Social Care*. Brighton: Pavilion.

Munro, E (2011) *The Munro Review of Child Protection*. London: HMSO.

Murray, C (2019) Beyond recognition: persistent neglect of young Traveller children's rights in Ireland. In Murray, J, Swadener, BB and Smith, K (eds) *The Routledge International Handbook of Young Children's Rights*. London: Taylor & Francis.

Murtagh, L (2019) Others and othering: the lived experiences of trainee teachers with parental responsibilities. *Journal of Further and Higher Education*, 43(6): 788–800.

Newberry-Koroluk, AM (2018) 'Little girls' and 'Bitching up': early-career social workers. *Afflilia: Journal of Women and Social Work,* 33(4): 435–52.

Nilsen, AB, Fylkesnes, S and Mausethagen, S (2017) The linguistics in othering: teacher educators' talk about cultural diversity. *Reconceptualizing Educational Research Methodology*, 8(1).

Nussbaum, M (2000) *Women and Human Development: The Capabilities Approach*. Cambridge, MA: Cambridge University Press.

Nygren, K, Walsh, J, Ellingsen, IT and Christie, A (2019) What about fathers? The presence and absence of the father in social work practice in England, Ireland, Norway and Sweden: a comparative study. *Child & Family Social Work*, 24: 148–55.

Oakley, L, Kinmond, K, Humphreys, J and Dioum, M (2019) Safeguarding children who are exposed to abuse linked to faith or belief. *Child Abuse Review*, 28(1): 27–38.

Office of National Statistics (ONS) (2011) *Census*. London: HMSO.

Office of National Statistics (ONS) (2020) *Religion and Health in England and Wales*. Available online at: www.ons.gov.uk/peoplepopulationandcommunity/culturalidentity/religion/articles/religionandhealthinenglandandwales/february2020#main-points (accessed 25 February 2020).

Oguz, E (2017) Teachers' perceptions and practices/experiences of social justice in Turkey. *Journal of Education and Practice*, 8(21).

O'Leary, P, Abdalla, M, Hutchinson, A, Squire, J and Young, A (2019) Child Protection With Muslim Communities: Considerations For Non-Muslim-Based Orthodoxies/Paradigms in Child Welfare and Social Work. *The British Journal of Social Work*, bcz088. doi.org/10.1093/bjsw/bcz088

Orstein, AC (2017) Social justice: history, purpose and meaning. *Social Science and Public Policy*, 54: 541–48.

Ortega, RM and Coulborn Faller, K (2011) Training child welfare workers from an intersectional cultural humility perspective: a paradigm shift. *Child Welfare*, 90(5): 27–49.

Osman, S and Carare, RO (2015) Barriers faced by the people with dementia in the Black and minority ethnic groups in accessing health care and social services. *Journal of Gerontology & Geriatric Research*, 4(1).

Owens, J (2015) Exploring the critiques of the social model of disability: the transformative possibility of Arendt's notion of power. *Sociology of Health and Illness*, 37(3): 385–403.

Oxhandler, HK and Pargament, KI (2014) Social work practitioners' integration of clients' religion and spirituality in practice: a literature review. *Social Work*, 59: 271–9.

Parker, J (2010) *Effective Practice Learning in Social Work*. London: Sage.

Parker, J and Crabtree, S (2018) *Social Work with Disadvantaged and Marginalised People*. London: Sage.

Pease, B (2011) Men in social work: challenging or reproducing an unequal gender regime? *Affilia: Journal of Women and Social Work*, 26(4): 406–18.

Pease, B (2016) Critical social work with men: challenging men's complicity in the reproduction of patriarchy and male privilege. *Social Alternatives*, 35(4): 49–53.

Pile, H (1997) *The Asylum Trap: The Labour Market Experiences of Refugees with Professional Qualifications*. London: World University Service (UK)/Low Pay Unit.

Preston-Shoot, M (2007) *Effective Groupwork* (2nd edn). Basingstoke: Palgrave Macmillan.

Prilleltensky, I (2008) The role of power in wellness, oppression, and liberation: the promise of psychopolitical validity. *Journal of Community Psychology*, 36(2): 116–36.

Pruitt, LJ (2019) Closed due to 'flooding'? UK media representations of refugees and migrants in 2015–2016 – creating a crisis of borders. *The British Journal of Politics and International Relations*, 21(2): 383–402.

Ramsundarsingh, S and Shier, ML (2017) Anti-oppressive organisational dynamics in the social services: a literature review. *British Journal of Social Work*, 47(8): 2308–32.

Rapp, CA and Goscha, RJ (2011) *The Strengths Model: A Recovery-Oriented Approach to Mental Health Services* (3rd edn). New York: Oxford University Press.

Rattray, RS (1954) *Religion and Art in Ashanti*. London: Oxford University Press.

Raven, BH (1965) Social influence and power. In Steiner, ID and Fishbein, M (eds), *Current Studies in Social Psychology* (pp. 371–82). New York: Holt, Rinehart, Winston.

Rawls, J (1999) *A Theory of Justice*. Cambridge, MA: Belknap Press.

Razack, N (2001) Diversity and difference in the field education encounter: racial minority students in the practicum. *Social Work Education*, 20: 219–32.

Refugee Council. *Refugee Asylum Facts*. Available online at: www.refugeecouncil.org.uk/information/refugee-asylum-facts/ (accessed 18 July 2020).

Ridgway, V (2019) Social work students' perceptions of ageing. *Practice*, 31(2): 117–34. doi: 10.1080/09503153.2018.1473356

Rigby, P (2011) Separated and trafficked children: the challenges for child protection professionals. *Child Abuse Review*, 20: 324–40.

Robinson, K (2014) Voices from the front line: social work with refugees and asylum seekers in Australia and the UK. *The British Journal of Social Work*, 44(6): 1602–20. doi.org/10.1093/bjsw/bct040

Rotabi, K, Bromfield, NF, Lee, J and Abu-Sarhan, T (2017) The care of orphaned and vulnerable children in Islam: exploring kafala with Muslim social work practice with unaccompanied refugee minors in the United States. *Journal of Human Rights and Social Work*, 2: 16–24.

Schiffer, K and Schatz, E (2008) *Marginalisation, Social Inclusion and Health.* Available online at: www.drugsandalcohol.ie/11927/1/Correlation_marginalisati on_web.pdf (accessed 18 July 2020).

Schraer, R (2016) Recommend me or you'll never see your children again: social worker struck off for abuse of power. Available online at: www.communitycare.co.uk/2016/02/03/recommend-youll-never-see-children-social-worker-struck-abuse-power/ (accessed 14 July 2020).

Schroots, JJ (1996) Theoretical developments in the psychology of aging. *Gerontologist*, 36(6): 742–8.

SCOPE (2019) *Disability Facts and Figures.* Available online at: www.scope.org.uk/media/disability-facts-figures/ (accessed 25 July 2020).

Scourfield, J, Tolman, R, Maxwell, N, Holland, S, Bullock, A and Sloan, L (2012) Results of a training course for social workers on engaging fathers in child protection. *Children and Youth Services Review*, 34: 1425–32.

Shaia, WE (2019) SHARP: a framework for addressing the contexts of poverty and oppression during service provision in the United States. *Journal of Social Work Values and Ethics*, 16(1): 16–26.

Shakespeare, T (2006) *Disability Rights and Wrongs.* Oxford: Routledge.

Sheikh, S and Teeman, D (2016) *A Rapid Evidence Assessment of What Works in Homelessness Services.* SCIE. Available online at: www.basw.co.uk/system/files/resources/what-works-homelessness-services.pdf (accessed 2 June 2019).

Sherwood, DA (1998) Spiritual assessment as a normal part of social work practice: power to help and power to harm. *Social Work & Christianity*, 24(2): 80–9.

Sin, C (2007) Older people from white-British and Asian-Indian backgrounds and their expectations for support from their children. *Quality in Ageing and Older Adults*, 8(1): 31–41.

Sin, C and Fong, J (2009) The impact of regulatory fitness requirements on disabled social work students. *The British Journal of Social Work*, 39(8): 1518–39.

Skehill, C (2009) An integrative approach to teaching gender and social work. In Leskosek, V (ed.), *Teaching Gender in Social Work.* London: ATHENA, pp. 15–34.

Slay, H and Smith, DA (2011) Professional identity construction: using narrative to understand the negotiation of professional stigmatised cultural identities. *Human Relations*, 64: 85–107.

Slee, R (2018) *Inclusive Education Isn't Dead, It Just Smells Funny.* London: Routledge.

Smith, A (2010) Queer theory and native studies: the heteronormativity of settler colonialism. *GLQ: A Journal of Lesbian and Gay Studies*, 16(1/2): 41–68.

Smith, R (2008) From child protection to child safety: locating risk assessment in the changing landscape. In Calder, M (ed.), *Contemporary Risk Assessment in Safeguarding Children.* Lyme Regis: Russell House Publishing.

Social Work England (SWE) (2020) *Qualifying Education and Training Standards 2020.* Available online at: www.socialworkengland.org.uk/media/1642/socialworkengland_ed-training-standards-2020_final.pdf (accessed 21 January 2020).

Solomos, J (1999) Social research and the Stephen Lawrence Inquiry. *Sociological Research Online*, 4(1). Available online at: https://journals.sagepub.com/doi/pdf/10.5153/sro.236 (accessed 2 March 2020).

Spicer, N (2008) Places of exclusion and inclusion: asylum-seeker and refugee experiences of neighbourhoods in the UK. *Journal of Ethnic and Migration Studies* 34(3): 491–510.

Spijkerboer, T (2013) Moving migrants, states, and rights human rights and border deaths. *Law & Ethics of Human Rights*, 7(2): 213–42.

Stanley, T (2017) Working more reflexively with risk: holding 'signs of safety and wellbeing' in mind. In Cooper, A (ed.), *Adult Safeguarding.* London: Jessica Kingsley.

Stone, C (2018) Transparency of assessment in practice education: the tape model. *Social Work Education*, 37(8): 977–94.

Stones, S and Glazzard, J (2018) *Supporting Student Mental Health in Higher Education.* St Albans: Critical Publishing.

Stonewall (2017) *LGBT in Britain: A Trans Report.* Available online at: www.stonewall.org.uk/lgbt-britain-trans-report (accessed 15 July 2020).

Stryker, S (2017) *Transgender History: The Roots of Today's Revolution* (2nd edn). New York: Seal Press.

Stuckler, D, Reeves, A, Loopstra, R, Karanikolos, M and McKee, M (2017) Austerity and health: the impact in the UK and Europe. *European Journal of Public Health,* 27(4): 18–21. doi. org/10.1093/eurpub/ckx167

Swain, J and French, S (2000) Towards an affirmation model of disability. *Disability & Society,* 15(4): 569–82.

Sweeney, S and Matthews, Z (2017) *Friends, Families and Travellers: A Guide for Professionals Working with Gypsies, Roma and Travellers in Children's Service.* Available online at: www.gypsy-traveller.org/wp-content/uploads/2017/03/A-guide-for-professionals-working-with-Gypsies-and-Travellers-in-the-public-care-system.pdf (accessed 10 March 2020).

Swinton, J (2001) *Spirituality and Mental Health Care: Rediscovering a 'Forgotten' Dimension.* London: Jessica Kingsley.

Szymanski, D (2005) Feminist identity and theories as correlates of feminist supervision practices. *The Counseling Psychologist,* 729–47.

Taylor, E (1998) A primer on critical race theory. *Journal of Blacks in Higher Education,* 19: 122–24.

Taylor, S, Vreugdenhil, A and Schneiders, M (2017) Social justice as concept and practice in Australian social work: an analysis of Norma Parker addresses, 1969–2008. *Australian Social Work,* 70(1): 46–68.

Tedam, P (2012) The MANDELA model of practice learning: an old present in new wrapping? *Journal of Practice Teaching and Learning,* 11(2): 60–76.

Tedam, P (2013) Developing cultural competence. In Bartoli, A, Kennedy, S and Tedam, P (eds) *Anti-Racism in Social Work Practice.* St Albans: Critical Publishing.

Tedam, P (2014) When failing doesn't matter: a narrative inquiry into the social work practice learning experiences of Black African students in England. *International Journal of Higher Education,* 3(1): 136–45.

Tedam, P (2015) Black African students' experiences of social work practice earning in England: a critical race inquiry. University of Northampton (unpublished doctoral thesis).

Tedam, P and Adjoa, A (2017) *The W Word: Witchcraft Labelling and Child Safeguarding in Social Work.* St Albans: Critical Publishing.

Tedam, P and Zuckowski, I (2014) The MANDELA practice framework as a tool for strengths-based social work education. In Francis, AP, Venkat, P, Clark, M, Mariscal, ES and Ponnuswami, I (eds), *Advancing Social Work in Mental Health through Strengths-Based Practice.* Brisbane, Australia: Primrose Hall Publishing Group, pp. 158–71.

Tervalon, M and Murray-Garcia, J (1998) Cultural humility versus cultural competence: a critical distinction in defining physician training outcomes in multicultural education. *Journal of Health Care for the Poor and Underserved,* 9(2): 117–25. doi:10.1353/hpu.2010.0233

Tew, J (2006) Understanding power and powerlessness: towards a framework for emancipatory practice in social work. *Journal of Social Work,* 6(1): 35–51.

Thiara, R, Hague, J and Mullender, A (2011) Losing out on both counts: disabled women and domestic violence. *Disability and Society,* 26: 757–71.

Thomas, RR (1995) Adversity framework. In Chemers, MM, Oskama, S and Costanzo, M (eds), *Diversity in Organizations: New Perspectives for a Changing Workplace.* Thousand Oaks, CA: SAGE, pp. 318–19.

Thompson, N (1995) *Age and Dignity: Working with Older People.* Aldershot: Arena.

Thompson, N (1997) *Anti-Discriminatory Practice* (2nd edn). Basingstoke: Macmillan.

Thompson, N (2001) *Anti-Discriminatory Practice* (3rd edn). Basingstoke: Palgrave Macmillan.

Thompson, N (2006) *Anti-Discriminatory Practice* (4th edn). London: Palgrave Macmillan.

Toowoomba Catholic Education (2006) *Social Justice Commission.* Available online at: www.twb.catholic.org.au/ministry/social-justice-commission/ (accessed 15 July 2020).

Trevithick, P (2000) *Social Work Skills: A Practice Handbook.* Maidenhead: Open University Press.

Troman, G (2008) Primary teacher identity, commitment and career in performative school cultures. *British Educational Research Journal*, 34(5): 619–33.

Trotter, C (2015) *Working with Involuntary Clients* (3rd edn). London: Routledge.

Tuckman, B (1965) Developmental sequence in small groups. *Psychological Bulletin*, 63(6): 384–99.

UNCHR (2016) 20 per cent of those arriving in the first two months of 2016 were women according to the latest UNHCR data. Available online at: http://data.unhcr.org/mediterranean/regional.php

United Nations (2008) *Convention on the Rights of Persons with Disabilities and Optional Protocol*. New York: United Nations.

United Nations (2015) *World Population Ageing*. Available online at: www.un.org/en/development/desa/population/publications/pdf/ageing/WPA2015_Report.pdf (accessed 15 July 2020).

United Nations Refugee Council (1951) *Who is a Refugee?* Available online at www.unhcr.org/1951-refugee-convention.htmlns (accessed 18 July 2020).

Valenti, K (2017) Family group conferencing with BME families in Scotland. *Practice*, 29(2): 121–36. doi: 10.1080/09503153.2016.1173667

Vargas-Silva, C and Fernandez-Reino, M (2019) *EU Migration to and from the UK*. Available online at: https://migrationobservatory.ox.ac.uk/wp-content/uploads/2019/09/Briefing-EU-Migration-to-and-from-the-UK.pdf (accessed 15 July 2020).

Vigh, H (2009) Motion squared: a second look at the concept of social navigation. *Anthropological Theory*, 9(4): 419–38.

Wade, J (2019) Supporting unaccompanied asylum-seeking young people: the experience of foster care. *Child and Family Social Work*, 24(3): 383–90.

Walker, S (2011) Access denied: refugee children and the exclusionary logic of the education system in England. *Power and Education*, 3(3): 210–23.

Wayne, J, Bogo, M and Raskin, M (2010) Field education as the signature pedagogy of social work education. *Journal of Social Work Education*, 46(3): 327–39. doi:10.5175/jswe.2010.200900043

Webb, S (2017) *Professional Identity and Social Work*. London: Routledge.

Welch, M and Schuster, L (2005) Detention of asylum seekers in the UK and USA: deciphering noisy and quiet constructions. *Punishment and Society*, 1462–4745: 7(4): 397–417.

Wiles, F (2013) Not easily put into a box: constructing professional identity. *Social Work Education*, 32(7): 854–66.

Williams, P (2009) *Social Work with People with Learning Difficulties*. Exeter: Learning Matters.

Williams, C and Parrott, L (2013) From specialism to genericism: rising and falling to the challenges of responding to racial and ethnic diversity in social work education in Wales. *British Journal of Social Work*, 43: 1206–24.

Wilson, A and Beresford, P (2000) Anti-oppressive practice: emancipation or appropriation. *The British Journal of Social Work*, 30(5).

Yee, JY, Hackbusch, C and Wong, H (2015) An anti-oppression (AO) framework for child welfare in Ontario, Canada: possibilities for systemic change. *British Journal of Social Work*, 45(2): 474–92.

Young, G (1999) *The Death of Stephen Lawrence: The Macpherson Report*. The Political Quarterly Publishing Co., pp. 329–34.

Index

Added to a page number 'f' denotes a figure and 't' denotes a table.

EDITORIAL TEAM
KIDS MINISTRY PUBLISHING

Chuck Peters
Director, Kids Ministry

Jeremy Carroll
Publishing Manager,
VBS and Kids Discipleship

Rhonda VanCleave
Publishing Team Leader

Danielle Bell
Writer

Kayla Stevens
Content Editor

Sara Lansford
Production Editor

Alli Quattlebaum
Graphic Designer

Requests for permission should be addressed in writing to
Lifeway Press®
One Lifeway Plaza
Nashville, TN 37234-0172

ISBN: 978-1-535962-24-7
Item 005816334

Dewey Decimal Classification Number: 268.432
Subject Heading: Discipleship—
Curricula\God\Bible—Study
Dewey Decimal Classification Number: 248.82
Subject Heading: CHRISTIAN LIFE \ JESUS CHRIST—
TEACHINGS

Printed in the United States of America
Lifeway Kids
Lifeway Resources
One Lifeway Plaza
Nashville, Tennessee 37234-0172

We believe the Bible has God for its author; salvation for its end; and truth, without any mixture of error, for its matter and that all Scripture is totally true and trustworthy. To review Lifeway's doctrinal guideline, please visit lifeway.com/doctrinalguideline.

All Scripture quotations are taken from the Christian Standard Bible®, Copyright © 2017 by Holman Bible Publishers. Used by permission. Christian Standard Bible® and CSB® are federally registered trademarks of Holman Bible Publishers.